The Struggle for Iran

The Struggle for Iran

Christopher de Bellaigue

NEW YORK REVIEW BOOKS

New York

THIS IS A NEW YORK REVIEW BOOK

PUBLISHED BY THE NEW YORK REVIEW OF BOOKS

THE STRUGGLE FOR IRAN
by Christopher de Bellaigue

This edition published in 2007
in the United States of America by
The New York Review of Books
1755 Broadway
New York, NY 10019
www.nyrb.com

Library of Congress Cataloging-in-Publication Data

De Bellaigue, Christopher, 1971–
    The struggle for Iran / by Christopher de Bellaigue.
        p. cm. — (New York Review Books collections)
    ISBN-13: 978-1-59017-238-4 (alk. paper)
    ISBN-10: 1-59017-238-8 (alk. paper)
  1. Iran — Politics and government — 1997– 2. Iran — Strategic aspects. I. Title.
DS318.9.D43 2007
955.05'44 — dc22

                                                              2007004178

ISBN 978-1-59017-238-4

Printed in the United States of America on acid-free paper.

1 3 5 7 9 10 8 6 4 2

For my Father

Table of Contents

Acknowledgments

I AM INDEBTED to all who helped me during the almost seven years that I have served in Iran as a reporter. Mohammad-Hossein Khosh-vaght and his team at the Foreign Media Department of the Ministry of Culture and Islamic Guidance, Ali-Reza Shiravi and Efat al-Sadat Eqbali-Namin, were invariably courteous and helpful. Saeed Leylaz, Ali-Reza Alavi Tabar, Amir Mohebbian, Hossein Rassam, and Mohammad-Hossein Zeynali taught me much, over the years, about Iranian politics and society. Parviz Ismaili and Mohammad Atrianfar provided invaluable help on the essay about young Iranians. I should also like to thank my agent David Godwin, the editors of the essays that appear here, most notably Robert Silvers, and Michael Shae from New York Review Books, who edited this volume.

Introduction

REREADING THE TITLE essay in this collection, which dates from the autumn of 1999, I feel saucer-eyed all over again. I wrote it after my first visit to Iran, when I was twenty-nine, and the stiff and distant place that I had expected to find turned out to be irresistibly alive. Briefly, in the late 1990s, Iran was a young country again. People were tossing aside the fossils and relics around them, or at least holding them up to the light, expressing nothing less than a renewed faith in universal brotherhood—a resolve to speak and to listen, to treat others and to be treated with respect, to end the hostility that since the revolution of 1979 had soured Iranians' relations with each other and with foreigners. It was Iran's springtime and the youthful spirit of reform, watched over by the president of the past two years, Mohammad Khatami, seemed strong. I was hurrying through Tehran to meet men and women who, until very recently, had had little or no contact with the West, and who thrilled me with their belief that almost anything was possible. To me, they shone brightly next to the slick, buttoned-up professionals of our own "mature" democracies. It is at times like these that a journalist, free to meet whom he pleases and to draw his own conclusions for the benefit of an inquisitive audience a long way away, is convinced that his is the best of professions. And heightening my good humor during that first trip, I was falling in love at breakneck speed—I had a three-week visa, after all—with a distant, beautiful Iranian who would eventually become my wife.

Now, more than seven years on, a little fatter, a little balder, a long-term Tehran resident, the father of two half-English, half-Iranian children, I miss the optimism that I felt at that time. I assumed that the reform movement would succeed because enough people had told me it was Iran's destiny that it should. But as the world knows, and the essays in this volume recount, reform did not succeed; it died, slowly and painfully.

The simplest explanation for this defeat is that the giants I met in 1999 turned out to be, if not pygmies, then as frail and as human as their predecessors in Iran's century-long, unconsummated flirtation with democracy. Take, for instance, Ataollah Mohajerani, the culture minister who spoke to me smoothly, and not without condescension, during that first trip; the man behind Iran's opening up to culture and pluralism; a man giddy with his own success and daring. He was driven from office by his conservative opponents, and later forced into exile after a sexual indiscretion. (Nowadays he is to be found living quietly in an outlying suburb of London.) There is Abdolkarim Soroush, political philosopher, lay theologian, and student of Sufi verse, who provided ballast for the whole reformist enterprise. Soroush's intellectual reputation is intact and he can move around Iran more or less as he pleases, but he must pay the price, appalling to any public intellectual, of remaining silent in public. Above all, there is Khatami himself, whose presidency ended in 2005 and who is regretted only because he is so much nicer than his successor, Mahmoud Ahmadinejad. It's hard to find much honor in the defeat of these people—much easier, in fact, to discern the same strain of indifference, even contempt, that you find being shown by the elite for the rabble throughout much of Iran's history. They retreat without explanation, without apology. They announce speaking engagements

—literally, in the case of Soroush—that they don't honor. And that's the story of the reform movement: an engagement that dozens of men and a few women made, and then did not honor.

This, the conventional "Iranians deserve better" analysis, is convincing but incomplete. It leaves questions hanging in the air. If Iran's reform movement was as authentic as it claimed to be, why did Iranians entrust it to such a select group of leaders and their allies in the press and bureaucracy? If the yearning for democratic reform was so deep and strong, how did the people allow the project to collapse so cheaply? The answer, it seems to me, lies buried in a political culture where, on the one hand, people have never quite made the leap from being subjects to being citizens and, on the other, where men of principle very often lose their lives or their freedom. When I first visited Iran, political discussion among normal Iranians was so intense that I assumed people's engagement must be very deep. Then, gradually, as reform died, these people depoliticized themselves. They accommodated themselves to the new circumstances so deftly that I almost forgot how political they had once seemed. They went off politics, stopped talking about it, got on with their lives, and you could imagine them cursing themselves secretly for having been foolish enough to believe that this time, perhaps, after so many disappointments and false starts, Iran might leap forward and win a free public culture. They turned off and feigned indifference in order to avoid inevitable disappointment and stress. It's one reason why authoritarian regimes survive.

Time and again, as I followed the decline of the reform movement, I was told—confidingly, for it's not polite to say such things loudly—that Iranians, having nominated leaders to articulate their aspirations, are apt to watch events unfold from the comfort of their homes. (The revolution was an exception, according to this argument, and many Iranians show signs of regretting having mounted it.) Iran is a semi-democracy, but it's not a participatory semi-democracy. Khatami has often been accused of letting down his constituency, of not showing the mettle that would have inspired them. His allies counter that, on the contrary, he refused to battle his opponents at the top of the conservative establishment because he knew that once the backlash started, he would be on his own. The fate of one of Iran's few genuine dissidents, the journalist Akbar Ganji, who was recently freed after serving a jail sentence, supports this. Brave and inspirational, Ganji is now criticized by many for being too extreme in his criticism of the Islamic Republic. The people who loved his subversive articles did not follow him, or mount protests, or hang banners in their workplaces to protest his disgraceful incarceration. They remained silent and got used to reading much less interesting newspapers.

The essays in this volume describe a slow flattening of hopes and, at the same time, a countervailing—and not unrelated—rise in international tensions to such a pitch, at the time I am writing this, that international sanctions against the Islamic Republic are in place and likely to become heavier, and the probability of military strikes seems to be increasing. From the autumn of 2002, when I wrote the third essay in this collection, to the final piece, which is dated October 2006, the question of Iran's nuclear intentions was at or near the top of the world's agenda. Gradually, as the Bush administration and other governments reduced Iran, in their depiction, to an evil theocracy bent on acquiring nuclear weapons and threatening Israel, my challenge as a journalist came to be to resist succumbing to this caricature, to treat Iran as something more complex than a country of bad men holding yellowcake and repressing their people. The challenge was to put the Iranians' insistence on nuclear "independence" into a necessary context—the invasions of Afghanistan and Iraq, George Bush's inclusion of Iran in his "axis of evil"—and to relate that to the ending of hopes of internal reform.

I had an advantage in that my editor, for the majority of the essays that appear in this book, was Bob Silvers of *The New York Review of Books*. Awed, at first, by Bob's long experience and by the intimidating list of former and current contributors to the *Review*, I learned after a while to answer back to him during the editing process, and the best of these essays are, I think, those that occasioned the most spirited exchanges between us. Often, it was only after a much-scrutinized piece had gone to press that I would realize the value of Bob's ruthless filtering—his insistence on clarification here, his challenging an assumption there, and above all his success at preparing sometimes unpalatable ideas for an American audience. As much as his skill as an editor, it is his integrity and judgment, exemplified by the *Review*'s opposition to the invasion of Iraq, that has my admiration. That opposition was, I'm sad to say, exceptional, despite the wisdom after the event that has now revealed itself to dozens of other editors. The publication that Bob and the late Barbara Epstein set up is a monument to the curiosity and compassion of the American liberal tradition, and it has always been a source of pride for me to say, "I write for *The New York Review of Books*."

I have not done much to modify or update these essays, except to add footnotes where questions are left hanging or egregious mistakes were made. They stand in their chronological order, as a record, however flawed, of seven years spent watching Iran, and I hope that every one conveys a fleeting flavor of the moment it was written, of the hopes and anxieties of a particular time. There is a gap after the attacks of September 11, 2001, when those events and their aftermath caught the attention of us all. As a journalist, my gaze turned to Afghanistan, Pakistan, and, later, Iraq, and each time I returned to Tehran I found that the Islamic Republic had been similarly transfixed. Since September 11, it has seemed natural to put small, even parochial events into a much wider frame—to see what they mean in the context of America and its wrath. Nations, journalists, ordinary citizens—we have all done this, and the historians will tell us whether this has helped or hindered our understanding.

It seems right that here, under the *Review*'s rubric, my dissections of the nuclear issue rub shoulders with very different essays that have appeared in journals as varied as *The Economist*, *Harper's*, and *The Guardian*, and another, published here for the first time, describing the aspirations of young Iranians. It's tempting, when a superpower is weighing hostile action, to forget the human consequences of the various courses that might be taken, and this increases the usefulness of watching Iran from inside the country. It also explains why the US, whose diplomats, politicians, and academics observe events from a distorting distance, has such a poor feel for the place. Here, where I sit, people try to get on with their lives, and yet are constrained by lurking fears and by events, decided in the councils of their own and other countries, over which they have no influence. The worst thing about not being able to decide your destiny is the sense of impotence, the piling up of small humiliations. Iranians were young when I visited back in 1999. Now, they are old again, and resigned. For the outsider, that has its own charm, for disappointed Iranians make witty, lyrical company. Ultimately, though, there is a regret in the heart of Iran, and a rarely acknowledged need for friends, of which I hope I can always consider myself one.

—Tehran, March 2007

I

THE STRUGGLE FOR IRAN

November 1999

IN TEHRAN AT the end of September 1999 Mohammad Khatami rose to his feet to address some ten thousand students on the occasion of the one hundredth birthday of Ayatollah Ruhollah Khomeini, the leader of Iran's Islamic revolution of 1979. Khatami captured Iran's presidency two and a half years ago with promises to extract democratic freedoms from the hard-line clerical establishment that has dominated Iranian politics for the past two decades, and to improve ties with the West. The students who came to listen to him, drawn from Tehran's half-dozen universities, wanted to express their support for these goals, but in his speech Khatami often seemed to be reading from a different script altogether. His attack on the "spineless imitators of the West" and his call for piety, for example, would not have been out of place in a tirade by one of Iran's hard-liners. Why, then, when the President had finished and sat cross-legged among the other dignitaries, was he loudly cheered, with female students holding up his photograph, their male counterparts bellowing his name?

There are two main reasons for this apparent anomaly, and both shed light on the President's reform movement. The first is the need felt by Khatami to play down the potential that he has to change Iran dramatically. His stated goals of democratic accountability and the rule of law in a civil society may seem bland. In Iran, however, they are a direct challenge to the politically powerful clerics who have shaped the Islamic Republic since its inception. Khatami has to contend with a suspicious parliament, a doctrinaire judiciary, and with Ayatollah Ali Khamenei, a conservative Supreme Leader drawn from the ranks of the senior clergy who has been given powers unthinkable in a Western-style democracy. As a medium-ranking cleric and former minister, Khatami comes from the very establishment that he challenges, but he risks political oblivion if his position strays too far from that of his opponents.[1] Such caution colored the response of Mohammad-Ali Abtahi, Khatami's longtime adviser, when I asked him about the absence of policy statements in the President's speech: "The less he says, the better."

A second characteristic of Khatami's movement is the political acumen of its supporters. Along with most other young Iranians, a great many of Iran's one-million-odd students helped to vote him into power until 2001. They are eager for political reform. They, too, appreciate the influence exerted by Khatami's opponents, and the need for prudence. Their activism is more considered than was that of their parents' generation, whose violent opposition to the Shah hastened his downfall in 1979. In July, Khatami disappointed his more impatient supporters when he condemned the violent protests of reformist students at Tehran University against the clerical establishment. Nevertheless, the event which had provoked these protests, the death of a young man during an attack on reformist students by militant Islamists supported by the police, was more significant, since it illustrated the frustration hard-liners felt at Khatami's enduring popularity. For the moment, reform-minded Iranians tend to remain indulgent of their President's soft-pedaling.

Khatami's skill as a public speaker helps to explain their indulgence. True, his speeches often contain conventional anti-Western themes, but he gets across more radical ideas, too. Just as his address

---

1. See Shaul Bakhash, "Iran's Unlikely President," *The New York Review*, November 5, 1998.

to the students at the end of September contained traditional invective, it was also disturbing to conservatives, calling as it did for increased student participation in politics, and expressing admiration for Western technological advances. Khatami cleverly fends off charges of betrayal by quoting—very selectively—pronouncements of Ayatollah Khomeini himself that seem to support a more open society. The President won sustained applause with an attack on those who "suppose that the more retarded a society is, the better protected its religion will be." Like every successful Iranian politician, Khatami refrains from identifying his opponents. But everyone knows who they are.

The President's enemies look for leadership to the Shiite clerics who have been labeled, with a nod to Western political nomenclature, *muhafazakaran*—conservatives. The conservatives claim, with partial justification, to be the heirs to the political legacy of Ayatollah Khomeini, whose quasi-divine persona continues, ten years after his death, to exert a strong hold over his people. The conservatives—many of them clerics—and their allies have around 120 representatives in Iran's heterogeneous, 270-seat parliament, and they have, until recently, relied on support from Ayatollah Ali Khamenei.

Iranians wishing to know what these conservatives are thinking need only follow the sermons they deliver at prayers each Friday. In general, such sermons follow a predictable course, with strong attacks on "liberals" (by which they mean Khatami and his supporters), "nationalists" (a blanket term that can refer to closet monarchists, socialists, and secularists), and other lackeys of the West. They are suffused with images of martyrdom, a traditional Shiite motif lent contemporary resonance by the deaths in the 1980s of at least 300,000 Iranian soldiers during eight years of war with Iraq. One of the best-known practitioners of such sermons is Ayatollah Ahmad Jannati.

Like Ali Khamenei and Mohammad Yazdi (who this summer stepped down as Iran's top judge), Ayatollah Jannati is a middle-level ayatollah whose temporal power exceeds his clerical authority. His influence derives from his position at the top of the Council of Guardians, a twelve-member, conservative-dominated body which can turn down parliamentary legislation and candidates for election to public office if they do not adhere to Islamic tenets. Before the 1996 parliamentary elections, it vetoed the candidacy of well over a third of 5,359 registered aspirants, most of them associated in some way with the (then-nascent) reform camp. A year later, it cleared the candidacy of only four of the 238 Iranians who wanted to run for president. It is likely that the Council of Guardians will use its veto to eliminate candidates in next February's parliamentary polls, in an effort to prevent pro-Khatami candidates from winning control of Iran's narrowly conservative chamber. In the meantime, Ayatollah Jannati uses his Friday sermons to drum up indignation against the supposed excesses of the current government.

In late September, I was among several thousand men who gathered to hear the ayatollah talk beneath a gigantic awning inside the gates of Tehran University. Congregations here have dwindled since the early days of the revolution, when up to 100,000 students and other ideologues came to be thrilled by firebrand clerics. Twenty years later, however, the speeches are pretty much the same. On September 24, Ayatollah Jannati's voice cracked as he denounced the student authors of a short play alleged to lampoon the twelfth imam—the final heir to the succession of the Prophet Muhammad—whose reappearance at the end of time will establish a reign of justice and truth. While the congregation shouted "Death to America"—the all-purpose villain, whatever the crime—the ayatollah demanded retribution for those who had given the "green light" for the play's publication. Like the President, Ayatollah Jannati does not identify his adversaries, but it was clear whom he meant: the *dovom Khurdadis*, Iran's prominent reformist politicians, journalists, and intellectuals.

* * *

4

The *dovom Khurdadis* take their name from the Persian solar calendar date on which Khatami won his momentous election victory twenty-nine months ago: the *dovom Khurdad*, 1376. Plenty of *dovom Khurdadis* have impressive revolutionary credentials. At least three were heavily involved in the defining revolutionary event, the takeover by students of the US embassy in Tehran in 1979–1980: Ibrahim Asgharzadeh, one of eight reformers elected in February to Tehran's ten-member municipality; Abbas Abdi, co-founder of *Sobh-e-Emruz*, a pro-Khatami newspaper; and Mohammad Musavi Khoeniha, cleric and former publisher of *Salam* (whose banning provided a spark for events that led to July's student unrest). Many of them have proud war records, too; Hamid Reza Jelaeipour, another prominent reformist journalist, spent much of the 1980s fighting the Iraqis, and lost three brothers in the war.

To be a *dovom Khurdadi*, you do not need to prove exclusive allegiance to Khatami. Ataollah Mohajerani and Gholam-Hossein Karbaschi, both of whom are now closely associated with the President, were loyal to Akbar Hashemi Rafsanjani, Khatami's immediate predecessor, whose relations with the *dovom Khurdadis* are currently cool. Yet both men have proved invaluable to Khatami, Mohajerani as a liberal minister of culture and Islamic guidance—the same portfolio held by Khatami until he was forced from office in 1992 for alleged permissiveness. Karbaschi, then mayor of Tehran, is said to have persuaded his friends in the construction industry to bankroll Khatami's election victory. Karbaschi himself is now in jail on charges of embezzlement—a martyr to the reformist cause, his supporters say.

A striking thing about the *dovom Khurdadis* is that they are rather few—perhaps fifty politicians, journalists, clerics, and intellectuals. Some are related to others. Mohsen Kadivar, for instance, a progressive and controversial Islamic intellectual, is the brother of Jamilah Kadivar, a former Tehran councilor who recently resigned so that she could run in next February's parliamentary elections. Kadivar's candidacy will have the backing of Mohajerani, who is her husband. The *dovom Khurdadis* publish their political tracts with half-a-dozen like-minded publishing houses, and they are connected with several reformist newspapers. In the offices of one such newspaper, *Sobh-e-Emruz*, you may catch a glimpse of Saeed Hajarian, the newspaper's publisher and a senior reformist politician, discussing editorial policy with Abdi, whose research group conducts polls for the government. Reza Tehrani, whose progressive theological magazine, *Kiyan*, is required reading for reformists, may have dropped by from his office around the corner. *Sobh-e-Emruz* often features open letters from the minister of culture and Islamic guidance—in some ways Mohajerani is the quintessential *dovom Khurdadi*.

To appreciate Mohajerani's importance to the reform movement, it helps to visit one of the newspaper kiosks that stand on the street corners of Iranian towns. Before his appointment, these kiosks sold just a handful of newspapers, most of them conservative, and all of them competing in a highly restricted market. Nowadays, you may see dozens of people at the kiosks reading the headlines of several dailies which have begun publishing in the past two years. Even in very pious towns like Mashhad, news vendors attest to the popularity of centrist newspapers like *Hamshahri* (declared circulation 460,000) and the reformist *Khurdad* (approximately 120,000) and *Sobh-e-Emruz* (around 110,000) over conservative mouthpieces like *Keyhan*, whose readership is rumored to have dropped from 200,000 in the 1980s to less than 100,000.

The combined circulation of Iranian newspapers and magazines is now 2,750,000, twice what it was a couple of years ago. The new newspapers tend to be color tabloids, while *Keyhan* (along with *Resalat*, a second conservative paper) remains foreboding and bulky —"good for vegetable peelings," in the opinion of a woman in Isfahan. *Hamshahri* owes at least some of its popularity to its reputation as the best place for classified advertisements. In general, however, Iranians tend to like the new newspapers because they like their politics. If you buy a copy of *Sobh-e-Emruz*, you will find that its twelve pages contain little news. The paper and its similarly inclined competitors are polemical sheets, reproducing the speeches of politicians they admire and lambasting those they do not. They have fed what Faribah Adelkhah, a Paris-based anthropologist, calls "a society engaged in full-scale internal debate."[2]

Mohajerani has made the new press possible. Whereas his conservative predecessor was inclined to refuse applications for permits to establish newspapers and magazines, Mohajerani readily gives his assent; his ministry has allowed hundreds of new publications to start up. The minister has encouraged other cultural activities, too, many of them previously unthinkable. It was Mohajerani's men who allowed the release of the unprecedented fifty-odd Persian pop albums recorded in Iran during the past two years, and his ministry permitted (after a four-year wait) the screening of the movie *Two Women*, a boldly unconventional story of the degradation of a young woman trapped in a traditional marriage. It is no wonder that many anti-Western conservatives loathe Mohajerani. He speaks favorably of the novels of Milan Kundera; his daughter plays the piano; his lively wife promises representation "for the women of this country" if she gets into parliament.

But for all Mohajerani's regard for Western culture and the relative emancipation of his wife, it would be a mistake to visit his office expecting an Iranian version of the Westernized elite one finds in the bureaucracies and parliaments of other, more secular Muslim states —Turkey and Egypt, for instance. Mohajerani offers his visitors a learned critique he wrote of *The Satanic Verses* and goes on to argue that the reform movement is underpinned as much by a progressive

---

2. Fariba Adelkhah, *Being Modern in Iran*, translated from the French by Jonathan Derrick (Columbia University Press, 2000).

Islamic theology as it is by imported Western ideas. In May 1999, he gave an important insight into this theology when he replied in parliament to hard-line deputies who were trying to have him impeached. In a speech that was praised for its eloquence and daring, he defended the principle of freedom of speech not in Western but in Islamic terms: "Why does the Koran carry the harshest criticisms of the Prophet?" he asked. The answer was, "It was not in the nature of the Prophet to stifle discussion of opposing points of view." The minister survived.

A talk with Mohajerani highlights a second aspect of the reform movement, which appeals to many young Iranians: the idea of a still-developing Islamic revolution. "We have only twenty years of experience, and it will take time for the revolution to find its equilibrium," he says, reflecting the view of the President himself, who has called the revolution a "point of departure." The political dynamism promised by the reformers contrasts sharply with the passivity of many of their opponents. The conservatives maintain that the revolution needs only fine-tuning, and that the responsibility of ordinary people is to remain "vigilant" in the face of "enemies" both at home and abroad. Surprisingly, the reformist view has been cautiously endorsed by some members of the very senior clergy. When I asked Ayatollah Makaram Shirazi, one of seven Shiite clerics to be recognized as grand ayatollahs, about the fidelity of Khatami's government to the ideals of Ayatollah Khomeini, he replied, "The goals of the republic remain those of the Imam [Ayatollah Khomeini], but the means of reaching them can change." Does this suggest the beginning of an Islamic pluralism?

Khatami, the president, whose peculiar circumstances oblige him to be the opposition leader as well, clearly hopes so. He has defined liberty as "the freedom to oppose." Emboldened by this implicit endorsement, progressive clerics and lay philosophers have taken up an old but long-suppressed argument over the role of the *vali-e-faqih*, the position of Supreme Leader now occupied by Ayatollah Khameini.

Conservatives, taking their cue from Khomeini as he neared the end of his life, believe the *vali-e-faqih* to be the representative of the twelfth imam and, as such, exempt from temporal accountability. Progressives, who quote Khomeini's more ambiguous earlier pronouncements on the subject, believe that the *vali-e-faqih*'s legitimacy is temporal, and that he should be subject to democratic checks and balances.

Mehdi Bazargan, the nationalist Islamist who formed a short-lived government just after the revolution, described the institution of the *velayat-e-faqih*—literally, the "guardianship of the Islamic jurist"— as a garment stitched for Ayatollah Khomeini. In a recent biography of Khomeini, the London-based journalist Baqer Moin recalls the difficulty experienced by the Assembly of Experts, the group of clerics that selects the Supreme Leader, when it came to finding his successor: "There was no other jurist in the land who could lay claim to all his qualifications, especially on the political front."[3] For the institution and its supporters, this remains the case. In *Iran: Comment sortir d'une révolution religieuse*,[4] their survey of Iran's politics and society two decades after the revolution, Farhad Khosrokhavar and Olivier Roy argue that Ayatollah Khamenei's appointment as *vali-e-faqih* robbed the position of "its revolutionary élan, and of all charisma" ("*de son élan révolutionnaire, et de tout charisme*"). Many Iranians agree. How, they ask, can the current Supreme Leader be considered a divine representative, when Shiism's top clerics considered him insufficiently learned to merit recognition as a grand ayatollah?

The men who have reheated the debate over the *velayat-e-faqih* are well known. Despite his belief in the value of the institution itself, Ayatollah Hossein-Ali Montazeri, Khomeini's designated successor until he fell from grace shortly before the Supreme Leader's death in 1989, has cited Islamic law in defense of his proposition that the

---

3. *Khomeini: Life of the Ayatollah* (London: I. B. Tauris, 1999).

4. Paris: Seuil, 1999.

vali-e-faqih should be directly elected. (The Assembly of Experts, which chooses the *vali-e-faqih*, is elected by universal suffrage, but only after candidates have been rigorously vetted by the Council of Guardians.)

Mohsen Kadivar, Mohajerani's brother-in-law, favors only a supervisory role for the *vali-e-faqih*, and accuses conservative clerics of gathering powers more suited to the monarchy they replaced. Other clerics question the theological validity of an Islamic state itself, while Abdolkarim Soroush, a prominent lay intellectual, looks forward to the evolution of an Iran both democratic and religious—a "true Islamic Republic."

Many Iranian progressives also hold contentious views about *ijte-had*—the interpretation by authorized theologians of the application of Islamic law. In general, the progressives think that *ijtehad* should be subject to revision. "Dynamic" *ijtehad*, they argue, would be a way of getting rid of those onerous interdictions and constraints which, while sanctioned by Islam, seem out of step with modern life. In *Islam and Gender*,[5] a recent study of theological responses in Iran to emerging female emancipation, Ziba Mir-Hosseini, an Iranian-born anthropologist, gives prominence to dynamic *ijtehad*, recalling that Ayatollah Khomeini, in his fatwas that overturned earlier bans on music and the sale of chess sets, himself legitimized it. Anxious not to seem out of step, many conservative theologians pay lip service to dynamic *ijtehad*, but they have so far prevented it from having an effect on legislation. If it were adopted sincerely in lawmaking, however, dynamic *ijtehad* could have enormous consequences, and not just for Iranian Islam.

Conservative institutions and groups have attacked the proponents of these progressive notions. In April, Kadivar was jailed for eighteen months for commenting on the contradiction between the revolution's

---

5. Princeton University Press, 1999.

aims to serve the people and the subsequent concentration of power in the hands of clerics. Ayatollah Montazeri, who two years ago questioned the competence of Ayatollah Khamenei to be *vali-e-faqih*, languishes under what amounts to house arrest in Qom. Mohammad Shabestari declines to be interviewed "in the current climate," a seeming reference to the murders last year of several progressive intellectuals, and the wife of one of them, at the hands, it later emerged, of government agents. Not surprisingly, the liberal Dr. Soroush, whose classes at Tehran University were canceled last month after the university received threats by Islamic bullies, declines to expand on his "true Islamic republic," quoting a helpful *hadith* (saying) of the Prophet: "Hide your money, your relations, and your ideas."

The President would doubtless disapprove, but this remains a sensible maxim in today's Iran, since the reformers have often been powerless to protect those whom they encourage to speak out. During the past few months in particular, the President has looked impotent in the face of a relentless judicial campaign to muzzle the press, which in the absence of a pro-Khatami majority in parliament is the main outlet for the reformist message to ordinary Iranians.

July's unrest at Tehran University and elsewhere reinforced the power of the pro-Khatami press as an instrument of reform; it was partly the banning of Khoeniha's *Salam*, the oldest and best-established of these newspapers, and partly the ratification of the draft of a restrictive press bill that brought reformist students into the streets. This in turn prompted the deadly attacks by hard-liners on reformers. In September, it was the turn of *Neshat*, another reformist daily, to be banned (for, among other things, questioning the Islamic view of capital punishment). Latif Safari, *Neshat*'s publisher, was sentenced to two and a half years in prison, although he remains free pending appeal.

The list of aggrieved journalists now grows larger week by week. In September, Mashallah Shamsolvaezin, who was *Neshat*'s editor in chief (and now edits a hastily put-together replacement), was in court for "insulting the sanctity and tenets of Islam," and Abdullah Nouri, a cleric, former interior minister, and proprietor of *Khurdad*, was found guilty by a clerical court of charges which may result both in a prison sentence and in his being banned for life from politics. Nouri has attracted wide attention not only for courageously challenging the authority of the court but for suggesting that the Supreme Leader is subject to the law, just as other citizens are, and that religious doctrine supports democratic values.[6] *Sobh-e-Emruz* may be next; Saeed Hajarian is expected to be summoned soon to face some seventy charges on behalf of his newspaper. What is more, when they are called before Tehran's special court dealing with the press, few editors or publishers expect a fair trial. "The decision to close the paper has been taken elsewhere," one courtroom observer told me on the final day of the *Neshat* trial, "and we're here to watch the court rubber-stamp it."

The other institution which is currently making life difficult for Khatami and his supporters is Iran's parliament. Since many deputies abstain on crucial votes, not wanting to risk taking controversial positions, conservatives can quite often enact repressive legislation with the votes of just a minority of deputies. They are currently putting in final form the same press bill whose draft ratification brought the students onto the streets in July. If enacted, this bill would make it harder for banned newspapers to reopen under a different name (as *Neshat* has effectively done). It would make journalists legally answerable for what they write (at present, the publisher is liable), and transfer some press offenses to juryless courts.

All in all, the news for reformers is bad. The *dovom Khurdadis* are under heavy pressure.

* * *

---

6. *Nouri was jailed for insulting Islam and spent three years behind bars before he was pardoned by Ayatollah Khamenei in 2002. He has since kept a low political profile. [Added 2007]*

The virulence of the judicial and parliamentary campaign against the reformers lends weight to an important *dovom Khurdadi* argument: Iran's conservatives are clamping down on reformers because they themselves are losing a battle of ideas. Senior clerical conservatives are dismayed by declining mosque attendances and the support expressed by young Iranians for the "dialogue of civilizations" called for by the President. They find particularly disturbing the fascination of young Iranians with Western culture, and with the US in particular. The seminaries of Qom and Mashhad have been divided by the progressive theology promoted by clerics like Ayatollah Montazeri and lay philosophers like Dr. Soroush, and by persistent doubts over the fitness of Ayatollah Khamenei for the position of *vali-e-faqih*.

Wandering through the cloisters of the seminary at Qom last month, I met students who described themselves as far more "open-minded" than their predecessors who studied there a generation ago; they are enthusiasts, they say, of both dynamic *ijtehad* and the films of Steven Spielberg. In private, some senior clerics fear that the insertion of religion into the bureaucracy, the courts, and the parliament has been to the detriment of Shiism's essential mysticism. Farhadid Khosrokhavar and Oliver Roy argue convincingly that the revolution has reduced the "transcendence" of the religious sphere. Islam has become banal.

As the conservatives' ideology has lost its suppleness, so the organizations and groups closely associated with them have seen their authority diminish. Iranians are much less committed revolutionaries than they were during the Khomeini years, when the Islamic regime was for export, and a holy war with Iraq and its Western backers was under way. Volunteers in the Basij civil defense force and members of the better-trained, paramilitary Pasdaran no longer have the prestige they had during the war; the civil defense force has no defined peacetime role, and reformist ideas are said to have gained currency in the Pasdaran. The Komitehs, the associations of vigilantes notorious for their enforcement of Islamic restrictions on dress and behavior—what

Moin calls the regime's "eyes and ears"—are less heavy-handed and, consequently, less feared than they were. Some senior conservatives appear to be withdrawing the protection they traditionally provided to the Ansar-e-Hezbollah, a loose collection of thuggish hard-liners whose founding inspired that of Lebanese Hezbollah.

Although the future of these highly ideologized organizations and associations looks uncertain, the vastly more influential economic superstructure erected by the revolutionary authorities during the 1980s remains intact. Under this system, the public sector was enlarged to the point where it now accounts for 80 percent of Iran's economic activity. Besides benefiting from fiscal laxness which has cut tax revenues to "half of what can legitimately be expected," in the IMF's view, loyalist bureaucrats and some of the merchants called *bazaaris* were also given access to hard currency at a privileged rate of exchange, fostering speculation and discouraging investment in production. These inducements stiffened support for the revolutionary government, but they also created centers of influence whose concerns the authorities could not ignore. In the 1980s, for instance, the opposition of many of Iran's more than two million civil servants and of key *bazaaris* forced President Rafsanjani to drop plans to privatize parts of the public sector and to permanently abolish multiple exchange rates. Clearly, economic interest groups will have something to say about the pace and nature of reform.

Among the most powerful of these are Iran's charitable institutions and foundations, some of them inherited from the Pahlavi era. Others were set up to manage assets confiscated from the former regime and its supporters. They are run by clerics and lay ideologues appointed by the Supreme Leader, and their senior positions have traditionally been filled by former members of organizations like the Pasdaran. With considerable power over the major industries and exempt from taxation, they have developed into vast holding companies with sidelines in social services. The most-cited example is the Foundation for the Disinherited and War Disabled. In 1997, the foundation's 30,000-odd employees were responsible for controlling production of 28 percent of the textiles manufactured in Iran that year, as well as 42 percent of the cement, 45 percent of the soft drinks, 28 percent of the tires, and 25 percent of the sugar. "When you step into the foundation's headquarters," says one diplomat lucky enough to receive an invitation, "you feel the power."

For an idea of the autonomy enjoyed by some of Iran's charitable institutions, a visit to Mashhad, capital of the northeastern province of Khorasan, is instructive. This city of more than two million people owes its importance to the shrine complex that has grown up around the tomb of Imam Reza, the most important Shiite figure to be buried within the borders of modern Iran; its prosperity depends on the millions of pilgrims who visit the shrine every year. The shrine is run by the Astan-e-Qods-e Razavi, a charitable institution seized by the new government soon after the revolution, and informally abbreviated to Astan-e-Qods. When asked to identify the most important man in the city, Mashhadis do not name the mayor but rather the cleric who has spent the past two decades heading the Astan-e-Qods: Ayatollah Vaez Tabassi.

For a visitor to Mashhad, the source of the ayatollah's authority soon becomes apparent. Since the revolution, the Astan-e-Qods has grown from a modest concern into a conglomerate employing 19,000 people. Thanks in part to the generosity of pious Shiites, the foundation owns most of the city's real estate, renting out shop space to bazaaris and land to many of the city's eight-hundred-odd hoteliers. According to the head of the Astan-e-Qods international relations department, the land occupied by the shrine has grown fourfold since 1979; at the moment, the vast skeletons of two future administrative buildings flank the open space at its entrance. Since the Astan-e-Qods is a religious institution, its commercial activities are not taxable; requests to learn the cost of the shrine's splendid new library are politely deflected. It is virtually impossible to guess the size of Ayatollah Tabassi's empire. But everyone recognizes its power.

It is hardly surprising, then, that Iranian presidents try to avoid offending institutions like the Astan-e-Qods, and Khatami is no exception. Challenging these institutions directly could easily backfire, nudging them further into the conservative sphere from which they came, and setting up a popular cause around which demoralized hard-liners could rally. Furthermore, the Astan-e-Qods and the Foundation for the Disinherited and War Disabled are not immune to the currents of change in Iran. It is possible that Khatami might never have to confront them. If he waits, they might drop into his lap.

A similar prognosis might be advanced for the *bazaaris*, who control some 10 percent of the economy, and whose influence helped Ayatollah Khomeini to strengthen his grip on power after the revolution. Conservative-minded guilds retain the authority to shut individual bazaars to make a political point—they shut the Tehran Bazaar for a few hours on September 27, in protest against the student play to which Ayatollah Jannati had taken exception. But many of the *bazaaris* I spoke to that day had pulled down their shutters reluctantly. They ignored invitations to hear Major General Yahya Safavi, the Pasdaran commander in chief, denounce the liberals in a nearby shrine. Although most guild leaders are conservatives, many of their members voted for Khatami in 1997.

What seems clear is that a popular yearning for reform has prompted an evolution even among conservatives. This view gets additional support when one examines the President's dealings with the most influential of them all, Ayatollah Khamenei. The ayatollah is no *dovom Khurdadi*. As Supreme Leader, he is in overall charge of the hard-line judges who have banned four reformist newspapers in the past twelve months. This spring they charged thirteen Iranian Jews and a handful of Shiites with spying for Israel (they have yet to come to trial), and they recently sentenced to death four students involved in July's unrest.[7] Plenty of issues divide the Supreme Leader and his President—not least the President's popular mandate. In 1997, Khatami won more than 69 percent of the vote from an exceptionally high turnout and, in February 1999, reformist-minded candidates scored a resounding victory in the republic's first municipal election. Nevertheless, their relationship has much more to it than the "barely concealed tension" described by Khosrokhavar and Roy. Khatami's studied moderation and his repeatedly expressed support for the institution of the *velayat-e-faqih* have not gone unrewarded.

The Supreme Leader has shown the most flexibility in foreign policy. Had the President not had the ayatollah's support, his assurance that the Rushdie fatwa would not be pursued would have carried little weight, and relations with EU countries would likely not have improved as dramatically as they have. It would have been far more difficult for the President to make a visit to Italy this spring, and another—acknowledged to be a success even by Iran's conservatives —to France in October. Nor would European diplomats be saying that Iran is no longer committing terrorist acts abroad, and that it is now more cooperative with international monitors investigating its capacity to make biological and chemical weapons.

In some foreign policy matters, however, the President has not won substantial concessions, and may have judged it unwise to try, especially in Iran's relations with the US, whom many Iranians still regard as the regime's most implacable enemy. Since 1997, Khatami's vague but friendly call for a "thoughtful dialogue" between Iranians and Americans has received a cautious welcome in Washington. Instead of advocating the collapse of the revolutionary regime, the US now proposes face-to-face talks. Khatami, however, cannot afford to

---

7. *In 2000, ten of the Iranian Jews were given jail sentences of between four and ten years. None of the students who were arrested for involvement in the 1999 protests was executed, but there have been reports that some of them were badly tortured. [Added 2007]*

reciprocate until the US unfreezes several billion dollars' worth of Iranian assets and lifts sanctions against Iran, which were renewed by President Clinton this month. Expressions of goodwill on Khatami's part would hardly amount to the rapprochement "as equal partners" that Iranians demand, and would provoke damaging domestic protests. The speeches of Ayatollah Khamenei remain full of anti-US rhetoric.

Closer to home, though, the President has had better luck. Although Khamenei's condemnation of the student violence this summer lost him points with some reformers, equally significant was the Supreme Leader's unprecedented condemnation of the students' attackers, some of whom were hezbollahis. Since then, the ayatollah has sacked several virulent hard-liners from his entourage, praised Khatami's contribution to the "rebirth of Islam," and approved a modernizing shake-up in the Foundation for the Disinherited and War Disabled. He has ceded to the President practical control over the police and Intelligence Ministry, and endorsed the unprecedented arrest of several intelligence officials who were suspected of the murders of the progressive intellectuals. (The leading suspect died mysteriously in prison, and the trial of the remaining suspects has yet to start.) The Supreme Leader may even have had a hand in the relatively light prison sentences handed down in the beginning of November to the authors of that controversial campus play. If we bear in mind that Ayatollah Khamenei spent much of the 1980s as Ayatollah Khomeini's president and close confidant, we can see how much he has changed his position.

In doing so, he has permitted the emergence of a pragmatic Iranian conservatism, which sees the wisdom in reaching an accommodation with the country's dominant political current, Khatami's pragmatic Iranian reformism. Such an accommodation is certainly not smooth, as can be seen from the prosecution of several *dovom Khurdadis* on flimsy charges; but both sides are profiting from it. The conservatives avoid pitting themselves more visibly against the wishes of the majority of Iranians. Khatami, for his part, is shielded against Iran's most uncompromising hard-liners, who press the Supreme Leader to use his constitutional and moral authority to derail the reform movement.

Twenty-nine months of reformist rule have given Iran a vigorous press and a less doctrinaire foreign policy. But Khatami's achievements in government have been modest. In the words of Adelkhah, the Islamic Republic is "continuing basically along the same course" it has followed since the revolution. About many aspects of Iranian life, a voter might ask: Are the *dovom Khurdadis* really reformers at all?

Take women's rights. Back in 1997, millions of Iranian women hoped that the new government would dismantle the many impediments to equality of the sexes which were erected by the revolutionary authorities. In the intervening period, however, the only legislation enacted in favor of women was a law indexing the *mehrieh*—the sum of money pledged by husband to wife in case of divorce—to the rate of inflation. Mehrangiz Kar, a prominent lawyer with a particular interest in women's rights, describes this law as an "aspirin," criticizing the indifference among reformists to the legal plight of Iranian women.

The practical results of reformist efforts to deepen representative government have disappointed many Iranians, too. By shouldering a long-standing (and long-ignored) constitutional responsibility to hold municipal elections, Khatami, it is true, gave substance to his pluralist rhetoric. The councils that were elected last February, on the other hand, have left voters cold. "We're told to be pleased that we have our representatives in the council," said one taxi driver in the small town of Kelardasht, a few miles south of the Caspian Sea, "but our council has no power." The new municipalities have no budget and, except for the right to choose the mayor, few responsibilities.

The government's worst omission, however, is economic. In depressed south Tehran there is less talk of civil society than of unemployment (independently estimated to affect 15 percent of the workforce) and inflation (which hovers around 25 percent). The economy is not providing enough jobs to accommodate the 800,000-odd Iranians who enter the workforce each year. As a result, according to one foreign economist, more than 50 percent of Iranian university graduates cannot find a job.

The problem has been compounded by confusion over Khatami's economic convictions. He has declared that economic reforms are contingent on political change, but no one knows what he means by economic reforms. Many of his advisers wish to preserve the state's dominance over the economy, and the President himself has said nothing to suggest that he is drawn to free markets. As a result, few independent analysts are inclined to believe recent government promises to cut inflation and unemployment, to reduce Iran's dependence on oil revenues (which currently account for some 85 percent of Iran's hard-currency earnings), and to privatize 30 percent of the economy.

In spite of this gloom, few of the Iranians who helped elect Khatami in 1997 show signs of missing the austere certainties of conservative rule. While some experts predict that many citizens will not vote in February, huge and exuberant crowds greet the President wherever he goes. In February, say reformers, the momentum of the parliamentary election campaign will carry reform-minded Iranians to the polling stations.

There are good reasons to support such a view. Although their record in government has been mixed,. Khatami and his supporters demonstrably occupy the center of Iranian politics. Furthermore, they promise to mount a strong defense of their biggest achievement, which was summed up by the same man in Kelardasht who had been criticizing the practical outcome of February's municipal elections. When I asked whether life under reformist rule had changed, he replied, "Before Khatami, we would have been unable to have this conversation."

So far, the Iranian taste for debate has had one beneficiary: Khatami himself. Conservative strong-arm tactics, combined with the President's own precarious position, have persuaded his supporters to exercise restraint. This, however, will only remain the case as long as Iranians perceive the *dovom Khurdadis*, in or out of government, as an embattled opposition. If pro-reform candidates gain control of parliament next February, they may demand that a wider range of issues be debated. This may not be in Khatami's interest. An expanded debate would oblige Khatami and his circle to confront the repressed heterodoxy inside their own movement. On the few occasions that Khatami and his close allies had to do this, as in the aftermath of this summer's student arrests, they have taken defensive positions, which have alienated their less patient supporters. In October, too, Mohajerani, that staunch advocate of freedom of expression, was forced to concede that if they were found to have insulted the twelfth imam on purpose, the student playwrights should be "punished." The minister insists that the liberty he and the President speak of is "in complete accord with Islam." Nevertheless, they look uneasy when this notion is put to the test.

If reform-minded candidates win in February, they are likely to be tested further. As Iran's foreign policy becomes more open, for instance, Western-influenced arguments about human rights will be increasingly heard. At present, airing such arguments can earn you a jail sentence or worse. Does the President's support for "freedom to oppose" include those who demand greater liberties than those he himself seeks? What if the reformers were to demand that religiously sanctioned laws that discriminate against women be annulled; that Iran's charitable institutions be privatized; and that the constitutional basis of the Islamic Republic be scrutinized?

It is possible that these questions will never get asked. Iran's progress toward greater openness is not assured. If Iranian conservatives wanted to stop progress toward reform they would have to take harsh measures against ordinary Iranians, but they are still capable of this. It is possible that the fragile détente between the President and the Supreme Leader could break down, and pragmatic conservatism could give way to old-fashioned repression. The cause of reform could suffer setbacks, sidelining Khatami; it might reemerge in new, and perhaps more radical, forms.

That would be tragic, since Mohammad Khatami represents most of his people very well. His goal—a version of Islamic government answering to both a yearning for freedom and an allegiance to God—seems to be theirs.

2

BOOM IN QOM

May 2002

THE SHIA SEMINARY town of Qom, seventy-five miles south of Tehran, is bleak and set in semidesert, with a dried-up river going through it. It has few orchards; it is not renowned for any fruit or pickle. Most of the vegetables you find here have traveled long distances. The townspeople produce a sickly caramel, sometimes embedded with shards of pistachio, called *sohan*. To escape the soporific effects of the heat the seminarians work in subterranean libraries. In the case of bachelor scholars, widows and impoverished women attend to their physical needs. Some people have likened Qom to Oxford or Cambridge, for the seminarians wear black gowns and inhabit cells inside brick-built colleges that look in on themselves. There, the resemblance ends. Never in English history were the universities as mighty as the seminaries of Qom are today.

Qom rose to prominence as a modern seminary town after Britain seized what is now Iraq from the Ottomans at the end of World War I. When the clerics of Najaf, an important Shia shrine town in southern Iraq, incited revolt against the British, they were expelled; some of these clerics ended up in Qom, which a prominent ayatollah was reviving as a center of religious learning. Qom's development was still not assured; from 1925, the Shah of Iran, Reza Pahlavi, regarded Islam in general and clerics in particular as hindrances to his efforts to modernize Iran. He introduced military service for some clerics and banned all but the senior clergy from wearing the traditional gown and turban. He came to Qom to horsewhip a senior ayatollah who had criticized the Queen's immodest mode of dress.

Clerical resentment of the monarchy increased under Reza's son, Mohammad Reza, but the theologians of Qom were divided on whether Islam required that they actively oppose tyranny or concentrate on their primary duty: studying Islamic law and transmitting it to believers. In the 1960s, the activists came under the influence of Ayatollah Ruhollah Khomeini; and in 1979, after the Shah fled and Khomeini returned from exile to set up the modern world's only clerical state, Tehran was its capital but Qom was its heart.

Since then, Qom has been booming. The clerical population has risen from around 25,000 to more than 45,000, and the nonclerical population has more than tripled, to about 700,000. It is very hard to calculate the vast sums of money that flow, in the forms of alms and Islamic taxes, to Qom's ten senior ayatollahs—called "Objects of Emulation" because their fellow clerics have pronounced them qualified to act as models whose behavior and rulings laymen and lesser clerics can follow. (Every believer is free to choose the "Object of Emulation" he or she admires most, whether they are inside or outside Iran.) These donations, along with state help for favored institutions, have pushed up the number of seminary schools in Qom to fifty-odd, and the number of research institutes and libraries to around 250. These institutions produce hundreds of books and journals every year, and they use the Internet to disseminate and publicize their findings on subjects like Islamic law and history, philosophy, and political economy. The municipal council is buying and destroying buildings that stand in the path of a grand boulevard that has been projected to lead from the shrine of the sister of one of Shiism's twelve imams to a grand modern mosque five kilometers away.[1]

Shortly before the revolution, a highway was laid between Qom and Tehran, making it easy for politicians and bureaucrats to go back and forth; if you have a reckless driver, the trip from south Tehran will take you barely an hour. This spring, Syria's foreign minister, on a visit to Iran, made an unpublicized nocturnal trip to Qom; he wanted clerical support for his request, prompted by the US and Lebanon, that Iran downgrade its relations with Hezbollah. (He got an ambiguous answer.) The Intelligence Ministry is said to have consulted clerics in Qom on the wisdom of exploring better relations with the US. (Here, too, the response was vague; Bush, who included Iran in the "axis of evil," has alarmed many clerics, but some have warned against giving the impression that Iran is buckling under pressure.) If the US brings down Saddam Hussein, the thousands of Iraqi clerics currently in exile in Qom will have a strong influence on their country's future.

The word "Qom" has come to stand for the nationwide clerical establishment, since other seminary towns are subservient to it; and the influence of Qom is particularly evident at the center of power in Tehran. Iran's Supreme Leader, its president, parliament speaker, and top judge are clerics. So are both the head and half the members of the twelve-man Council of Guardians, the powerful monitoring group whose clerical members are appointed by the Supreme Leader; it acts, in effect, as the upper house of parliament and can annul legislative acts. A significant minority of the thirty-eight members of the Expediency Council, appointed by the Supreme Leader to resolve disputes between parliament and the Council of Guardians, are clerics. The

---

1. The twelve imams were all male descendants of the Prophet, through Ali, the Prophet's nephew and son-in-law. Shias believe that the imams were entrusted the leadership of the Islamic community, and that the twelfth of them, who disappeared in 874, would later miraculously return to establish an era of divine justice and truth.

Assembly of Experts, which chooses, appraises, and can, in theory, dismiss the Supreme Leader, is made up of eighty-six clerics who have been elected by universal suffrage—but only after candidates first have been vetted by the Council of Guardians. Although most provincial governors are not clerics, in each province the assent of the Supreme Leader's representative, invariably a cleric, is required for most of the important decisions he makes. The same is true of the heads of universities.

Lower down, clerical dominance is less institutionalized, but nonetheless striking. The thousands of seminarians who leave Qom after completing the six years of study that generally qualify them to wear the clerical gown and turban have a head start in the race for jobs in the bureaucracy. Their children tend to be granted places at the best schools. If they are suspected of breaking the law, they are tried by other clerics, usually behind closed doors. In some parts of the government and bureaucracy, such as the judiciary, an old-boy network favors appointments from particular seminaries. The senior echelons of the intelligence ministry and judiciary contain many graduates from Qom's Haqani seminary.

Although the revolution has made the clerical calling more powerful and more privileged, not all clerics have been happy about this. Far from bringing about the end of the old debate over clerical involvement in politics, Khomeini's revolution intensified it. At the revolution's outset, most of the half-dozen "Objects of Emulation" who were living in Iran and Iraq either opposed the principle of clerical rule or remained silent about it. Qom's subsequent resistance to attempts to impose on it a uniform reading of political Islam has much to do with the pluralistic tradition of the seminary. Seminarians are free to join the study circles of the "master" they most admire. He can teach pretty much what he wants, provided he does not disseminate contentious views outside the seminary.

For the past decade, the prestige of the clerics among most Iranians has been falling. This is clearly illustrated by the decline in clerical representation in parliament. In the first parliament after the revolution, clerics made up 51 percent of the total number of deputies. They now make up 12 percent. In the early 1980s, clerics were generally treated with elaborate courtesy. Nowadays, clerics are sometimes insulted by schoolchildren and taxi drivers, and they quite often put on normal clothes when venturing outside Qom. Some are willing to give up the official privileges that they believe cause the public to resent them. I talked in Qom to clerics who said there was now increasing sympathy for Abdolkarim Soroush, a brilliant lay theologian and philosopher who argues that religion must sever its links with worldly power if it is to retain its authority. Far from improving the status of the clergy, these clerics say, involvement in government has debased it.

A small but important part of George Bush's "axis of evil" speech seemed aimed at these clerics. In Tehran, people thought it was crass of the US president to lump Iran together with Saddam Hussein's Iraq; they remember when America sided with Saddam during the Iran–Iraq War of the 1980s. Some professed astonishment at Bush's suggestion that Iran sponsors terrorism and is trying to produce weapons of mass destruction. In Qom, however, reactions were more concerned with the US president's observation that "an unelected few repress the Iranian people's hope for freedom." Although Bush was referring to Iran's malfunctioning democracy in general, his comments recalled to many people the continuing influence of the Ayatollah Khomeini and particularly the political sectarianism that Khomeini used to entrench clerical rule: the *velayat-e-faquih*," or "the guardianship of the jurist."

As early as the late 1960s, Khomeini was putting forward a novel interpretation of Shia doctrine, defending a rudimentary version of the kind of religious government he eventually installed. Using deductive reasoning and a tendentious interpretation of the sayings attributed to the Prophet and the twelve imams, Khomeini argued that religious government should not be allowed to lapse simply because there were no imams to provide it. Instead, he said, Shiism's leading clerics, the senior scholars of Islamic law, should assume judicial and executive authority, pending the return of the twelfth imam. The "guardianship of the jurist" proposed by Khomeini can be understood as an expansion of the "guardianship" that Islam proposes in the case of orphaned minors, with the whole Islamic community in the role of orphan and the ruling jurist in the role of the adoptive parent. On his return from exile, following the Shah's flight in 1979, Khomeini said he was invoking "the guardianship that I have from the holy lawgiver [the Prophet]" to appoint an interim government. He announced that opposition to this government would be "blasphemy."

Khomeini, many people believe, may have abhorred electoral democracy, but he was forced to compromise with nonclerical Islamists who had been influenced by modern democratic notions. According to Daniel Brumberg, the author of a meticulous examination of Khomeini's legacy,[2] the 1979 constitution, which turned Iran from a monarchy into an "Islamic republic," was "an ideological mishmash...probably unmatched in the history of constitutionalism." It provided for the direct election of a president and a parliament, and separated the legislative, judicial, and executive branches. But it made all officials answerable to the appointed Supreme Leader and made no clear provision for the settlement of disputes between the elected lower house of parliament and the appointed upper house, the Council of Guardians. The constitution was marred by what Brumberg describes as a "chaotic division of powers" between different institutions and organs of government, and it was silent on how these competing institutions should coexist. According to some articles of the

---

2. *Reinventing Khomeini: The Struggle for Reform in Iran* (University of Chicago Press, 2001).

constitution, sovereignty belonged to God; but the principle of holding elections suggested a recognition of popular sovereignty as well. Khomeini dominated the patchwork government of Iran until his death in 1989. He alone had the theological expertise, political flair, and popularity that he himself had laid down as criteria for Islamic leadership. Sometimes contemptuous of Western-style elections, he could claim that he had a popular mandate, illustrated by the vast numbers of people who greeted and visited him after he returned from exile. This reminds Baqer Moin, his excellent biographer, of a pledge of allegiance.[3] Khomeini's appeal was exploited by his entourage. They attributed to him a pseudo-divinity that, in turn, endowed his pronouncements with binding authority, allowing him to interfere in public life wherever he wanted. Khomeini was able slowly to discredit a very senior dissident ayatollah, Kazem Shariatmadari, even though Shariatmadari's theological standing was equal to his own. A word from Khomeini obliged the Council of Guardians to lift their veto on any law he favored. His "decree" led to the execution, without due process, of thousands of political prisoners.

It was clear that the aura of authority surrounding the guardianship of the jurist would diminish with his passing. Already in 1988, the creation of the Expediency Council had relieved future Supreme Leaders of the burden of adjudicating disputes between parliament and the Council of Guardians. (On May 26, for example, the Expediency Council ended a long process of mediation between parliament and the Council of Guardians on a foreign investment bill, which has now become law.) A few weeks before Khomeini died, a special assembly convened at his behest removed the constitutional stipulation that the Supreme Leader had to be a theologian of the highest rank, i.e., an Object of Emulation. From now on, hundreds of lesser clerics were theoretically eligible to be the Supreme Leader, provided

---

3. Baqer Moin, *Khomeini: Life of the Ayatollah* (I. B. Tauris, 1999).

they had the necessary piety, courage, and "good managerial skills." The requirement of popular recognition and approval—the pledge of allegiance, as it were—was dropped as a criterion. Having been the preserve of a revered divine whom millions believed to be an intermediary between themselves and God, the guardianship of the jurist could now be conferred on a middle-ranking theologian who had much less popular support.

The changes were designed to prepare the way for the appointment of Ali Khamenei, the president, as Khomeini's successor. Barely two months before he died, Khomeini had dismissed Ayatollah Hossein-Ali Montazeri, the well-known and much-respected cleric whom he had earlier designated as his successor. Apparently Khomeini felt that Montazeri was too independent in his thinking and too pluralistic in his outlook. Many in Qom were dismayed by Ali Khamenei's appointment. Although he was known to be an experienced politician and to have shared many of Khomeini's views, he was only in the upper-middle rank of clerics and had been hastily named an ayatollah. Many Iranians were troubled by the idea that a man they had elected to the mundane office of the presidency, knowing they could oust him, had become the unchallengeable vice-regent of God.

The death of Khomeini would have been a good time to trim the Supreme Leader's powers and require that he be elected. But Khomeini's eleventh-hour constitutional amendments pointed the other way; the revised constitution increased the Supreme Leader's formal powers, and described his authority, with an explicitness absent from the original, as "absolute." Furthermore, Khomeini, in some of his last statements, implied that the Supreme Leader could make any decision he considered to be in "the interests of Islam and the country." In the eyes of some, this gave him the authority to create divine injunctions.

Ayatollah Montazeri's house in Qom is a few hundred yards from the city's shrine, but he hasn't visited the shrine for years. He is not allowed to see people, except his family, and cannot leave home except in an emergency. His allies talk to him on the telephone; they can also ring the front doorbell and chat with him over the intercom. Through these contacts, Montazeri keeps abreast of current theological debates as well as rulings that have been issued by other senior clerics and the political situation in Tehran. He issues his own rulings on religious matters, and replies to theological questions posed by his followers, whether through the Internet or through cassettes that are distributed by his sons. Last year, he posted a long memoir on the Internet. It was immediately denounced by the conservative establishment, and around a dozen of his supporters were arrested for helping him prepare it.

Montazeri is a ruddy-faced man with the accent of his native Najafabad. His modesty is such that if you get into casual conversation with him, you might mistake him for an itinerant preacher. In fact, Montazeri is an Object of Emulation who is acknowledged to be brilliant, even by those who disapprove of him; as a young seminarian, he was well known for his ability to recall, word for word, lectures that he had heard weeks before. He talks bluntly, lives plainly, and equates Islam with social justice. Not for him is the political plotting for which some other clerics are known. Before his social life was restricted, he would happily share his bread and cheese with, say, a farmer who had come from Najafabad to complain about a venal official. Once the farmer had gone, Montazeri would send off an angry letter to the official's superior.

This, at least, is the portrait drawn by his supporters. It is meant to counter the derogatory claims of some of his peers, particularly the *Book of Pain*, which was written by Ahmad Khomeini, the Ayatollah Khomeini's now deceased son, after Montazeri's dismissal by his father.[4] According to Ahmad, Montazeri's stubbornness and naiveté

---

4. Ahmad Khomeini, *Ranj-nameh* (Book of Pain) (Tehran, 1989).

were his downfall. At the height of the Iran–Iraq War, he argued for reconciliation with internal enemies, and this was said to have benefited counterrevolutionary groups like the People's Mujahideen, called "the Hypocrites" by the followers of the Ayatollah Khomeini. "My intention in this letter," wrote Ahmad, "is not—God forbid!—to suggest that you accepted the ideas and ideology of Hypocrites and Liberals." Of course, Ahmad wanted to suggest just that.

By the standards of revolutionary Iran, Montazeri is considered a democrat. That wasn't always the case. In the days following the revolution, he argued that Shia Islam should be named the state religion, despite Iran's large Sunni minority. He had an important part in making the principle of the guardianship of the jurist part of the constitution—which he demanded be "far removed from every Western principle," and he did not defend Ayatollah Shariatmadari when Khomeini humiliated him for criticizing the institution of the guardianship of the jurist. Before his dismissal, his supporters intimidated people with the slogan "Opposition to Montazeri is opposition to God." One of them, Mehdi Hashemi, upset officials by maintaining his own connections with the Lebanese Hezbollah and the Afghan Mujahideen. In 1986, Hashemi disclosed secret efforts by Akbar Hashemi Rafsanjani, who was running Iran's war effort against Iraq, to buy arms from Iran's sworn enemy, the US, through the good offices of a second enemy, Israel. Rafsanjani got his revenge, and Hashemi was executed.

For all that, one can find a strain of pluralism and compassion running through Montazeri's career. He sent private letters to Khomeini in 1988, protesting the summary execution of thousands of imprisoned supporters of the People's Mujahideen. His criticism of Rafsanjani for prolonging the war seems to have arisen from genuine anger at the appalling loss of life. As Khomeini's dauphin, he tried to pierce the wall that Khomeini's possessive entourage had erected around him. According to Gholam-Hossein Nadi, a fellow cleric and long-standing ally, "other people would go before Khomeini and flatter him." Montazeri, on the other hand, "told the truth and passed on the complaints of the people."

Private complaint could perhaps be tolerated, but Montazeri went public after the end of the war with Iraq, criticizing the regime's "mismanagement" and "the denial of people's rights." There is, he said, "a great distance between what we have promised and what we have achieved." He accepted his dismissal with grace, perhaps relief, but it came as a shock to people who associated him with revolutionary ideals. During the early and mid-1990s, Rafsanjani, who had succeeded Khamenei as president, carried out economic reforms apparently designed to benefit people who were already privileged. At the same time, the politically influential people around Khamenei were putting slavish emphasis on the Supreme Leader's "absolute" authority.

In 1997, Mohammad Khatami, a cleric advocating increased democracy, was elected president by a large majority. Word got around that the Supreme Leader, who was said to have lent veiled support to Khatami's conservative rival during the campaign, was imposing his influence on the composition of the new government. At the same time, some clerics were suggesting that Khamenei be declared an Object of Emulation. Invoking his authority as author of the 1979 constitution, Montazeri, in a speech that created a sensation, asserted that the Supreme Leader's duty was not "to interfere in everything" but "to oversee the country." He attacked Iran's "monarchical setup." He openly suggested that Khamenei was unqualified to be an Object of Emulation, and unqualified to be Supreme Leader as well.

The speech confirmed Montazeri's status as the senior theological advocate of democracy within the Islamic Republic. At the same time, it ruined him politically; his private college in Qom was closed, his office ransacked, and he was put under house arrest. With one exception, Montazeri's fellow Objects of Emulation were too timid to defend him. His enforced isolation ended hopes that he and Khatami might join forces; the elected president could hardly come out in support of the man who had been attacked and dismissed from public life by the Supreme Leader.

The cause of reform suffered as a result. Montazeri's disgrace made it impossible for reformers in Tehran to call on him for support in their struggle with the Council of Guardians, which routinely humiliates them by disqualifying Khatami supporters from seeking office, and by vetoing all legislation that would increase democracy or protect rights. Montazeri would have made a useful ally in the continuous confrontations between Khatami's supporters and the judges who have jailed scores of reformists, including editors, writers, economists, and mayors, among others; virtually all of the top judges are anti-reform clerics and all of them Montazeri's theological inferiors. If Montazeri had been free to argue with Khamenei in 2000, he might have tried to dissuade him from ordering the closing of more than a dozen reform-minded publications, and from suppressing parliamentary discussion of plans to make the press freer.

In April 2002, Ali-Reza Amini, a conservative cleric in Qom, told me dryly that some of the reformers who argue today for a referendum on limiting the Supreme Leader's powers were, in Khomeini's time, convinced of the Supreme Leader's absolute authority. Amini's comment reminded me of a nagging question that occurs to me as I observe some of Iran's reformers. Are they driven by a desire to reduce the power of the Supreme Leader, or are they mainly concerned to limit the power of Ali Khamenei?

For several weeks after Bush's "axis of evil" speech, Iran was overcome by an irrational fear of imminent US attack. People talked of little else. There was renewed debate about the merits of reopening relations with the US. (This has now ended, amid claims by reformers that secret contacts with US officials had been initiated by influential members of the regime, without the government's knowledge.) In the

face of the external threat, a temporary understanding was reached
between reformers and conservatives. Fewer newspapers were closed.
Some jailed reformers—including all but one of Montazeri's imprisoned allies—were set free. It was said that the head of the clergy court
had promised Montazeri that he would regain his freedom if only he
would stop issuing controversial statements.

The immediate fear has passed. Montazeri is still under house
arrest. (He may have upset conservatives with a statement that was
published in newspapers on April 22, in which he implicitly dissoci-
ated himself from Khamenei's insistence that Israel be eliminated and
endorsed the coexistence of Palestinian and Israeli states.) Reform-
minded newspapers are now being closed down again. Despite a constitutional clause that guarantees parliamentary immunity, a senior
deputy in parliament who had been demanding more press freedom,
among other reforms, has been sentenced to a six months in prison.
Playing chicken with the judge, he has refused to appeal his sentence.

Bush's shadow remains. Unease over his intentions, and the politicians' calculations of gain that may result from provoking or mollify-
ing him, will complicate next year's parliamentary elections—which
the Council of Guardians might easily spoil by disqualifying scores of
sitting members. Uncertainty about US policy will complicate the
search, already beginning, for a suitable reform candidate to replace
Khatami, who must step down after his second term ends in three
years. It may lend urgency to the underlying national debate about
the power of unelected clerics who have defied the expressed will of
the voters.

When I was in Qom this spring, a friend there observed that it is
hard to find a conservative cleric who hasn't changed his views on the
legitimacy of the guardianship of the jurist. To one degree or another
they all now felt the office should change so as to reflect a society that
is seeking a less paternalistic sort of government. According to Sadeq
Haqiqat, a reform-minded cleric, "as democratic thoughts gain ground,

it's impossible" for the religious authorities to resist efforts to modify the principle of the guardianship of the jurist. "It must evolve." Even conservatives like Ali-Reza Amini agree it can change. He seems exasperated, furthermore, by the obstructionism of the Council of Guardians; "its political coloring," he says, "has weakened the guardianship of the jurist."

Four years ago, a friend of Haqiqat's, Mohsen Kadivar, published a book in Iran, *Government of the Guardian*, that opened new perspectives in the debate over theologically based power.[5] Kadivar examined the ten sayings attributed to the Prophet and to the imams that are commonly presented as documentary evidence for the necessity of clerical rule. According to Kadivar, a well-regarded scholar, eight of these sayings may not be authentic. Even the two sayings he considers "authoritative" cannot, he argues, be used to justify the clerics' assumption of political power. Rather, they confer on jurists the responsibility to "propagate, publicize, and teach Islamic rulings.... There is no authoritative evidence for the absolute guardianship of the appointed jurist."

It said something for the openness of Iranian society that Kadivar's book could be published. Many Iranians agree that the guardianship must change. And yet it does not. "In order to change," Ali-Reza Amini says, "there needs to be consensus, and there is no consensus." As much as conflicting ideas, the problem comes down to people who loathe one another; their personal hatred precludes the emergence of workable compromises. The recent war in Afghanistan provided an example of the current internal political conflict. The fall of the Taliban was openly celebrated throughout Iran. Khatami's government cooperated with the US-led coalition, providing it with intelligence and also providing considerable help to the Northern Alliance; it is now enthusiastically trying to help in Afghanistan's reconstruction.

---

5. Mohsen Kadivar, *Hokumat-e Velayi* (Government of the Guardian) (Nashrani, 1998).

Its efforts, however, were undermined by a small number of hard-line conservatives who apparently helped al-Qaeda and tried to undermine Hamid Karzai's government in Kabul.

In this poisonous atmosphere, it is hard to imagine that the reformers can persuade the conservatives to give up power voluntarily. A popular explosion remains a distant prospect; most people do not want another revolution, and the police and revolutionary guard are disciplined and loyal. Unless the reformers can muster allies in the conservative establishment, or find new ways to bring public pressure on it, Iran seems fated to an unyielding form of Islamic rule.

3

THE LONELINESS OF
THE SUPREME LEADER

December 2002

ON NOVEMBER 22, 2002, I was a guest at a barracks of the Islamic militia (officially called the Basij, or the Mobilization of the Oppressed) in a suburb of Tehran. Some thirty militiamen in their late teens and early twenties had gathered to celebrate the birthday of Ali Ibn-Abu Taleb, the Prophet's nephew and son-in-law, the first imam of Shia Islam. Before the ceremony started, a middle-aged man entered the room, holding a copy of *Keyhan*, the main newspaper of the conservative establishment. From the polite greetings he received and the superior manner of his responses, it was clear that he was a figure of authority. Without noticing me, the only foreigner in the room, he sat on the floor, cross-legged, and began speaking.

At the time, Iran's politics had been convulsed by nationwide student demonstrations protesting against the death sentence that had been given to a freethinking academic, Hashem Aghajari, for apostasy. The demonstrations—which began the day after Aghajari's sentence was made public, on November 6—were supported by the reformist government of President Mohammad Khatami, and were mostly confined to university campuses. Although none of the demonstrations is thought to have attracted more than five thousand participants, they were Iran's most serious protests since 1999, when the suppression of riots at Tehran University left one student dead. Alarmed by the scope of the current demonstrations, the Supreme Leader, Aya-tollah Ali Khamenei, ordered a review of the verdict against Aghajari, but he issued a warning as well. If trouble continued, he would not hesitate to deploy "popular forces." He was partly referring to the Ansar Hezbollah, a fellowship of Islamic thugs who take orders from senior conservatives. But most of the regime's "popular forces" are members of the Islamic militia, such as the young men I was visiting.

In this modest Tehran suburb, Khamenei's words hung in the air. The speaker assured the militiamen that the Islamic Republic faced mortal danger. They should not, he urged, suppose that the campus demonstrations were spontaneous expressions of dissent; they had been meticulously planned by Iran's enemy, America. America's aims, he said, were to make Iran seem divided and, eventually, to bring down the Islamic regime. "Do you think," he asked rhetorically, "that America intends to stop after it has dealt with Iraq? Do you think that's the sum of George Bush's ambitions for the region?"

Supported by America, he said, Israel also posed an immediate danger. Its ambition was to expand as far as the Euphrates, putting it on Iran's doorstep. Everyone knew, he said, that over the years Iran had supported the oppressed Palestinians and opposed Israel. In a week's time, on Jerusalem Day, which falls on the last Friday in Rama-dan, and was used by the late Ayatollah Khomeini as a means of showing Iran's solidarity with the Palestinians, it was vital that Irani-ans exhibit their resolve.

"This Jerusalem Day," he went on, "must be different from other Jerusalem Days." Any member of the militia who did not participate in the state-sponsored marches, he said, would be guilty of "the great-est betrayal of Islam." The Americans and their lackeys, the British, would be observing the marches; they would seize on signs of falter-ing zeal. Unless Iran made an impressive show of unity and strength, he concluded, "we might as well recite the *fateheh* [prayer for the dead] over the corpse of the Islamic Republic."

The following day, Khamenei delivered the sermon during Friday prayers at Tehran University. He castigated the Americans for coveting the material wealth of the Islamic world, and accused them of supporting the "unprecedented violence" being inflicted by Israel on the Palestinians. In an oblique reference to the protesting students, he declared that anyone who accused the Islamic Republic of despotism was either "the agent of the enemy, or its dupe." Another part of the sermon seemed to have nothing to do with America or the students, although in fact it was a reply to both. Khamenei recalled the thousands of Iranians who "had been persecuted and whipped" by the Shah's "diabolical regime." They had not endured these persecutions, he said, "in order to bring about Western democracy." Then, referring to the Iran–Iraq War of the 1980s, he said, "Those mothers who swelled with pride at the sacrifices they made—at losing two or three sons, a son-in-law, a husband—they weren't pursuing Western democracy." "Back then," the Supreme Leader continued, "the people longed for spiritual development and material welfare under the shelter of Islam, and for the boon of the sovereignty of Islamic law. Now, too, that remains the case."

If Khamenei's office or other institutions under his control have based their rhetoric on opinion polls, their findings have been kept from the public. In fact, the conservative establishment seems terrified by any attempt to find out what Iranians actually want, to judge by the trial that began in December of Behrouz Geranpayeh, Hossein-Ali Ghazian, and Abbas Abdi, all of them pollsters and public opinion researchers. The public prosecutor accused Ghazian, who runs a polling institute with Abdi, of having contacts with "agents associated with foreign intelligence and security services." He told the court that Geranpayeh, who runs another polling organization, had given "a false picture of public opinion," sold information to foreigners, and been in contact with "counterrevolutionaries." According to the editor of *Keyhan*, the authorities had "unearthed the ultimate base of American espionage, and the operations center for a fifth column."

Public prosecutors hope to use classified documents, allegedly found in one of the polling institutes, to implicate other reformists in the affair. Another explanation for the trial may be that the public opinion surveys of the two polling institutes were unpalatable to conservatives, particularly their findings that 74 percent of people living in Tehran favor the restoration of official dialogue with the US, and that 64 percent want full bilateral relations. (Geranpayeh had also polled people in Tehran on their favorite leaders, and found that President Khatami came near the top of the list, with conservative leaders trailing far behind.) It is possible that Abdi, who is an influential political strategist, is being punished for publicly urging reformists to refuse to cooperate with the authorities as a means of pressuring conservative institutions to give up some of their power. As an indication of conservative thinking, the most enlightening part of the charge sheet was its reference to the crime, allegedly committed by one of the polling institutes, of gathering "precise and comprehensive data about the views [and] beliefs of people across the country."

There is a widespread belief that the judiciary will arrest reformists in parliament if they decide to carry out their long-standing threat to call for a referendum on the arbitrary powers of the senior conservative clerics. The sole empirical evidence available for the Supreme Leader's account of Iranians' desires may be the referendum held a few weeks after the 1979 revolution which asked, "Should Iran be an Islamic Republic?" More than 98 percent of the replies were positive. But Iran has changed a lot since then.

Taken together, the Supreme Leader's sermon and the pep talk given to the militiamen are revealing. The conservatives have rarely felt so embattled; they blame America—along with Israel and Britain —for their recent vulnerability. Moreover, they have identified the ideology that threatens them. It is not the nostalgic monarchism that animates many Iranian exiles who are drawn to Reza Pahlavi, the elder son of the late Shah, who is living in the US. Nor is it the Islamic-leftist movement that was popular as well as murderous in the early years of the Islamic regime. It is something else, inchoate but ominously associated with the enemy: liberal democracy.

At present, there are few declared liberal democrats in parliament or among the ministers and bureaucrats who make up Khatami's reform movement. Most of the reformists continue to argue for the "Islamic democracy" that Khatami has been trying, ineffectively, to install since he became president five years ago. Khatami's followers present Islamic democracy as a third way—between religious dictatorship, which is what Iran increasingly resembles, and secular democracy, which it has never known. Illegal arrests and the suppression of free speech; the disqualification of reformist candidates for office by the powerful Council of Guardians, half of its members appointed by the Supreme Leader; and the wholesale spiking of legislation by the same body—all of these stem, they claim, from a despotic and willful misinterpretation of the constitution established under the Ayatollah Khomeini in 1979 and later amended, not the constitution itself.

But Khatami's "Islamic democracy" seems to be running out of steam. This isn't because it cannot work—that hasn't been proved either way. It is because the Islamic conservative leadership hasn't given it a chance to work. Parliament's reformist majority is making a final effort to save Islamic democracy by working to ratify two legislative bills that were put forward by Khatami. The first of these would, in theory, allow him to end such constitutional violations as the trial without jury of political prisoners and the arbitrary vetoing of legislation by the Council of Guardians. The second would curtail the Council of Guardians' power to disqualify reformist candidates from public office. (The council, it is widely believed, intends to abuse this privilege before the next parliamentary election, scheduled for 2004.) Conservative deputies have in effect been filibustering the legislation by proposing hundreds of amendments to it; but Mustafa

Tajzadeh, a prominent reformist and former senior government official, expects that parliament will pass both bills by the end of April.

It seems unlikely, however, that the bills will be ratified by the
Council of Guardians, and then implemented. If they are, this would
signal a profound shift in Iran's politics, and President Khatami's
prestige would rise. If the bills are vetoed, or their implementation is
obstructed, Islamic democracy will be further enfeebled. Khatami, his
allies insist, would submit his resignation. (He would probably be
accompanied by members of the cabinet, and perhaps by some parliamentary deputies.) Whether or not the Supreme Leader accepts
Khatami's resignation, Iran could fall into political crisis.[1]

Khatami, because he has twice been overwhelmingly elected to
office, represents the Islamic Republic's last claim to popular legitimacy. His friendships with European leaders might have a moderat-
ing effect on George Bush, who has been urged by Ariel Sharon to
take aggressive measures against Iran, once Iraq is dealt with. Anything other than outright victory for Khatami would signal his political eclipse, and a huge setback for Islamic democracy. The President's
former supporters would have to search for new ways of expressing
their aspirations; many will probably turn toward Western models.

Earlier this year, Akbar Ganji, a courageous journalist who was
jailed in 2000, ostensibly for attending a controversial conference
abroad, posted his "Manifesto for Republicans" on the Internet. Ganji
used to be an Islamic democrat. But in his recent manifesto, which he
wrote behind bars, he accused many reformists of using democratic
jargon to disguise their essentially authoritarian tendencies. He con-
tradicted the preeminent reformist philosopher Abdolkarim Soroush,
who has argued that religious government, if it is authentic, cannot be
anything but democratic. The only way to avoid conflict between

---

1. *As expected, both bills were vetoed by the Council of Guardians, but Khatami did not
resign. [Added 2007]*

democracy and religious law, Ganji maintained, is for religion "to retreat from the domain of the state, into the private sphere." He called for a referendum on a new, democratic constitution.

Many of Ganji's demands—as well as his impudent lampooning of the Supreme Leader—were echoed during last month's protests. "We students," Akbar Attri, a leader of Iran's biggest student body, the Office to Foster Unity, told me, "gave up our hopes in Khatami a long time ago. Iran has mixed religion and democracy, and found that it doesn't work." According to Abdullah Momeni, a colleague of Attri's, there is a qualitative difference between the student actions and the Khatami government's own protests in the Aghajari affair. "The government," he told me, "protested against the severity of the sentence against Aghajari. We were opposing the fact that someone can be tried for apostasy."

In a recent issue of *Aftab* ("Sun"), a monthly magazine, Ali-Reza Alavi Tabar, a prominent progressive and a professional colleague of Ghazian's and Abdi's, outlines three stages on the road to full democracy. Iran, he writes, hasn't reached the first of these, which would be to force conservative leaders to be more accountable by accepting critical scrutiny of activities and institutions over which they enjoy absolute control, like broadcasting and the powerful religious foundations. The second stage, according to Alavi Tabar, would be to establish a more democratic interpretation of the existing constitution. This is, in fact, the effect that Khatami hopes his two bills will have. The final stage would be more radical. It would involve building a consensus to change the constitution, and to substitute a new definition of government that would either sharply diminish the influence of religious authority or establish a secular democracy. If this were done, he makes clear, the institution of the Supreme Leader, set up by the Ayatollah Khomeini, would not survive.

At present the liberals who want democracy unrestricted by Islamic law and the Islamic democrats need each other. During the recent protests, Khatami's education minister put pressure on the university authorities to allow campus demonstrations, and he made sure that uniformed policemen protected students from physical attack by hezbollahis, and from arrest and torture at the hands of plainclothes members of Iran's myriad intelligence organizations. Student leaders were unhappy when the Khatami government reacted to Khamenei's order to review the death sentence of Hashem Aghajari by withdrawing its support for the protests; but they delayed further demonstrations until December 7, which is National Student Day. The few students who have been arrested since then, during revived on-campus demonstrations, are now in the hands of the Intelligence Ministry, which is dominated by reformists. They seem to have been arrested for breaking the peace, not for political crimes, and there have been no allegations of torture or mistreatment.

Khatami is defending people who are more radical than he is. At the height of the unrest, the National Security Council—which he chairs but which contains many leading conservatives—issued an order that forbade the arrest of prominent student activists. The edict was signed by the Supreme Leader, but was soon violated. On November 25, four student leaders, including Attri and Momeni, were arrested by agents of the Revolutionary Court, the arm of the judiciary that deals with political offenses and alleged crimes against national security, and is known for the harshness of its sentences. Khatami was furious. He ordered the students' immediate release, and was, surprisingly to some, obeyed. He then refused to consider the demand of a senior military official that some 140 student activists—who had been identified as subversives—be arrested.

The much-respected reformist Mustafa Tajzadeh told me that this was a triumph for the students. Following the 1999 disturbances, he points out, students were tortured and condemned to long jail sentences. This time, none of the four arrested students complained of physical mistreatment. The case against them now looks as if it has been shelved; the student movement is intact, and its most important leaders are free. This is surely owing to Khatami and the support—

however unwilling—that he is getting from Khamenei and some of his fellow conservatives who are anxious to avoid chaos.

Not all conservatives are as pragmatic as the Supreme Leader, however. According to Tajzadeh, ultra-hard-liners in the judiciary, the Intelligence Ministry, and the security forces—"a cancerous tumor" on the country—are searching for an excuse to launch a coup d'état against the President, in the hope of installing a strong dictatorship. They oppose the secret negotiations that are taking place between Iran and the US concerning limited bilateral cooperation against Iraq. Tajzadeh suggests that they may have been behind the admission of al-Qaeda operatives into Iran.

On November 30, these hard-liners were criticized by a conservative newspaper, *Jumhuri Eslami*, in a remarkable article, "The Loneliness of the Supreme Leader." The newspaper acknowledged that Khamenei is being undermined by people who are even more authoritarian than he is. The article specifically attacked Abdulnabi Namazi, the prosecutor-general, for flagrantly defying Khameini's order to review the Aghajari verdict. (His defiance forced Aghajari's lawyer, against his client's wishes, to lodge an appeal in early December.)

The extreme conservatives, most of them senior clerics, would like Aghajari's sentence to be confirmed by a court of appeal. Ominously enough, the panel of judges who are to oversee this court includes two very conservative judges, both of whom are notorious for having sentenced reformists to death in the past. It is rumored, furthermore, that a powerful conservative ayatollah has issued a fatwa sentencing Aghajari to death; this will make it hard, even for a lenient judge, to reverse the earlier verdict. If Aghajari is executed, the ultra-conservatives would welcome the opportunity to violently suppress the intense campus demonstrations that would inevitably follow.[2] The hard-line

---

2. *After spending two years on death row, Aghajari was freed in 2004, allegedly after a behind-the-scenes intervention by President Khatami. [Added 2007]*

leaders have small numbers of fanatical supporters in the judiciary, the Revolutionary Guard, the plainclothes squads, and the intelligence organizations. They proclaim their loyalty to the Supreme Leader, but this seems a marriage of convenience.

At the height of the student protests in November, a US-based Persian-language television channel broadcast what it said was a "live" conversation with several young Iranian men who claimed to be speaking from Tehran. The young men announced that the capital was in chaos, and that they were preparing to seize control of it. The interviewer breathlessly urged them on. "Go, my dear ones!" he said. "Don't sit there glued to the television screen!"

Such fantasies have long given heart to the Iranian diaspora. Now they color the judgment of the press and television in the US. During the recent protests, several mainstream US publications gave their readers the impression that Iran was in the throes of a revolution. On November 15, CNN interviewed a spokesman for a US-based Iranian dissident group, the Student Movement Coordination Committee for Democracy in Iran. I know this committee; they clutter my e-mail in-box with fictitious accounts of mass arrests, riots, and mayhem in Iran. They have referred to the recent protests as an "uprising."

In the November 25, 2002, online edition of *National Review*, Michael Ledeen claimed that "something like half a million" Iranians had taken to the streets on November 22 "to demonstrate their disgust with the regime of the Islamic Republic." On December 6, in the same publication, he misrepresented events as follows: "The revolution is being led by students, workers, intellectuals, and military officers and soldiers."

So far as I know, Ledeen hasn't visited Iran since the days of Iran-contra—in which, acting as a consultant to Ronald Reagan's administration, he played a small and inglorious part. His distorted analysis of events in Iran—which conflicts diametrically with my own experience—has unaccountably been given a platform by *The Wall Street Journal* and the *Financial Times*. It would be interesting to know the sources of the information he and other conservative American commentators have been circulating about Iran.

There is no revolution in Iran. Most Iranians are sullen but cautious; they were merely observers of the recent protests. The biggest demonstration to have taken place on November 22, the day that Ledeen claims half a million people took to the streets, and which I observed myself, was attended by around five thousand people. Most students in Iran had nothing to do with the campus demonstrations. Even activists like Attri and Momeni disclaim revolutionary ambitions and admit that they are not leading a mass movement. They are not armed. Few are willing to die for their beliefs. (In these two characteristics they differ from the revolutionaries of 1979.) They need protection, by the police and from Islamic bullies.

They can, however, act as a catalyst, and their cause is strengthened by the relative feebleness of the forces opposing them. In theory, in times of crisis the regime can call on eight million members of the militia. The reality is different. A few boys in the Basij barracks I visited are genuine ideologues. Many more joined the militia because of the special privileges they get for doing so—basijis do three months less military service than non-basijis, and have a better chance of gaining admission to a university. The same motives can be found in hundreds of Basij barracks across the country.

The militiamen turned out, as instructed, on Jerusalem Day. In central Tehran, several hundred thousand basijis and other dependents of the regime, men and women, thronged the streets. (Perhaps this is where Ledeen got his figure of half a million.) Their attendance was hardly voluntary. Many of the participants have jobs in conservative-sponsored state institutions and were instructed to attend. The mood was lighthearted. It was hard to imagine these people physically attacking fellow Iranians.

Such attacks can be expected only from a relatively small number of hezbollahis, hard-line basijis, and murderous ideologues like Saeed Asghar, who was convicted of trying to kill an important reformist in 2000, but was freed in time to direct much of the violence against students and other demonstrators during the recent protests. The violence may, in fact, be intensifying. On December 8, some three hundred Islamic thugs stormed onto the campus of Iran's Amir Kabir University and attacked about two thousand students who were participating in a peaceful political meeting there.

It is possible that a dramatic escalation of protest, or perhaps the death of a demonstrator, would shake more Iranians from their timidity and torpor. This may be the aim of the ultra-conservatives. Both Khatami and Khamenei are apprehensive about growing unrest. The Supreme Leader is being pressured by fanatics. Khatami not only faces strong conservative opposition to his bills in parliament; he is also being outflanked by democrats who draw their inspiration not from his benign reading of Islam but from Western political traditions. The center of Iranian politics—the ground that is currently occupied by the President and the Supreme Leader—is becoming more and more unstable. If this trend continues, radicals on both sides will have an impact way beyond their relatively small size.

4

BIG DEAL

January 2004

IN 2003, IT became clear that Iran had for years concealed an extensive nuclear program that had brought the country closer than many governments had suspected to the ability to build a bomb. But there was still dispute over exactly how advanced Iran's program was. Last summer, a senior Israeli intelligence official predicted that Iran would have its first nuclear bomb within four years. Others, particularly in Europe, regarded the end of the decade as a more realistic date. There was also uncertainty about Iran's nuclear aims. It seems likely that rather than attempting to build a bomb, the Iranians were assembling technology that would enable them to do so at short notice. By creating this capacity, they may have hoped to reduce their vulnerability to George Bush's hostility toward the Islamic Republic. About one thing, international observers were unanimous: when diplomatic pressure, particularly from the US, Britain, France, and Germany, succeeded in persuading the Iranian government to call a halt to the most controversial parts of its nuclear program in October 2003, the country was alarmingly close to producing the nuclear fuel that could be used to make a bomb.

During the Shah's regime, Iran signed the Nuclear Non-Proliferation Treaty (NPT), which permits the controlled civilian, but not military, application of nuclear technology. But evidence obtained by inspectors for the International Atomic Energy Agency (IAEA), the UN's nuclear watchdog, as well as Western intelligence findings, showed that Iran intended to invest at least one billion dollars, and probably much more, to become self-sufficient in the production of enriched uranium. States hostile to Iran maintained that a country that is rich in oil and gas would not have an interest in developing nuclear technology unless it wanted to make weapons.

Moreover, Iran had been building gas centrifuges—sophisticated machines that can be used for enriching uranium to the level needed to power nuclear reactors, and that can also be used to make fuel for nuclear weapons—which bore a close resemblance to a Pakistani design developed in the 1980s. Some Western intelligence officials also alleged that Iran had engaged the help of North Korean scientists to pursue advanced missile technology.

In September 2003, the IAEA delivered an ultimatum to Iran, demanding that it give up uranium enrichment, respond to requests for information, and allow agency inspectors a much freer hand to search for nuclear activities. The Iranian government then took the dramatic step of agreeing to disclose in full its nuclear activities. On October 21, it announced it would turn over previously classified documents about its nuclear program. It also agreed to sign an "additional protocol" to its existing agreement with the IAEA that would allow scientists from the agency to make intrusive spot inspections of any suspected nuclear sites. (According to the existing "safeguards agreement" which Iran accepted a few years after it signed the non-proliferation treaty in 1969, inspectors were only allowed to visit declared nuclear sites, and on advance notice. Iran's leaders also acceded to demands that they suspend uranium enrichment.)

The international pressures that led to Iran's agreement to the new protocol can be dated, at least in part, to August 2002, when an exiled opposition group, the National Council of Resistance of Iran (NCRI), began releasing, from the US and elsewhere, damaging information exposing Iran's progress toward achieving a fuel cycle—the capacity to make nuclear fuel either from natural uranium or from the plutonium that is a by-product of a nuclear reactor.[1] The NCRI revealed that the Iranians were constructing a big plant near Natanz, in central Iran, where uranium hexafluoride (UF6), the gaseous form of natural uranium, would be enriched by being spun in centrifuges at supersonic speeds. The cost of this plant, a Tehran-based proliferation specialist has estimated, is around one billion dollars. The same group revealed that Iran had completed a heavy-water production plant at Arak, also in the center of the country; reactors using heavy water designed for peaceful uses of nuclear energy can be manipulated to produce plutonium in weapons-grade concentrations.[2]

By building these facilities, Iran was not violating its "safeguards agreement" with the IAEA—the agreement obliged Iran only to inform the agency six months before introducing nuclear material into any of its production plants. But Iran was acting suspiciously. Why had it not announced its plans for nuclear facilities at Natanz and Arak? Iranian officials claimed that they had informed the IAEA both about Natanz and about their intention to build a heavy-water reactor at Arak. It turned out that they had told the agency only that they were building an enrichment facility, without disclosing the location; and they had said nothing about Arak.

---

1. The NCRI is a front for the People's Mujahideen, an Iranian opposition group to which Saddam Hussein granted safe haven, and which the US State Department and the EU consider to be a terrorist organization. Before its assets were blocked in the US last summer, the NCRI was able to release in America its most incriminating information about Iran. In December 2003, American administrators in Iraq announced plans to disperse some 3,800 Iranian Mujahideen members, who are currently held in occupied Iraq, to other countries.

2. Enriched uranium and separated plutonium both produce energy when they are fed into the appropriate type of nuclear reactor, and both can also be used as the fissile cores for nuclear bombs. Low-enriched uranium contains no more than 5.5 percent uranium 235 (U-235); in high enriched uranium, which is suitable for nuclear weapons, the proportion of U-235 is at least 90 percent.

Iran could have eased the mounting international concern caused by these revelations by the NCRI. A quick decision to sign and ratify the additional protocol providing for inspections on short notice of any suspected nuclear site would have satisfied most of the thirty-five members of the IAEA's board of governors. Faced with the hectoring of America and Israel—the latter generally conceded to be a nuclear state that has never signed the nonproliferation treaty—many countries, especially those not aligned with the US, defended Iran's right to develop a fuel cycle. But Iran's diplomacy was amateurish. Asked to sign the additional protocol, it stalled, reinforcing the impression that it had something to hide.

Under pressure from the US, the UK, and other nations, the IAEA and its director general, Mohamed ElBaradei, helped to work out a consensus among IAEA member states that Iran had engaged in illegal nuclear activity and posed a threat to international efforts to contain proliferation. Throughout 2003, ElBaradei, who used to be a member of Egypt's diplomatic service and has also taught at New York University Law School, tried to expose Iranian secrets with scrupulous fairness, going out of his way not to act like an instrument of the Bush administration, which, in early 2002, had declared Iran part of its "axis of evil." His reports did not lay out Iran's misdemeanors in neatly quotable accusations but presented them as part of a larger analysis. His exactitude infuriated American officials, but it ended by working in their favor. The IAEA's more incriminating findings had an integrity that even the nonaligned countries found persuasive. For instance, in a report dated August 26, the director general obliquely accused Iran of lying when it claimed that it had developed its uranium enrichment technology without first testing undeclared nuclear material. Such a test would be a violation of the safeguards agreement, which obliges its signees to inform the agency of any change in their nuclear inventory.

ElBaradei started building a consensus on the need to expose Iran's programs during his visit to Iran in February 2003, when he pronounced himself "impressed" by the sophistication of the Natanz facility. This backhanded compliment was the first of a series of the IAEA's increasingly explicit criticisms of the Iranian program. As the IAEA investigation went on, agency inspectors encountered more and more deception on the part of the Iranians. According to a Western diplomat in Tehran, Iranian officials were engaging in a combination of outright "lies" and

> admissions that were calibrated to get the international community off their backs.... What the Iranians claim is transparency is in fact enforced admissions.

Early in 2003, for example, the Iranians confessed to having secretly imported undeclared natural uranium in 1991, some of it in the gaseous form of UF6. But some of this UF6 could no longer be accounted for and the Iranians' explanation—that it had leaked from its containers—only increased suspicions. Later in the year, they admitted to having used this "leaked" UF6 to conduct several tests in 1999 and 2002.

By mid-September, the IAEA governors were sufficiently angry, and united, to issue their resolution demanding that Iran sign an additional protocol, reveal the full history of its nuclear program, and suspend its uranium enrichment activities. On October 21, when the British, French, and German foreign ministers visited Tehran, the Iranians, in what amounted to a reversal of their former position, said that they acceded to these demands. In the weeks following, documentary evidence that Iran turned over to the IAEA gave Western officials a startling picture of a nuclear program that had been developing for years virtually undetected. According to a recent article in *The Washington Post*, these documents provided "the outlines of a vast, secret procurement network that successfully acquired thousands of sensitive parts and tools from numerous countries over a seventeen-year period."

Diplomats interviewed by the *Post* said that the information provided by Iran confirmed the long-standing suspicion of many nuclear experts that Pakistan was one of the principal sources of Iran's nuclear technology. Other Western publications, including *The New York Times*, have also reported that there was a secret agreement, made in 1987, between Pakistan and Iran to exchange nuclear technology. By exposing the sources of both its supplies and its expertise, Iran has made it hard for itself to clandestinely reinvigorate its nuclear program.

For an Islamic regime that prides itself on making strategic decisions without first asking for the approval of foreign countries, least of all Christian ones, Iran's acceptance of the IAEA ultimatum on October 21, 2003, was a momentous retreat. Faced with the immediate prospect of isolation, and the more distant threat of Security Council sanctions, Iran chose cooperation over confrontation.

Iranians both in and out of government have felt they were targets of the US since Bush's "axis of evil" speech in early 2002. Pressure on Iran increased with America's invasion of Iraq and the Bush administration's refusal to publicly repudiate demands, from Israel and from some American neoconservatives, for "regime change" in Iran. These fears seemed further confirmed last summer when US officials told members of a Japanese consortium that they would be liable to secondary sanctions if they signed a long-pending $2.8 billion agreement to develop Azadegan, a big oil field in southern Iran. The Japanese have their own nuclear worries over North Korea and depend on America's protective shield. They did not sign the agreement, and even now remain reluctant to do so until the parliament in Tehran ratifies Iran's adherence to the additional protocol, something that will not happen until after February's elections. Both Japan and Iran hope that the mooted participation in the project of companies from other countries, like China and India, will have the effect of blunting US objections.

Until last autumn the Iranians' economic vulnerability was exacerbated by the growing sense among European officials that the EU's diplomatic approach to Iran had failed. The EU had been hoping to persuade the Iranian government to do four things: reveal its nuclear secrets, improve human rights in Iran, stop supporting groups that violently oppose peace initiatives in the Middle East, and cease opposing Israel's existence. In 2002, the EU opened negotiations on a trade agreement with Iran. By the summer of 2003, Iran's negotiations on the EU's four points were going nowhere. Negotiations on the trade pact stopped. Some European leaders talked of adopting a harder, more "American" line. Then came the IAEA ultimatum.

The Iranians might have taken a stronger stand against the ultimatum if they had received more diplomatic support from Russia. By the end of the 1990s, Russia had become Iran's acknowledged nuclear partner. Unlike Pakistan, whose apparent assistance remained covert, Russia was willing to risk American anger and openly supply Iran with nuclear technology. By 2002, despite American and Israeli opposition, Russian companies had come close to completing a nuclear reactor, worth more than $800 million, near the town of Bushehr on the Persian Gulf. Then, as allegations about Iran's secret activities grew, and Russia's defense of Iranian intentions became less tenable, Russia's position changed.

In public, Russian officials politely urged the Iranians to dispel the doubts about their nuclear program. In private, they stalled on their contract to build the reactor at Bushehr; they did so as a gesture to American officials, who argued that the Bushehr plant was essentially a military installation.[3] The Russians allowed technical hitches and

---

3. The US and Israel have consistently described the Bushehr reactor as capable of producing weapons. But in order to make a bomb using the plutonium by-product of a light-water reactor like Bushehr, the Iranians would need technology that they are far from attaining. To extract this plutonium, furthermore, the reactor would have to be closed down, which would be impossible to disguise.

quibbles over the price of equipment to delay the completion of the reactor, which, according to the original contract with Russia, was supposed to be completed in 2000. Now no one expects the Bushehr plant to come on line before 2005. The Russians have insisted that Iran agree to return, after using it, the nuclear fuel that it had contracted to buy from Russia, thereby ensuring that the used fuel could not be reprocessed to make weapons. A few days after the IAEA board of governors issued its ultimatum, Russia's atomic energy minister said that talks with Iran on buying and returning the spent fuel could take "a long time." In private, the Russians told the Iranians that they would not receive Russian fuel unless they signed the additional protocol.

Less than a month before the October 31 deadline set by the IAEA, Western officials continued to have doubts whether its ultimatum would have an effect. On October 9, ElBaradei told the *Financial Times* that although the Iranians had increased the flow and accuracy of their disclosures to the IAEA, information remained inadequate. A big problem seemed to be the inability of Iran's two major political factions to cooperate with each other. In theory, the Supreme Leader, Ayatollah Ali Khamenei, had assigned the Supreme National Security Council (SCNC), a bipartisan body of senior officials, to formulate Iran's nuclear policy. In practice, as with much other Iranian decision-making, there was an impasse between the allies of the Ayatollah Khamenei, the Supreme Leader, and the reformist president Mohammad Khatami.

Since his triumphant election to the presidency in 1997, Mohammad Khatami has taken a conciliatory line in relations with the West. He and his supporters in the government and parliament were keen to reach an amicable agreement with the IAEA, but he was stymied by his conservative rivals—the senior clerics who are protected by the Ayatollah Khamenei and have been appointed to positions of great power. As Khatami's government explored ways of increasing Iran's cooperation with the IAEA, senior clerics with links to Khamenei advocated withdrawing from the nonproliferation treaty altogether.

The conservative-led Revolutionary Guard resisted advice from reformists that military bases be opened to IAEA inspectors. Iranian diplomats, most of whom are from the reformist faction, were kept in ignorance of the discussions. "You had lobbyists from the foreign ministry," recalls the same Western envoy, "who knew less about the latest Iranian position than their foreign interlocutors."

By the middle of October, Khamenei had decided to end the impasse by favoring his fellow conservatives. Rather than assign the reformist president to negotiate on Iran's behalf, Khamenei gave Hassan Rohani, his representative on the SNSC, authority to do so. When ElBaradei visited Tehran on October 16, Rohani told him that "a decision had been taken to provide the agency, in the course of the following week, with a full disclosure of Iran's past and present nuclear activities." ElBaradei understood that Rohani's promise carried the authority of the Supreme Leader; it was therefore worth more than any number of assurances from the reformists. On Rohani's authority, the IAEA inspectors were given access to the military bases they asked to see, and the way to the October 21 deal was open. That deal showed that Khatami's influence over strategic decisions was declining. The three European foreign ministers saw the President only after they had successfully concluded negotiations with Rohani. The meeting with Khatami amounted to no more than a courtesy call.

A little over a month later, the IAEA governors responded officially to the changes in Iran's position and to the information that the Iranians had given them. They passed a resolution deploring the fact that Iran had on several occasions before October seriously breached its agreement to allow inspections. The resolution also obliquely threatened Iran with censure or punitive action from the United Nations Security Council if it continued to break its agreements.[4] But the

---

4. The clause in question states that if "any further serious Iranian failures come to light," the board of governors will "meet immediately to consider...all options at its disposal."

board also praised Iran's new readiness to cooperate with the IAEA and resisted America's urging that Iran's behavior be immediately referred to the Security Council. The Iranians were thus able to present the IAEA's otherwise damning document as a national triumph. In effect, the board agreed that the Iranians should not be punished for past misdeeds as long as they came completely and verifiably clean about them, and took convincing measures to ensure that they were not repeated. According to Rohani, the resolution marked the end of a state of "emergency" that had characterized relations between the Iranians and the IAEA.

In January 2004, diplomats in Vienna, where the IAEA has its headquarters, said that Iran had continued to acquire equipment that could be used to enrich uranium. Iranians were said to be quibbling over what the suspension of uranium enrichment activities means; just acquiring equipment, they argued, does not amount to uranium enrichment. Iran's alleged transgression, and Rohani's repeated insistence that Iran's suspension of uranium enrichment was "temporary," may be designed to win further diplomatic advantages in the future. In other respects, the IAEA board of governors seems confident that Iran is abiding by its new commitments, and that it has given up all enrichment and fuel-reprocessing experiments. The information that the Iranians have given the IAEA will be an invaluable guide to the methods and suppliers that have been used to secretly develop nuclear weapons. On December 18, Iran signed the additional protocol allowing spot inspections. In exchange, Iran hopes to receive help in pursuing its civilian nuclear program. This nuanced solution was first formulated in the communiqué that the three European countries issued with Iran on October 21. The document affirmed Iran's right to develop nuclear energy for peaceful purposes. Once concerns about its programs "are fully resolved," it said, "Iran could expect easier access to modern technology and supplies." That vague promise was designed to reassure Iran, which has made clear its anger at having been subjected to what it claims is an unjust embargo on nuclear technology needed for peaceful uses.

Britain, France, and Germany proposed allowing Iran to have a supply of nuclear fuel—probably from Russia—that could be used in light-water reactors and then returned to Russia. In Tehran, some foreign diplomats speculate that Iran may favor a different solution, one which would allow it to restart uranium enrichment as long as it was placed under permanent international monitoring. This sounds like ElBaradei's own position, stated in an article he wrote for *The Economist* in October, that sensitive nuclear processes should be permitted only in "facilities under multinational control."

Some hard-liners in the Bush administration, supported by Israel, have remained skeptical about Iran's new position. They argue that Iran should abandon all nuclear activity, not merely the uranium enrichment that Iran has undertaken to suspend. The plant at Bushehr, they maintain, should be closed down. The Iranians are reserving their right to resume enrichment activities. If they are ready to bargain away that right, they will be looking to the US to offer inducements, not the Europeans, for it is the US they fear.

By engaging Iran in talks, the EU hoped to help Khatami make his country more democratic at home and more acceptable abroad. Most Iranians, who twice elected Khatami president, share these goals, but they have been thwarted by the conservatives who continue to exert control over public life and have behind them the military and police forces. Conservative judges have suppressed freedom of speech. The appointed upper house has vetoed virtually every enlightened legislative act that the reformist parliament has passed since it was elected in 2000. In 2002, according to some sources, the conservatives, wanting to embarrass Khatami, steered a shipment of Iranian arms, ostensibly bound for Palestine, into the path of Israel's security forces.

The conservatives have demonstrated to the world that when

voters challenge their grip on power they achieve nothing. At first, foreigners enjoyed dealing with the reformists; Khatami himself is a cultivated and charming mullah. But frustration then set in. The reformists promised much, including more friendly international relations. The conservatives prevented them from delivering domestic reforms and took over international negotiations.

The first months of Iran's nuclear crisis followed this pattern. According to a senior government official that I spoke to, Khatami urged, earlier this year, that Iran sign the additional protocol. He was overruled by "certain people"—that is, Khamenei. Months later, however, the Supreme Leader endorsed not only the signing of the protocol but also other concessions that Khatami had not considered. Cynical Iranians have long suspected that the conservative faction, despite its opposition to Khatami's ideas about détente, might be willing to deemphasize or discard its radical anti-Americanism and anti-Zionism if it were to feel threatened. In the October 21 deal, the conservatives relinquished the secret nuclear programs that they previously thought would shield them from American hostility.

Among the conservatives are pragmatists who seek a more congenial place for Iran in the world. Above all, they seek an exit from the "axis of evil." On the whole, they do not subscribe to the liberal ideals that have made the reformists attractive to the West. Instead of democratizing the Islamic Republic, they are interested in preserving it and their place in it. They take heart from the example of Pakistan, where a military dictator has shown that he does not have to share values with the US; he has only to cooperate with it.

After seven years of Khatami's presidency, the anti-reformist campaign to undermine him is succeeding. In February's parliamentary elections, the conservatives will benefit from the apathy of the voters, especially among young people and women, who make up Khatami's core constituency yet perceive the dwindling of his power. On January 10, the Council of Guardians, a hard-line twelve-member body that has the power to vet candidates, disqualified some four thousand parliamentary candidates, including eighty-two sitting deputies, from standing in next month's elections. Under pressure from the President and some eighty protesting deputies, the Supreme Leader then recommended both that most of the disqualified deputies be declared eligible and that the cases of excluded candidates outside the parliament be reviewed.

It is likely that some of the most influential reformist deputies, including the President's brother, will be declared, once again, unfit to stand, but that many will have their eligibility confirmed. The absence from the election of leading reformists, however, will work in the conservatives' favor; and the next parliament may well be less reformist than the current one. In 2005, when Khatami's term ends, a rigged selection process will ensure that candidates to replace him will be conservatives and nonentities. Hassan Rohani's recent nuclear negotiations and his visits abroad make him seem like a president-in-waiting. Since October 21, for example, he has met senior EU officials in Brussels, and was received by Vladimir Putin in Moscow and Jacques Chirac in Paris.[5]

As for nuclear policy, the new system of UN inspections may discover more Iranian transgressions. But it would be uncharacteristically foolish for the conservatives to commit themselves to actions that they do not intend to carry out. Fulfilling their promises, moreover, is the only way that they are likely to achieve their immediate goal of softening, if not isolating, America's hard-line position within the IAEA. An image of reliability is vital, also, to the broader message

---

5. During Rohani's trip to Paris, the French daily *Le Figaro* published on January 17, 2004, an interview with him that was remarkable for the reasonableness of his tone. It was only a matter of time, he said, before Iran and the US reopened relations—what was needed was "bulldozers to destroy the wall that separates our countries." By sending conciliatory messages to the US, and by indicating Iran's willingness to discuss questions like peace in the Middle East, Rohani positioned himself as the authoritative voice of Iranian foreign policy.

that they want to convey—namely, that they, not Khatami, can make concessions on the military issues that interest the West. By doing so, they hope that concerns about human rights and democracy will not determine Western attitudes toward Iran.

The intended recipients of this message in Washington—or at least some of them—seemed, until recently, to be impervious to it. At least twice last year, the Bush administration was indirectly approached by well-connected Iranian conservatives who suggested that steps be taken to normalize relations between the two countries. US officials are said to have rejected the overtures, partly because of their distaste for Iran's theocracy, partly because they judged it inadvisable to deal with just one part of a split polity.

But American attitudes toward Iran may now be changing. In December 2003, in response to Iran's catastrophic earthquake, which killed more than 41,000 people, the US offered to send emergency relief and medical workers. The Iranians accepted immediately. But they turned down the Bush administration's offer to send a high-level humanitarian delegation to the afflicted region, perhaps because they worried that Iranians, who are generally pro-American, would give their guests an embarrassingly warm welcome. That rebuff has not stopped the US from temporarily waiving restrictions on the transfer of money to private organizations in Iran, thereby allowing Americans to donate directly to relief efforts.

In an interview that was published on December 29, 2003, in *The Washington Post*, Colin Powell praised the "new attitude" that Iran was showing on some issues. He was referring primarily to the Iranians' capitulation to the IAEA's demands, but also to other Iranian positions as well. Having vociferously opposed the American invasion of neighboring Iraq, Iran has been cooperating with the interim government there. Iranian leaders have a good relationship with Abdul Aziz al-Hakim, who holds the rotating presidency of the US-appointed governing council, as well as three other influential members of the council. It sends gasoline across the border and its cement makers are keen to take part in reconstruction. The Revolutionary Guard has good working relations with coalition forces that control the areas bordering on Iran. Iran's ability to disrupt Iraq, even if it wanted to, is complicated by its relatively feeble influence over Ayatollah al-Sistani, the country's preeminent Shia cleric.

The Iranians believe that they are doing the US a favor by detaining more than three hundred suspected al-Qaeda operatives. It will take US concessions before they acquiesce to long-standing American demands that the detainees be handed over to their countries of origin. In public, Powell indicates that the US may favor restoring the low-level dialogue that it used to have with Iran. This was cut off last spring, after the US linked three bombings in Saudi Arabia to some of the al-Qaeda militants that are now thought to be in Iranian custody. In private, Powell speaks of more substantive discussions.

Although he welcomed the aid that the US sent to the victims of the earthquake, Khatami was careful to distinguish between humanitarian cooperation and a political thaw. Having tried sincerely to bring about détente with Bill Clinton, who seemed amenable to improving relations, Khatami is said to feel personally affronted by Bush's hostility. In particular, he blames Bush's "axis of evil" speech for plunging Iran into an extended crisis that has played into the hands of his conservative opponents and has frozen hopes of domestic reform. As long as Bush is in the White House, it is unlikely that Khatami will expect the kind of dialogue that briefly seemed possible during Clinton's second term.

For their part, the conservatives officially say they are skeptical of America's willingness to improve relations. On January 10, 2004, Ayatollah Ali Khamenei said that there was "no sign of US animosity toward Iran decreasing." Other Iranian officials said Iran has no plans to start talks with the US—which does not mean that such talks are ruled out. What seems clear is that Khatami's rivals are waiting for their next opportunity to further consolidate their power. For them, it is enough that America appreciate that it was conservatives who made the decisive intervention that led to the October 21 deal. It is now up to the US administration to decide whether, and to what extent, it may relax its hostility to the Islamic regime and its efforts to weaken it, and press instead for the sort of dialogue that could lead to a lasting accommodation. That would bring the Americans into contact with the conservatives they despise. But these conservatives have privately let it be known that they are in favor of talks. Their surprising U-turn on the nuclear issue has demonstrated more clearly than ever that they, not the elected government, hold the real power in Iran.

5

STALLED

May 2004

WHEN SHE LEFT Iran for the US in 1997, Azar Nafisi found that she was able to write with a freedom that she had not known since she was last in America as a student in the 1970s. Long muffled by Iranian censorship, she took advantage of her liberty to write a damaging and eloquent account of the Islamic Republic. Damaging but indirect, for *Reading Lolita in Tehran*[1] is about reading well-known works of English and American literature in a totalitarian environment—about entering a fictional world whose morally ambiguous characters resist the leveling effects of ideology. In revolutionary Tehran, Nafisi writes, reading *Invitation to a Beheading*, *Pride and Prejudice*, and, of course, *Lolita* offered "a critical way of appraising and grasping the world." In a political system that aims ruthlessly to homogenize, to impose a code of behavior and thought, fiction can be a weapon of resistance.

During the decade or so that she spent teaching English literature at Tehran University and at Allameh Tabatabai University, also in Tehran, in addition to two years of private instruction of a class of young women, Nafisi was engaged in resistance. By setting very demanding standards of Islamic virtue from its citizens, the Islamic

---

1. *Reading Lolita in Tehran* (Random House, 2003).

Republic has made criminals of millions of them. Nafisi was expelled from Tehran University for declining to wear the *hejab*, the Islamic head- and body-cover that the Iranian authorities have made mandatory. Later, at Allameh Tabatabai, she wore the *hejab* with contemptuous sloppiness; she ate ham and drank vodka after both had been banned; she had the temerity to try to shake the hand of a male student; and she taught *Lolita* to her private class, despite its perversion of what Islam, no less than any other religion, regards as a sacred relationship between a guardian and his juvenile charge.

Nafisi regards *Reading Lolita in Tehran* as an optimistic book about the "transformative power of literature." It contains a description of an exuberantly democratic classroom "trial," suggested by Nafisi herself, of *The Great Gatsby*, which has offended her Islamist and leftist students. The account of the trial goes on for pages, but some brief quotes can suggest its flavor. One of the Muslim students, Mr. Nyazi, states a case for the prosecution. "The only sympathetic person here," he says, "is the cuckolded husband, Mr. Wilson. When he kills Gatsby, it is the hand of God. He is the only victim. He is the only genuine symbol of the oppressed, in the land of...the Great Satan!" A young woman, Zarrin, defends the book:

> Careless is the first adjective that comes to mind when describing the rich in this novel. The dream they embody is an alloyed dream that destroys whoever tries to get close to it. So you see, Mr. Nyazi, this book is no less a condemnation of your wealthy upper classes than any of the revolutionary books we have read.

Nafisi writes:

> I discovered later that most students had supported Zarrin, but very few were prepared to risk voicing their views, mainly because they lacked enough self-confidence to articulate their

points as "eloquently," I was told, as the defense and the prosecutor. Some claimed in private that they personally liked the book. Then why didn't they say so? Everyone else was so certain and emphatic in their position, and they couldn't really say why they liked it—they just did.

Nafisi describes the intimacy that developed in her private class, where discussion of troubled characters like Daisy Miller and Catherine Sloper led "my girls" to share their problems. (These mostly have to do with men, or the state, or both.) She finds solace in a friendship with a mysterious academic. But to my mind *Reading Lolita in Tehran* is mostly a sad book, "a mournful feast," as Nafisi writes in another context. Censorship, of art and behavior, casts a shadow. So does the despotism exercised by men over women who, in the case of Nafisi and her girls, are helplessly aware of what is going on. Nafisi pays for her awareness "at night, always at night, when I returned. What will happen now? Who will be killed? When will they come?"

A description of a walk taken by a student, Sanaz, recalls the experience of many Iranian women:

It is in her best interest not to be seen, not be heard or noticed. She doesn't walk upright, but bends her head to the ground and doesn't look at passersby.... The streets of Tehran and other Iranian cities are patrolled by militia, who ride in white Toyota patrols, four gun-carrying men and women.... They patrol the streets to make sure that women like Sanaz wear their veils properly, do not wear make-up, do not walk in public with men who are not their fathers, brothers or husbands.... The streets have been turned into a war zone, where young women who disobey the rules are hurled into patrol cars, taken to jail, flogged, fined....

As a student, Nafisi had opposed US meddling in Iran, cheered the Shah's flight, and returned home full of optimism. The revolution soon soured. Freedom was subordinated to an intolerance that took the form of radical Islam; this intolerance permitted, through the promulgation of benighted laws, Iranian men to assume absolute authority over their wives, daughters, and sisters. For a great many Iranian women, this may have been seen as a correction of the excesses of the Shah's time, when the carousing of the nouveaux riches had raised fears of Western-style degeneracy. For a great many others, revolutionary but secular-minded, it was a ghastly surprise.

"The worst crime committed by totalitarian mind-sets," Nafisi writes, "is that they force their citizens, including their victims, to become complicit in their crimes." She is reminded of the condemned Cincinnatus C. in *Invitation to a Beheading* and the waltz that he dances with his jailer. When the waltz ends, Nabokov writes, "Cincinnatus regretted that the swoon's friendly embrace had been so brief." Nafisi writes:

> The only way to leave the circle, to stop dancing with the jailer, is to find a way to preserve one's individuality, that unique quality which evades description but differentiates one human being from the other.... There was not much difference between our jailers and Cincinnatus's executioners. They invaded all private spaces and tried to shape every gesture, to force us to become one of them, and that in itself was another form of execution.

By 1997, Nafisi had decided that the only way to leave the circle was to leave Iran, and that prompted people she knew to seek an escape route. Nafisi's epilogue alludes to the emigration of several of her students. Since she has written very critically about the Islamic Republic, it is unlikely that she will be allowed to return safely to Iran, even for a short holiday. That puts her in a position that is privileged but also difficult. Exiles are able, as Iranians in Iran are not, to tell the full truth about the Islamic Republic. However, the longer they spend away from Iran, the less acquainted they are with it, and the more their accounts are open to question.

I know the period that Nafisi deals with in *Reading Lolita in Tehran* only through books and conversations with people, including my wife, who lived in Iran at the time. Nafisi's portrayal is grimly authentic. On the other hand, I have direct experience of life in Iran since the election of a reformist president, Mohammad Khatami, which happened a month before Nafisi emigrated, and I disagree with aspects of Nafisi's portrayal of this newer Iran.

In articles and lectures written in the US, Nafisi describes the Khatami presidency as marking hardly a break with the past, and the Islamic Republic as being no less fanatical and vicious. She portrays normal Iranians as more politically conscious and willing to act with dynamism than they are. Such misapprehensions are common among Iranian exiles; they justify a vilification of the regime without regard to the nuances of its behavior, while offering an unrealistic hope of change through the power of its people.

In an article that she wrote last year for *The Wall Street Journal*, Nafisi suggested that Khatami's landslide election victory in 1997 was "more a vote against the rulers of the Islamic Republic than in support of an obscure cleric with impeccable revolutionary credentials."[2] That was not my impression from a rally of several thousand people I attended in 1999. Even then, more than two years after he came to power, it was remarkable how admired, even revered, the President was. He was, as I wrote, "loudly cheered, with female students holding up his photograph, their male counterparts bellowing his name."[3] As late as 2001, when Khatami's efficiency as a reformer was widely

---

2. "The Books of Revolution," *The Wall Street Journal*, June 18, 2003.

3. See Chapter One, "The Struggle for Iran."

questioned, I watched 12,000 people in the provincial town of Kerman, including young women close to hysteria, give him a welcome that might elsewhere be given to a pop star.[4]

In her *Wall Street Journal* article, Nafisi referred admiringly to Iranians "breaking into riots to see films by great directors, Iranian or Western." In the early 1990s, a decision to suspend the screening of two films by Mohsen Makhmalbaf, one of Iran's most famous filmmakers, led to rioting by people who had hoped to see the films. But the decision to suspend the screenings had been prompted by much more serious rioting, by violent Islamist groups, outside movie theaters where the films were playing. It is not uncommon for fists and insults to fly during the annual Tehran Film Festival. Seats are hard to come by and the festival organizers are notoriously incompetent. But these minor fracases do not amount, as Nafisi put it, to "the Iranian people ... revealing their civilizational aspirations."

In an interview that she gave in 2003 to *The Atlantic*, Nafisi lamented that following the terrorist attacks of September 11, scant attention was paid to the fact that "40,000 Iranians came out to the streets in Iran under threat of jail or torture and lit candles in sympathy with the American people."[5] There were several vigils in Tehran after the attacks. Some five thousand people took part in the biggest, on September 18, according to an Iranian cameraman whose pictures of the event appeared on the BBC. *The New York Times* put the number of participants at three thousand. None of the other vigils attracted more than a few hundred people.

Nafisi told her interviewer that "there is a lot happening in the universities. ... Universities now are the hotbed of the movement for democracy." This was no longer true in 2003, and it is not true now.

---

4. See my "Khatami's Admirers Lose Patience with Failure of Reforms," *The Independent*, February 24, 2001.

5. "The Fiction of Life," *Atlantic Unbound*, May 7, 2003.

In the wake of serious student rioting in 1999, the authorities decapitated the student movement by jailing its leaders and, it is widely believed, torturing some of them. Those demonstrating students were associated with President Khatami's reform movement, but that has now lost much of its support, and there is no longer a political current that reflects the aspirations of large numbers of young people. Many students are fatalistically convinced of their inability to influence the running of their country. There is less "happening" in the universities than at any time since the revolution.

The state uses repression more cunningly and selectively than it did, and the Iranian people are much more apathetic than Nafisi imagines them to be. This is why the Islamic Republic, for all the dislike that so many Iranians feel for it, is proving to be one of the Middle East's more durable regimes.

On the afternoon of March 8, 2004, I was among about five hundred people, most of them young women, who had gone to Tehran's Laleh Park to hear speeches against domestic violence. Upon reaching the park's small amphitheater, we learned that the Tehran governor-general's office had rescinded the permit that it had issued earlier for the event. The organizers were arguing that the permit remained valid. The police told the women to go home; many of them clapped their hands mockingly. At around six, the organizers encouraged everyone to go home, and left the park. I went back to my car. Some of the women stayed behind, clapping and shouting slogans.

Shortly afterward, I was told later, members of the Basij, an official militia, arrived and beat some of the protesters with batons. There were no serious injuries. The police arrested three protesters. Alerted to the arrests, the organizers traced the detainees. They were freed the following day. And that was how International Women's Day was marked in Tehran, a city of seven million inhabitants.

A few days later, Nooshin Ahmadi Khorasani, a founder of the

Iranian Women's Cultural Center (IWCC), the main organizer of the March 8 event, posted an article on the IWCC Web site. When I first met her, in 1999, Ahmadi Khorasani was editing one of the Islamic Republic's first feminist magazines, *Jens-e Dovom* (The Second Sex), which is now called *Fasl-e Zanan* (The Season of Women). The fourth issue of *Fasl-e Zanan* is currently being scrutinized by the censors at the Ministry of Culture and Islamic Guidance. For the past year and a half, Ahmadi Khorasani and her colleagues have been trying, through a touring workshop, to get women to discuss domestic violence. They plan to start a women's library in Tehran as well.

Ahmadi Khorasani's article was partly a reply to criticisms that had been made against the organizers of the March 8 event. These had been transmitted on Iranian Web sites abroad and echoed privately by some women in Iran. One article, by Shadi Amin, an exile in Germany, criticized the event's organizers for leaving the amphitheater and praised the boldness of those who stayed. These young women were victorious, in Amin's view, because they had aired their grievances in defiance of the state.

In her article Ahmadi Khorasani admitted that the women's movement is deeply vulnerable. "We are not heroes," she wrote. She criticized those who use "very radical slogans in private"; in 2000, many of the same radicals did not dare to sign an open letter criticizing the arrest of Mehrangiz Kar, Iran's most forthright woman lawyer, for her challenges to government repression. "We have come to realize that we have to go forward one step at a time, and that, if we suddenly leap forward one hundred paces, we'll look over our shoulders and find not one of those women behind us."

To Ahmadi Khorasani, the March 8 event was not a triumph. It was only in 2002 that the IWCC finally won permission to hold a Women's Day celebration in the open air. After a successful (and peaceful) meeting that year, the IWCC had adopted a modest aim, to hold open-air events every March 8, and to increase the number of participants. Because of this year's violence and arrests, Ahmadi Khorasani fears that next year no permit will be issued.

In 2003, while working on an article about Iranian women, I had trouble finding a women's movement.[6] This came as a surprise; I had expected the Islamic Republic's famously reactionary laws to have provoked more active opposition.[7] In the provincial town of Ghazvin, for instance, young activists told me that awareness of women's issues was only beginning to emerge, and that this had much to do with social changes. For example, a growing number of people are choosing their own spouses, rather than accepting their parents' choice. More women are not marrying. The spread of girls' schools has dramatically increased the number of educated women.[8] These developments, activists say, are starting to have political consequences.

Another Tehran-based activist I talked to advises young feminists: "Don't get too excited...this is about taking very slow steps" and not about provoking a backlash. Her point is that free activists, even if they are cautious, achieve more than jailed ones, or some of those in exile.

The case of Mehrangiz Kar, the forthright lawyer who was arrested in 2000, is salutary. At the time of her detention, following her attendance at a controversial conference in Berlin, Kar was Iran's most influential women's rights activist. She was shockingly direct in her advocacy of secular reforms. Having served a short prison

---

6. See my special report, "Women in Iran," *The Economist*, October 18, 2003.

7. A selection of the most benighted: Polygamy is legal for men. The courtroom testimony of two women is worth that of one man. It is virtually impossible for a woman to divorce her husband without his consent. Women wanting to go abroad must have the permission of the nearest male family member. Lapidation, although currently subject to a moratorium, remains a prescribed punishment for adulteresses.

8. In 1975, women's illiteracy in rural areas was 90 percent, and more than 45 percent in towns. Now, the nationwide literacy rate for girls aged between fifteen and twenty-four has reached 97 percent. In 2002, for the first time, female students in state universities outnumbered male ones.

sentence, she was allowed to leave Iran for cancer treatment. A second trial, to prosecute her for "insulting religious sanctities" and for "calling into question the *hejab*," had yet to convene. Kar did not return to Iran, and so her influence has waned.

Activists of all kinds must tread a thin line between confrontation and what impatient exiles call "appeasement." No one negotiates this path with more skill than Shirin Ebadi, who won the Nobel Peace Prize in 2003. Ebadi was a judge during the monarchy. After the revolutionary authorities ruled that women were unfit to be judges, she worked as a lawyer and human rights activist. She is famous for accepting politically charged cases of murder, repression, and domestic violence. She has been in jail. When I saw her, in April, she told me that she had twice narrowly escaped assassination.

On those occasions, Ebadi was lucky, but her survival as an influential activist is partly attributable to her caution. She does not demand reform according to secular principles, but according to an innovative reading of Shia jurisprudence. The piecemeal reform of Islamic laws that she proposes would mean using "rationality," which she describes as "the scales for the weighing and apprehension of the holy word," to determine which anachronistic laws should be discarded.

I met Ebadi a few days after hearing criticism of her from some female students. They felt that she should be using her position as a Nobel laureate to put forward more radical ideas. I had heard that more extreme criticism was circulating among exiled women. Some had accused Ebadi, absurdly, of being an apologist for the regime. Ebadi told me, "There's no reason for me to speak more radically. The Nobel Prize hasn't changed my beliefs."

Ebadi had an intriguing explanation for Iranians' apathy: their "unwise" habit of "building up heroes." (In this criticism, she resembles Ahmadi Khorasani, although Ahmadi Khorasani is unlike Ebadi in many ways, not least in her rejection of religious arguments, in favor of secular ones, to advance women's rights.) When people pin their hopes on a few heroes, Ebadi believes, they feel that they "have no responsibility but to sit around at home and, at most, cheer their hero." A few days after she won the Nobel Prize, she recalled with amazement, some of her supporters were urging her to stand for the presidency. "They expect their hero to shout their own slogans for them.... Until you roll up your sleeves, you won't achieve anything."

The reform movement that brought Khatami to power was destroyed both by the President's opponents, the conservative clerics who are accountable only to themselves, and by his own timidity. Early in his tenure, conservative judges tried the cases of prominent reformists and banned reformist publications. In 1999, their vigilantes put down student unrest with much brutality. From 2000 onward, the Council of Guardians, a supervisory body whose members are appointed by the conservative Supreme Leader, Ayatollah Ali Khamenei, vetoed virtually all reformist legislation ratified by parliament. The same body disqualified more than two thousand reform-minded candidates from standing in February's general election. The conservatives won a strong majority.

Khatami had been a hero, but his constituents deserted him when it became clear that he was unable, or unwilling, to challenge these despotic actions. Khatami is a cleric, and many people have had enough of clerics. He is also a politician, and they feel let down by politicians. To show their dissatisfaction, most urban Iranians did not vote in February's elections.

Still it is worth recalling Khatami's achievements. During his presidency, the Islamic Republic adopted conciliatory positions in its foreign affairs, except with respect to the US and Israel. Iran's nuclear program is widely perceived as being military in intent, but Iran is no longer interested in threatening its neighbors, even Israel. Iranian officials hope that the "strategic ambiguity" with which their nuclear program is conceived will make them less vulnerable to outside pressures, and force the US to negotiate with them. At home, Khatami halted the use of extrajudicial killings as an instrument of policy. Before he took office, Intelligence Ministry agents were said to be murdering dissidents and intellectuals at a rate of one per month. (The recent murder of a detained Canadian-Iranian journalist was appalling, but an aberration.)

Iran has changed in other ways, particularly in Tehran. On summer evenings, I step out of my house into a one-way street full of slow-moving cars. The groups of young women in some of them have little in common with Nafisi's terrorized student Sanaz, who tries "not to be seen, not to be heard or noticed." They wear fuchsia or violet headscarves, and are dazzlingly made up. Through open car windows, they flirt with boys in adjacent cars. The boys wear sunglasses (though it is dark) and goatees; some are drunk. Their car stereos broadcast illegal pop music written and performed by Iranian exiles in Los Angeles. The Islamic Republic is bothersome but at least for a while it can be avoided. Such scenes can be observed elsewhere in Tehran and, less flamboyantly, in other large towns.

A few weeks ago, I visited a member of the English literature department at Allameh Tabatabai University. He told me that he was free to teach whatever books he wanted, provided they conformed to a prescribed syllabus. The previous term, he told me, he had taught Ian McEwan's *Black Dog*; no one had objected to its elaborate description of sexual arousal. He had also taught *A Portrait of the Artist as a Young Man*, with its account of Stephen Dedalus's experiences with a Dublin prostitute. As with many other universities, he told me, a new rector of Allameh Tabatabai was appointed after Khatami's election; the rector is more liberal-minded than his predecessor.

In April at the movies I saw the comedy *Marmulak* (Lizard), by Kamal Tabrizi. Parviz Parastui, one of Iran's finest actors, plays a criminal who escapes from prison dressed as a mullah, only to find himself adopted by a rural community as their prayer leader. In the film, the clergy is the butt of jokes that, a few years ago, would have got Tabrizi thrown into jail. *Marmulak* had the most successful opening in Iranian film history. It has been the target of conservative attacks, which prompted its producer, in mid-May, to withdraw it from movie theaters. Although this decision dismayed many Iranians who had given the film an enthusiastic reception, there have been no reports of riots in protest of this self-censorship.

Artistic censorship has become less intrusive, but the authorities remain vindictive toward people they distrust. In April, Bahman Farmanara, a distinguished filmmaker, announced that the Ministry of Culture and Islamic Guidance had prevented him from making a film about two elderly men who talk about Iranian history. Aging writers are made to pay, through severe censorship of their work, for the politics of their youth. In conservative quarters, the old fear of Western cultural contamination persists. Western films that are broadcast on TV carry distorted subtitles that reflect badly on Western society.

Khatami will step down next year. The conservatives will, by rigging the vetting process that candidates undergo, ensure that his successor is one of them. Whoever he is (women cannot stand for the presidency, even though Shirin Ebadi's supporters wish they could), he is unlikely to revive the fearful conditions that Nafisi describes in *Reading Lolita in Tehran*. Little of the progress made during Khatami's tenure would have been possible without the acquiescence of the Supreme Leader. Khamanei and other key conservatives are more pragmatic than their rhetoric suggests.

Confronted by a youthful population that is indifferent or hostile to revolutionary ideology, conservatives have been forced to tolerate "un-Islamic" dress and behavior, sexual morals, and films. So long as their families approve, it is possible for women in big cities to live relatively independent, Westernized lives. The authorities are much less interested than they used to be in what goes on behind closed doors.

The conservatives draw a line between social liberalization and political freedom. (This distinguishes them from Khatami, who is a democrat by conviction.) This was clear when they smashed the student movement after the 1999 riots. Periodic riots since then, some of them involving or inspired by students, have been put down with ease. The position of the conservatives was evident in the systematic way they used jail, threats, and the dissemination of sexual and financial slurs to hound out of public life people who might inspire followers. Mehrangiz Kar is one of many examples. The quality of debate has suffered. Politics is getting to be boring. At the beginning of his tenure, Khatami admirably expressed his people's desire for peaceful evolution. Now, for the first time since the revolution, Iran barely has a public figure, let alone a leading politician, who reflects popular desires.

Khatami will leave behind him a society whose troubles are reflected in soaring figures for divorce, drug addiction, and prostitution, and whose young people long to live abroad. The President has not succeeded in his stated aim of fostering civil society; Iran's pathetically few independent nongovernmental organizations—the IWCC is one —already suffer tedious, low-level harassment. After Khatami leaves office, they will be even more vulnerable.

From the comfort of satellite TV studios in Los Angeles, Iranian commentators summon young Iranians out onto the streets. Exiles in Europe urge women to shed their *hejab*. But Iran is entering a period of stagnation; it is hard to predict whether, far less when, the sullenness and cynicism of young people will turn to anger.

6

THE SPIRIT MOVES IN TEHRAN

October 2004

IT TOOK A year's mediation by a go-between before Mr. B admitted me to one of his classes on the mystical poems of Rumi. Mr. B has been teaching poetry in Tehran, the Iranian capital, for more than twenty years, but I was the first British journalist who had asked to be his student. I was not surprised when he refused me, for many Iranians regard journalists as unreliable, and resent the British for their history of meddling, spying, and otherwise obnoxious behavior in Iran. Several months passed before the intermediary, who is a friend of my Iranian wife, convinced Mr. B that I am not such a terrible person. The next problem was that his classes were full. My wife teased me: "They say that Rumi has to summon you; it isn't enough for you to want him. You should have known he wouldn't summon a Brit." Then, last January, Mr. B started a weekly class that was to be held in the home of some people called Roshan, and suggested that I join.

It is quite common for educated Iranians to host classes in their houses, mostly on spiritual, literary, and historical subjects. These classes are a small rebellion against efforts by the state to regulate the way that people think and act. Twenty-five years after the 1979 revolution that installed an Islamic republic, it is impossible to hold an intimate and relaxed poetry class in, for instance, a rented room in some public building. The authorities might balk at any gathering of men and women together. The women would be unable to remove their *hejab*, the Islamic head- and body-cover that must, according to Iranian law, be worn in public. (In private, many Westernized Iranian women do not observe the *hejab*; it is widely observed in traditional and poorer families.) Eavesdroppers might monitor the class's content, checking for subversive political undertones. Another advantage of private classes is that the host produces tea, cake, and fruit for the participants. This warms the atmosphere.

A few days before the first class, I visited a friend, Ali Dehbashi, in the offices of *Bukhara*, the literary magazine that he edits. Dehbashi is famous for promoting Persian letters. His office is lined with signed photographs of Iran's leading writers. (And, unexpectedly, John Updike, to whom Dehbashi was introduced by an Iranian professor at Columbia University.) He is the editor of a collection of essays about Rumi, one of several recent Iranian books on the subject. Since the 1990s, he told me, Iran has been experiencing a Rumi revival. Rumi's poems, he said, are popular among "people who want to keep their God," but are "not excessively religious." They are "a place to breathe." Dehbashi is not surprised by the depth and duration of the Rumi revival. "Historically," he told me, "mysticism has arisen in response to doctrinal pressure."

The history of the Islamic Republic is full of doctrinal pressure. After taking power, Iran's cleric-politicians advocated a dry, legalistic interpretation of Shia Islam. (Some 90 percent of Iranians are Shia.) They insisted that Iranians obey the letter of Muslim law; they did not emphasize the generally compassionate spirit that underlies it. They shut down lodges where mystical Islam was promoted, and silenced mystic holy men, called sheikhs, who disapproved of linking religion with worldly power. They encouraged people to use the recommendations of the most senior ayatollahs—they are called Objects of Emulation, and there are about a dozen of them in Iran—as their moral compass, rather than their own faith and conscience. They promoted a mood of perpetual mourning for the eleven imams, descendants of the Prophet who were murdered, most Shiites believe, at the behest of early Sunni caliphs. During the appalling conflict between Iran and Iraq in the 1980s, they extended this mourning to include hundreds of thousands of martyred warriors.

One evening, I drove from my home in north Tehran to a township full of tall apartment blocks that must have seemed vaguely futuristic when they were started, in the last years of the Shah's rule. A middle-aged woman without the *hejab* opened the door of an apartment on the fourteenth floor, and introduced herself as Mrs. Roshan. I was the first to arrive. She ushered me into a sitting room lined with straight-backed chairs, and introduced me to her husband, a bald man who greeted me gravely. She gave me tea and *kak*, a kind of mille-feuille, and we looked out at the lights of the neighboring apartment blocks. There was a shadow in the background, which I took to be the foothills of the Alborz Mountains. I felt vaguely uncomfortable, as though I had barged into a house that belonged to people who did not know who I was, or why I was there.

The other participants started arriving. The men hung up their coats and greeted the others, placing their right hands over their hearts and making barely perceptible bows. The women shed their headscarves and came in rearranging or patting down their hair. Some of them were lavishly made up. There was a married couple whose solicitous mutual regard betrayed them as newlyweds. There was a young woman with a plaster on her nose from an aesthetic operation; and there was a young man, pale and brainy-looking, who helped himself to a surprising quantity of *kak*. Mr. B's students seemed to be affluent. I learned later that we would have to pay around $4 per class, which is beyond the means of most Iranians. We all held copies of the *Masnavi-ye ma'navi*.

Masnavi-ye ma'navi means "The Spiritual Rhyming Couplets." It was composed in the thirteenth century by Jalal al-Din Muhammad

b. Muhammad al-Balkhi. Western readers know him as Rumi, from his long residence in Rum, so called because it had been the heart of the Eastern Roman (or Byzantine) Empire. (Rum corresponds roughly to Anatolia, the landmass that dominates modern Turkey.) He was born in 1207 in what is now Tajikistan, at the northeast tip of the area where Persian culture was dominant, but his father, a religious scholar, moved his family west when Rumi was a boy. They settled in Konya, the capital of the Seljuk Sultanate, in Rum. After receiving theological training in Syria, Rumi returned to Konya, where he achieved modest fame as an Islamic legal expert and preacher.

In 1244, an ageing mystic, Shams of Tabriz, arrived in Konya and struck up a rapport with Rumi. Shams deplored the Islam that Rumi had learned in the seminaries. He pitied "the multi-talented scholar, well versed in...the principles and details of the law! They have no relationship to the path of God and the path of the Prophets." The two men spent several months in seclusion and Shams guided Rumi toward an ecstatic realization of God. Shams taught Rumi to whirl, accompanied by music or an invocation. In 1247, Shams disappeared. (Lurid accounts of his murder by Rumi's students, who were jealous of Shams's influence over their master, persist to this day. Franklin Lewis, a Rumi specialist at Emory University in Atlanta, suspects that Shams left Konya when he had nothing left to teach Rumi.) Grief-struck by Shams's absence, Rumi composed odes that ascribe divine qualities to him. In the late 1250s or early 1260s Rumi started his great narrative and didactic work, his manual for life, the *Masnavi-ye ma'navi*.

Rumi is thought to have spent at least a decade intermittently composing the *Masnavi* before his death in 1273. (If you refer in conversation to the *Masnavi*, the rhyming couplets, Iranians assume that you are referring to Rumi's *Masnavi*, and not the *Masnavi* of another poet.) At more than 25,000 lines, each one roughly twice the length of a line of traditional English poetry, the *Masnavi* is very long. Its length seems to corroborate the belief of some scholars that Rumi composed much of it extemporaneously, in the presence of his scribe and muse, Hosam al-Din, and that he made few subsequent revisions.

The *Masnavi* contains thousands of stories and anecdotes, many of them drawn from the Koran and other, pre-Islamic and foreign narrative traditions, interspersed with Rumi's advice on belief, behavior, and the correct path toward spiritual perfection. Rumi's poetry can transport the reader to a kind of rapture. However, he warned against the blinding effects of outer beauty, and urged his readers to seek the wisdom inside his wit. "The letters are the vessel," he says in the *Masnavi*, "therein the meaning is (contained) like water." I know people who say that they have grasped this meaning, and that their temperament and view of the world have been changed.

Mr. B is a man of medium height, with thick gray hair and a beard of the same color and density. When I first saw him, he was wearing pressed corduroy trousers and a long woolen waistcoat over a white shirt. He bowed slightly as he came into the class and gestured for us to sit down. (It is customary in Iran to rise when your teacher enters.) When he smiled, his eyes shone darkly. Flushed by Mrs. Roshan's well-heated sitting room, he used a neatly folded handkerchief to dab his temples. He began the class with the words, "In the name of God, the compassionate and merciful." He referred to Rumi as "His excellency, our master."

During our first few classes, Mr. B introduced Rumi to us in a general way. I got the impression of someone who was profoundly spiritual and also profoundly religious, but opposed to fanaticism. Although the *Masnavi* addresses Muslims, it is tolerant of other faiths. In Mr. B's telling, it treads a pragmatic path between the competing ideas of predestination and free will. Rumi rejects the extreme asceticism of other mystical traditions, arguing that an engagement with the material world is not only necessary but also may be beneficial. "If you hoard a coin in your pocket," Mr. B told us, "it is material. As soon as you give it, out of charity, it becomes spiritual."

As someone who is married and recently became a father, I was reassured by Rumi's approval of earthly love. In an ode, he describes love between human beings as a bridge to heavenly love. I was attracted to the cosmic unity that Rumi presents as a means of reconciling the form of things with their spiritual essence. Although he was observant of Islamic law, Mr. B told us, Rumi believed that an observant person who is ignorant of Islam's spirit is "more dangerous than an irreligious person." In that person, "pieties take the place of faith."

In the *Masnavi*, Rumi hints that he can only communicate some parts of his awesome message; most people are incapable of understanding the whole. Mr. B seemed to share Rumi's spiritual elitism. He referred disparagingly to "the common people," for whom "only religious ordinances are important." It occurred to me that there might be something self-congratulating about our class. Perhaps, by reading fleet-footed mystical poetry, we were distinguishing ourselves from the literalness of the common people.

The classes developed a pattern. I would sit on a chair with my back to the window. The brainy-looking young man, a newly qualified civil engineer called Ali, sat on my left. The seat opposite was occupied by a middle-aged woman called Mrs. Malayeri. She dressed with a casualness that is rare among Iranian women. She usually wore jeans and a T-shirt, and little makeup. I sometimes imagined that she was a Western woman, transplanted to Iran.

For the first hour and a half, Mr. B would speak about themes that showed up in the section of text that we were reading. We would take notes. (I am slow and clumsy at writing Persian, and would copy from Ali the bits that I had missed.) Then there would be a break for tea and fruit. During the break, I would sometimes talk to Ali, or to Mrs. Malayeri. (It turned out that she is a yoga teacher. We have friends in common.) During the second, shorter part of the class, Mr. B would read from the text, quoting in Arabic from the Koran, and from other Iranian poets, to support points being made by Rumi.

Once, while Mr. B quoted and his eyes shone, I remembered that Mrs. Malayeri had told me that poetry flows in the veins of Iranians, even those who are not bookish. I looked up. The girl with the plaster over her nose had closed her eyes. Mrs. Malayeri was smiling. I smiled too. It was what Rumi had warned against, the blinding effect of beauty.

The class ended joyfully. We thanked Mr. B. The woman with the plaster asked if anyone intended to drive in the direction of Elahiyeh. Elahiyeh is the neighborhood where I live, so I offered her a ride. She introduced herself as Simin and added that I was very kind to offer to take her home. She hoped that my wife would not mind.

As we walked to my car, Simin switched from Persian to English. She told me that she had attended primary school in the English city of Leeds; her father had been finishing his university studies there. After getting an MA in English literature, she was planning a Ph.D. thesis on aspects of epic writing. She taught English at a language institute and came to class straight from work. She wore a shapeless black pinafore of the kind that the authorities deem suitable for the workplace.

For the next several weeks, I took Simin home after class and we would talk on the way. She was hungry for information about the literary scene in Britain and the US. She complained that the *London Review of Books* was hard to find in Iran. Her favorites were the Metaphysical poets; she loved Donne. I sometimes disappointed her when she spoke about this book or that. She had read more English classics than I had.

Our route took us along looping freeways that were built in the past decade and a half, during Tehran's dramatic period of expansion, past housing developments that have accommodated an influx of rural migrants. To the north, the lights stopped abruptly where the mountains were too steep for construction. To the south, they stretched for miles, into the scrub and semidesert that mark the beginning of the Iranian plateau.

It struck me that as recently as five or ten years ago, Simin and I might have been punished for sharing a car at night. A group of Islamic militiamen, uncouth village kids, might have flagged us down and demanded to know the nature of our relationship. If they had not believed us, they would have taken Simin away for a virginity test. If I had been recalcitrant, I might have been flogged.

That was before the baby boomers, the millions of Iranians who were born in the first decade after the revolution, grew up and reacted against official definitions of personal morality. The authorities responded by allowing social liberalization. Nowadays, cars are rarely pulled over. Women in cities no longer get hassled for wearing bright colors and makeup. In the streets, girls and boys brazenly hold hands.

At twenty-seven, Simin almost qualifies as a baby boomer. Society is changing so fast that she divides Iranians into mini-generations, each with mores of its own. "For women of my age," she told me, "sex before marriage is taboo. It's regarded as a tragic flaw that affects the whole family. But today's teenagers think differently. For many young girls, keeping their virginity before marriage is irrelevant." (Although the law forbids sex outside marriage, the authorities generally turn a blind eye to it.) Simin would like to get married but she has not met the right man. Like the vast majority of Iranian girls, she will go on living with her parents until then.

Simin has no recollection of life before the revolution. In schools, on TV, in speeches made by politicians, the authorities have tried to mold young Iranians' view of themselves and their history. The official view glorifies the revolution, Shia Islam, and the clerical elite. It denigrates Iran's pre-Islamic past and its rich tribal and secular culture. This approach has led to what Simin called "a loss of identity."

I recently discussed this phenomenon with Farideh Gheirat, a prominent lawyer who is concerned by the challenges that face young Iranians. Gheirat told me that "young people are incapable of conceptualizing Iran without thinking of the Islamic Republic."

Many are indifferent or hostile to the official ideology, but ignorant of other aspects of their heritage.

Simin's thirst for knowledge has protected her from a "loss of identity." She attends a weekly class on a great epic poem, Firdawsi's *Shahnameh*, whose roots lie in the mythology and legends of pre-Islamic Iran. For Simin, reading the *Shahnameh* is "a way of reminding ourselves of our glorious past." I asked her what she gets from the *Masnavi*. She replied that she likes to juxtapose it with Western literature. "It shows that the human spirit seeks the same thing, using different means."

This idea is reassuring to Simin, given the hatred and incomprehension that increasingly color relations between Islam and the West. Westernized Iranians like Simin inhabit a precarious middle ground. When I asked her about George Bush's war on terror, she said, "I have no sympathy for the Islam that's being attacked, but nor do I agree with the attackers."

In many ways, Iran is an exceptional Muslim country. Islamist and anti-Western feelings are declining. Shia Iranians loathe and fear the chauvinistic Sunnism that is espoused by groups like al-Qaeda. Young Iranians associate Shia militancy with the Islamic Republic, and the Islamic Republic is no longer popular. Although many Iranians were upset when US troops recently engaged their Iraqi enemies around Shia shrines in Najaf and Karbala, most regard America as a preferable neighbor to the hated Saddam.

Talking to Simin, I realized that, for many Iranians, poems like the *Masnavi* provide refuge not only from the Islamic Republic's interpretation of Islam, but also from aspects of Western culture. Simin referred to a Western-style consumer mentality that Iran's middle classes have embraced. The *Masnavi*, she said, teaches that "if you want spiritual calm, you won't achieve it by building up material possessions." She depicted it as a riposte to the value that society increasingly places on wealth and status.

Consumerism has emerged strongly during the four years that I have been in Iran. Iran has benefited from high oil revenues and many people are rich enough to buy expensive imported goods. In Elahiyeh and other well-to-do neighborhoods, young people parade Nokia cell phones, Nike sneakers, and Levi's jeans, and drive their fathers' luxurious Nissan sedans. (Iranian importers sidestep US sanctions by buying American goods through middlemen in Dubai and elsewhere.) Some people are worried by what they see as the spreading values of selfishness and materialism. Ali-Reza Alavi Tabar, a prominent journalist and intellectual, recently told me that he had been asked by poor neighbors to dissuade their teenage son from spending $30 on a pair of jeans. "I asked the boy," Alavi Tabar told me, "if he was aware that buying the jeans would mean less money for food at home. He shrugged and said he wanted the jeans."

One night, as Simin and I approached Elahiyeh, we passed a young woman in the street with a plaster on her nose. According to a plastic surgeon that I met several months ago, Tehran boasts more nose jobs per capita than most Western cities. (There is one monotonous model: retroussé.) I took the opportunity of asking Simin about her own nose operation. Given the mystical verses that we were reading—verses that value the content of a thing, not its form—I wondered whether Simin regretted her vanity.

She was not offended by my question. She ascribed the current craze to the new consumer culture. "In the 1990s, for the first time in so many years, we were exposed to Western products and magazines, and people learned to be aware of their appearance." Simin exempted herself from this reasoning; her nose, she told me, had been operated on for medical reasons. "I couldn't breathe easily in the summer," she said, "and my doctor said I should have it straightened."

It was daylight when we gathered for our next class. The Persian New Year celebrations, starting on March 21, had caused a three-week hiatus. The clocks had gone forward. The mountains rose before us, their white caps sparkling in the evening sun. Mr. B was full of the joys of spring. Rumi, he said, believed in "a renascence with every breath that you take."

Over the coming weeks, we read a story in the *Masnavi* about a king who falls in love with a handmaiden. When he brings her back to court, she falls ill. The king prostrates himself in a mosque and, entering a trancelike state, learns of the impending arrival of a wise physician. The following day, an old man presents himself at court.

Mr. B explained that the king represents the seeker of spiritual perfection. The old man is his "guide." Their meeting mirrors the epiphany of Rumi's encounter with Shams. "That was the greatest divine gift," Mr. B said. "Shams' physical aspect was human, but in reality he was something else." Mr. B meant that Shams had been infused with God's spirit.

Mr. B took off his spectacles and lay down his notes. He said, "There are people who forget the words of the Koran, which says that God is closer to us than a vein running through our brain." He was referring to people who say that God cannot be apprehended directly by the believer, but only through the prophets and imams—and nowadays, by extension, through the clerics who claim to be their representatives. According to Mr. B, the journey to spiritual perfection must be accomplished from within: "It's only by knowing yourself that you can come to know God." Mr. B's words seemed to contradict the Islamic Republic's recommendation that ordinary people organize their faith around a few Objects of Emulation. He seemed to be challenging the notion that clerics are worth emulating.

Mr. B alluded to Rumi's view, expressed in the *Masnavi*, that a person who blindly imitates another person is like an ape. I thought of an Iranian academic, Hashem Aghajari. In a speech he made in 2002, he compared the unquestioning emulation by Shiites of senior ayatollahs to the mimicry of monkeys. For this, and other comments that were deemed insulting to the clergy and Islam, Aghajari was sentenced to death. (He remains on death row, though the judiciary is reportedly close to bowing to international pressure and releasing him).

Mr. B quoted Saadi, another great poet, "How can I thank God enough for the divine gift of being too weak to oppress?" Everyone broke into smiles. It was a moment of subversion, a delightful moment.

One evening after class, I approached Mr. B and asked if he had ever known someone like the old man in the story we had read. He replied that when he was a boy, growing up in the eastern province of Khorasan, he had read the poetry of a mystic shepherd called Baba Taher. Years later, as a student in Tehran, Mr. B had felt an irresistible pull toward a man who passed him in the street. The man was a sheikh, and Mr. B told him that he wanted to be his student. The sheikh said, "I've known you since you started reading the poems of Baba Taher."

I had heard that the Islamic Republic had relaxed its hostility toward mystic lodges. I tried to picture Mr. B in such a lodge, spiritually inebriated and dancing and repeating an invocation, but the image was irreconcilable with the mellow, cerebral Mr. B that I knew. There was a border between the two, but I, a debutant, was a long way from the border. Mr. B told me, "For every one hundred people I teach, perhaps three are able to cross over into another kind of consciousness."

Over the next few weeks, we inched through the story of the king and the handmaiden. (At this rate, it will take us about eight years to complete the *Masnavi*.) The old man determines that the maiden is lovesick for an ironmonger in a distant city. On his instructions, the king uses promises of wealth and advancement to entice the ironmonger to leave his family and come to court. United with her lover, the maiden recovers, only for the old man to feed the ironmonger a potion that debilitates him. The ironmonger becomes ugly and the handmaiden stops loving him. In the end, the ironmonger dies.

According to Mr. B, the story relates a struggle inside us. The handmaiden, he said, is worldly love that has become "unhealthy" because of its reliance on physical infatuation. She is cured when her lover loses his looks. The ironmonger represents our covetous and materialistic self. His death is "a triumph over the devil in all of us." Mr. B advised us to concentrate on the meaning behind the story, not its literary merits. He wanted us to think of the *Masnavi* as being beyond literature.

During the break, I took my tea over to Mrs. Malayeri. She was thinking about Mr. B's advice. "He's telling us to concentrate on the gift," she said, "rather than the hand that's holding it."

I asked Mrs. Malayeri how she had become interested in Rumi. It goes back, she told me, to a personal calamity that happened shortly after the revolution. (Mrs. Malayeri is a divorced mother of two, but that is all that she told me about her private life.) She sought solace in Indian mysticism, Zen Buddhism, and yoga. In those days, yoga was regarded with suspicion by the authorities, and classes were held semi-clandestinely. After six or seven years of study, and two visits to India, Mrs. Malayeri regretted that she was ignoring sources of wisdom in her own culture. "I asked myself, 'Malayeri! Where are you?'" That "Where are you?" led her from Eastern philosophy to poems, including the *Masnavi*, that she had read in her youth.

As a young woman, Mrs. Malayeri had supported the revolution, and had been dismayed when the rhetoric of freedom was replaced by a radical, Islamic intolerance. I know many people who had similar experiences and are now embittered. With Mrs. Malayeri, I had the impression of someone who was content, despite the disappointments that she had experienced.

At the height of the Iran–Iraq War, at the height of the intolerance, she refused a chance to emigrate to Australia. "There's something here that's very strong," she said. "When I'm away from Iran, I miss it terribly." I asked what she missed. She said it was hard to explain. I said, "something in the soil," and she smiled, unable to find the words.

I was reminded of what Farideh Gheirat, the lawyer, had said about young Iranians' difficulty in distinguishing between Iran and the Islamic Republic. Mrs. Malayeri had a longer perspective. Her optimism seemed appropriate to our class. Rumi's world is full of optimism, partly because it promises redemption from fanaticism.

In Iran, fanaticism has been overwhelmed by a yearning for moderation. From the pulpit, senior ayatollahs perpetuate the old rhetorical hatreds—of the West and Israel in particular—but most Iranians see their sermons as a tired show, designed for foreign consumption. "Look at the brand of Islam that they tried to impose on us," said Mrs. Malayeri. "Even that didn't take root."

Mrs. Malayeri told me about the nearby apartment block where she lives with her twenty-eight-year-old daughter. (Her son is a student in the US.) In the old days, there were state-sponsored busybodies—people called them hezbollahis, a reference to the vigilante group, Hezbollah, to which many were affiliated. These people, Mrs. Malayeri said, would monitor their neighbors for un-Islamic behavior. They would watch for suspicious gatherings, such as parties with alcohol, that the police could raid. Those days are gone. Even the hezbollahi families, she said, "have accepted that we live in a certain way, and they live in a certain way."

I asked Mrs. Malayeri if she had voted in February's parliamentary elections. She raised and lowered her eyebrows very quickly—a wordless Iranian "no." She added, "I don't have anything to do with politics."

Twice, in 1997 and 2001, Iranians turned out in massive numbers to elect Muhammad Khatami as their president. But Khatami's plan to spread democracy was thwarted by a conservative elite made up of a few dozen clerics and their supporters in the judiciary, armed forces, and media. They jailed his supporters, banned reformist newspapers, and vetoed legislation that was passed in the pro-Khatami parliament. Under Khatami's influence, the Islamic Republic became more open and tolerant, but not more democratic.

Before February's general election, a conservative vetting body disqualified more than two thousand pro-Khatami candidates from running. Some 52 percent of the electorate went to the polls, a big drop from the 67 percent that turned out at the last parliamentary election, in 2000. Some cities experienced an unofficial poll boycott by young people. In Tehran, 32 percent of the electorate voted, a figure that would have been lower if the authorities had not mobilized civil servants and official militias. I recall the public enthusiasm that surrounded Khatami in 1999, the year that I first visited Iran. It has been replaced by apathy and cynicism.

A few weeks into the New Year, Khatami inaugurated the Tehran Book Fair. Khatami is a bookish cleric. (He is not an ayatollah, which means "sign of God" in Arabic, but has a lower rank, *hojjat-al-Islam*, which means proof of Islam.) He is a former culture minister and once headed the national library. After coming to power, he lifted many artistic restrictions and put a stop to the extrajudicial execution of intellectuals, which had happened with appalling regularity.

A few days later, I had a rendezvous at the book fair with Ali, the young civil engineer from Mr. B's class. I had got to know him over the past few months. Behind Ali's shy exterior, I sensed a young man's willfulness, and a keen academic intelligence. His self-confidence did not glow as it does in older people; it flickered. He criticized thinkers and philosophers with splendid precocity.

Ali told me that he had always been expected to follow a family tradition and become a civil engineer. A young man with a future in engineering, he told me, feels that his life is mapped out. "He anticipates that, in ten years, he will have a home and a car and social status." Ali and I joked that he also expects to marry a nice girl from a well-to-do family.

At university in the northern town of Rasht, Ali developed a passion for literature. He attended lectures that were unconnected to his engineering degree, and wrote poetry. The other engineering students made fun of his bookishness. ("Here comes Aristotle," they would say, and it is typical of Ali that he felt both insulted and flattered.)

After graduating, Ali returned to Tehran and, alongside his engineering job, started a part-time degree in Iranian literature. He longed to give up engineering and devote himself to books.

Ali was standing at an entrance to Tehran's open-air convention center. (It is organized around an artificial lake and has dozens of pavilions.) As we wandered around, I realized that the fair was attracting a variety of people. Seminarians in gowns and turbans compared purchases outside the Arabic-language pavilion. Through imitation designer sunglasses, young men ogled female students with bright scarves and tight cotton coats. At a refreshment stall next to a pavilion that specialized in religious books, some women in chadors unbuttoned lengths of black cloth, held books of Islamic ordinances, and sucked iced lollipops. Ali and I dawdled in the English-language pavilion. A young clientele perused dictionaries, novels, do-it-yourself guides, and books about philosophy and theology—I saw one book called *Religion without God*.

Unlike his conservative opponents, Khatami does not fear pluralism in dress, beliefs, or books. During his presidency, the Tehran Book Fair has grown and diversified. It has become a showcase for books that before 1997 would not clear the censors. Next summer, Khatami's second term of office will come to an end, and the clerical elite will ensure that only conservatives may stand to replace him. The 2006 book fair may have a different feel.

Ali and I bought French fries and ate them sitting on a lawn. Ali was preoccupied by his professional dilemma. If he abandoned engineering, his family would be disappointed. It would mean material uncertainty. (In Iran, as elsewhere, mediocre engineers are richer than brilliant academics.) On the other hand, he longed to turn his back on a society that judges people "not on what you think, but what you have."

I told Ali that I had recently met a graphic-design student who felt isolated because she was a practicing Muslim. "At university," she had told me, "I get odd looks for going into the faculty mosque to say my prayers." It was a terrible indictment of the Islamic Republic; a regime designed to promote faith was gradually destroying it.

Ali described the Islam that had been promoted at the boys' high school that he attended in the 1990s. The school would organize regular mourning prayers for the imams; the boys were expected to weep and beat their chests. Pious pupils were rewarded with good grades. Ali told me, "I couldn't accept that if I wept while saying a certain prayer, I would go to heaven."

Ali's religious beliefs, like his professional future, are not fixed. I asked if Rumi was having an effect. He said: "I've come to the conclusion that Rumi has something other than poetic power.... He sees something that others do not."

At our next class, Ali told me that he had consulted Mr. B about his dilemma. Mr. B had advised him to give up engineering only when he was certain that he could live with the consequences. After the class, Simin gave me some books, modern Persian novels that she thought I might like. She had taken off her plaster. Her nose was pert and downturned, and it suited her.

7

BUSH, IRAN, AND THE BOMB

January 2005

IN 2002, KENNETH POLLACK'S book *The Threatening Storm: The Case for Invading Iraq* helped to persuade some Americans that, sooner or later (preferably sooner), the US would have to unseat Saddam Hussein in order to safeguard its own security. Pollack put his case more cautiously, and more adroitly, than many Republican proponents of "regime change" in Iraq, but he turned out, like them, to be wrong about the threat that Saddam Hussein posed to the United States. He also failed, like them, to predict the grave repercussions of an invasion. In contrast to many hawkish members of the Bush administration, and a great many newspaper columnists and editors, Pollack had the grace to apologize for his errors. Now that the Bush administration is trying to decide how it should respond to a second hostile Middle Eastern state, Iran, which it suspects of seeking nuclear weapons, Pollack has written another long book, *The Persian Puzzle: The Conflict Between Iran and America*,[1] advising what should be done.

Although Pollack's judgment has been found lacking, he is more qualified than most to write about US policy toward the Middle East. Besides serving as director of Persian Gulf Affairs and Near East and South Asian Affairs on Bill Clinton's National Security Council, he

---

1. Random House, 2004.

has variously worked on policy toward Iran (as well as Iraq) for the CIA and for several think tanks and universities. Iran's recent efforts to acquire advanced nuclear technology justify his argument that now is the time to devote attention to the Islamic Republic. "If we do not take advantage of this window of opportunity to deal with Iran's nuclear program," he says, "someday we doubtless will regret not having done so."

The US and other nations, notably EU member states, Japan, Canada, and Australia, are alarmed by Iran's progress toward being able both to enrich uranium and to separate plutonium, processes that can produce fuel either for civilian power reactors or for nuclear bombs. Under the terms of the Nuclear Non-Proliferation Treaty (NPT), which Iran ratified in 1970, the Iranians are entitled to develop these technologies for civilian purposes, but the covert way that they have done so has aroused the suspicion that they intend to produce bombs, as well as energy for peaceful use. As part of its adherence to the NPT, Iran signed a "safeguards agreement" with the International Atomic Energy Agency (IAEA), allowing agency officials to monitor its activities regularly.

Beginning in the summer of 2002, however, in view of long-standing suspicions of nuclear activities that had remained hidden from inspectors, the agency brought the Iranian program under closer scrutiny. It has since established that Iran has egregiously breached the safeguards agreement which was designed to keep its nuclear activities transparent and limited to peaceful purposes. These breaches include Iran's failure to report the purchase and development of nuclear materials and to declare the existence of several of its nuclear sites.

Using the Iranian government's past behavior as a guide, some of its critics expect more breaches of the agreements. They are convinced that the government is lying when it insists that its nuclear program is exclusively for civilian purposes, and they believe that it intends to develop the capacity to build a nuclear bomb on short notice. To deny Iran that capacity, they are trying to persuade it to forswear the right, provided for under the NPT, to develop a nuclear "fuel cycle," the series of industrial processes required to produce fuel from uranium or plutonium, which can be used to produce either electricity or nuclear bombs.

Suppose for a moment that America had managed to impose stability in Iraq and installed a pro-US government there. One wonders what effect this success would have had on Pollack's thinking about Iran and its progress toward building nuclear facilities, and whether he and other former Clinton administration officials might now be arguing for the invasion of the Islamic Republic. Perhaps the only solace to be drawn from Iraq's current wretched condition is that such questions need not be asked.

In any event, the Pollack of *The Persian Puzzle* is a chastened man. His final chapter, "Toward a New Iran Policy," contains a section called "The Case Against Invading Iran," which draws partly on the example of Iraq. It argues that "the threat of Iran's acquisition of nuclear weapons" does not justify "what would be an extremely costly and risky invasion." Among the disincentives that Pollack cites are Iran's considerable size and its inhospitable terrain, and the hostility that he believes the Iranians would show toward their occupiers.

In Pollack's final chapter, he justifiably castigates European countries for allowing calculations of commercial advantage to influence their political approach to Iran. The Europeans, Pollack suggests, in the hope of better trade relations, like to offer the Iranians "carrots" such as the opportunity to enter a trade pact with the EU and strictly limited nuclear technology. On the other hand, George Bush, who in his first term included Iran in his "axis of evil," wields a stick in the form of his administration's hostility toward Iran, and its support for worldwide sanctions against the Islamic Republic, in addition to the trade sanctions the US now maintains. Pollack argues for a combination of the two approaches among the rich and powerful countries—

a common resolve, in other words, to reward Iran if it behaves well, and to punish it if it does not. It is unfortunate that Pollack finished his book before November 14, 2004. He would have had much to say about the accord Iran signed on that date with France, Britain, and Germany.

The November agreement was designed as a first step toward allaying suspicions that Iran's nuclear program is military in intent. Before the deal was made, France, Germany, and Britain, with EU backing, had threatened to support US moves to have the Iranian program referred to the Security Council as violating the Nuclear Non-Proliferation Treaty. Acceding to pressure, the Iranians accepted European demands that they suspend all activities related to enriching uranium and separating plutonium. Iran and the three European nations also agreed to start negotiations on "long-term arrangements" that would make it impossible for Iran's program to be diverted to military uses, and they also agreed to start negotiations on "technological and economic cooperation, and firm commitments on security issues." According to Javier Solana, the EU foreign policy chief, the agreement may mark "a new chapter" in relations between Europe and Iran.

The odd thing is that this new chapter was supposed to be opened almost exactly a year earlier. On October 21, 2003, Iran and the same three European countries signed an almost identical agreement, aimed at allaying identical suspicions. Back then, too, the Iranians were close to having their nuclear activities referred to the Security Council. Under pressure from the US, as well as from the Europeans and the IAEA, Iran committed itself "to suspend all uranium enrichment and reprocessing activities." This agreement would, it was hoped, prepare the way for "longer term co-operation" from which Iran would gain "easier access to modern technology and supplies in a range of areas." The Iranians agreed to provide the IAEA with a complete accounting of their nuclear program to date. Germany's foreign minister, Joschka Fischer, declared October 21, 2003, to be "an important day.... This will stabilize the region."

The new deal is similar, the parties are the same; but something clearly went wrong during the year that elapsed between the two accords. Although the 2003 agreement allowed the IAEA and its member states to learn a great deal about the Iranian program, it did not interrupt Iran's progress toward a nuclear fuel cycle to anything like the extent that the Europeans had intended. The Iranians exploited ambiguities in the text—in particular, over what constituted "enrichment and processing activities"—and carried on, in the words of one US official, "kicking the can down the street." They continued to assemble centrifuges, devices that enrich gaseous uranium by spinning it at high speeds. Later, under diplomatic pressure, they stopped assembling the centrifuges only to start again in the summer of 2004. They produced enough uranium and other "feed material" for the enrichment process to make several nuclear bombs, should they decide to do so.

The merit of the new deal is that its explicit and comprehensive definition of "enrichment related and reprocessing activities" makes it harder for the Iranians to be semantically evasive. If the Iranians produce more gaseous uranium, there is little doubt that the board of governors of the IAEA will refer their actions to the Security Council.

Many European diplomats complain that the US is obsessed with bringing Iran before the Security Council but it has not worked out what it wants to do once Iran is arraigned. These diplomats suspect that two permanent members of the Security Council, China and Russia, do not want Iran's case to come before the Security Council, and will try to divert the US and its allies from taking action to punish the Iranians.[2] As one reads between the lines of the latest report on the Iranian program by Mohamed ElBaradei, the IAEA's

---

2. In October 2004, China agreed to buy a considerable amount of Iranian natural gas and to develop an Iranian oilfield; in return for providing energy to China, Iran expects, and will probably get, Chinese diplomatic support. Russia, which has provided Iran with nuclear technology and equipment, as well as civilian aircraft and arms, would be embarrassed if Iran is referred to the Security Council.

director-general, issued on November 15, 2004, it is clear that he does not believe that there are grounds to bring Iran's case before the Security Council.[3] Before October 2003, he notes, he described Iran's cooperation with the IAEA as being marked by "extensive conceal-ment, misleading information and delays in access." Since then, how-ever, it has improved appreciably, he says.

ElBaradei's apparently sanguine view contrasts with the mood of pessimism expressed by Iran's most trenchant critics, and this contra-diction reflects the subtly different approaches of the IAEA officials on the one hand and its member states on the other. Whatever his private thoughts on the matter, ElBaradei is in no position to demand pub-licly that Iran give up its fuel cycle; under the NPT, a covenant that it is ElBaradei's job to uphold, Iran is entitled to develop such a cycle. Furthermore, Iran signed its 2003 agreement not with the IAEA but with Germany, France, and Britain, and so its violation of the spirit of that agreement does not necessarily amount to a violation of the safe-guards accord. During the past year, ElBaradei makes clear in his November 2004 report, the IAEA has resolved most of its doubts con-cerning the scope of Iran's declared nuclear program. Iran has made, in his words, "good progress" toward correcting earlier breaches of its safeguards agreement. ElBaradei believes that the NPT needs to be

---

3. "Implementation of the NPT Safeguards Agreement in the Islamic Republic of Iran," report by the IAEA Director General, November 15, 2004. This report was critical of Iran's past misdemeanors, but its generally optimistic tone infuriated the Bush administration, which has made no secret of its dislike for ElBaradei. According to *The Washington Post*, the Bush administration has eavesdropped on telephone conversations between ElBaradei and the Iranians, in an attempt to find evidence for the director-general's allegedly pro-Iran bias, apparently part of an effort to have ElBaradei replaced when his second term as director-general ends this year. ElBaradei has the support of most of the IAEA member states and, perhaps for this reason, the Bush administration has not proposed an alternative candidate; some administration officials now predict that ElBaradei will stay in place. ElBaradei originally incurred the administration's wrath when he questioned—with reason, it turned out—US intelligence on Iraq's WMD programs before the 2003 invasion of Iraq. According to Daryl Kimball, executive director of the Arms Control Association, a Washington-based arms con-trol policy group, "some in the Bush administration are simply seeking retribution."

amended to make it harder for countries to achieve fuel cycles. Until that happens, he can hardly demand that Iran abandon a goal to which it is legally entitled.

Within the frame of its accord with the IAEA, Iran is behaving better than before. In practice, Iranian intentions are more distrusted than ever.[4] Because of its subversion of the 2003 deal with the Europeans, Iran's critics on the IAEA governing board are even more convinced that the Iranians are determined to abuse their right to a fuel cycle, and to divert the fuel that it produces to military use. The critics' failure to expose Iran's recent breaches of the safeguards agreement has not lessened their suspicion that Iran is engaged in clandestine nuclear activities, or that, once it attains a fuel cycle, it may effectively be classified as a nuclear-armed state.

With the 2004 deal, gloomy European diplomats concede, the outside world gained time, if nothing else. Exactly how much time is not clear. The agreement is open-ended, but Iranian officials contend that the deal will not last very long—six months at the most, according to some estimates. Furthermore, Iran and its European interlocutors entered into the accord with different goals. To the Europeans, it is a first step toward the dismantling of Iran's fuel cycle facilities. To the Iranians, it is a first step toward convincing the Europeans to allow these facilities to become operational. On October 27, 2004, Ayatollah Ali Khamanei, Iran's conservative Supreme Leader, who has the final say on all policy issues, denounced as "illogical" any speculation that uranium enrichment will be suspended in the long term. He warned that Iran would "review" its current cooperation if the Europeans

---

4. Iran's decision at the beginning of 2005 to accede to pressure and open its vast military complex at Parchin, outside Tehran, to inspectors, illustrates this difference in perceptions. To Iran, the decision is more evidence of Iranian openness. The Americans, for their part, have long maintained that the Iranians are trying to develop a nuclear warhead at the site and assume that the Iranians have now covered their tracks there. If the inspectors find nothing at Parchin, the Americans will not be convinced that the Iranians are telling the truth when they say that they have no warhead development program at Parchin.

indulged in "illogical" threats. Shortly after the recent accord, the moderate President, Mohammad Khatami, described it as

> a guarantee for a guarantee. We guarantee that we will not be diverted toward nuclear weapons and, in return, they guarantee that...we will have a fuel cycle.

Within the frame of the November 14 deal, the EU trio and the Iranians have set up three working groups to discuss economic, technological, nuclear, and security cooperation. In exchange for granting Iran trade and other advantages, the Europeans, I was told, want Iran to suspend its nuclear fuel cycle activities permanently—requiring it to obtain any fuel it needs for civilian reactors from abroad—although they may not insist on a public announcement to that effect. Mindful of the fact that it is easier to obtain weapons-grade plutonium from heavy-water reactors than from light-water reactors, they will offer to sell Iran a light-water reactor if it abandons its current heavy-water reactor program. They will offer Iran a steady supply of nuclear fuel, suitable for light-water reactors, to be returned to the countries that supply it after use, provided that Iran abandons its own uranium enrichment plans and sticks to the development of nuclear energy for peaceful use.

As incentives, the Europeans offer to support Iran's pending application to join the World Trade Organization, and the EU and Iran will restart talks, suspended in 2004, on striking a trade and cooperation agreement. The EU will reiterate its current contention that the People's Mujahideen, an Iranian opposition group that is based in Iraq, is a dangerous terrorist organization, and the Iranians will do the same with regard to al-Qaeda.

A European diplomat said that his efforts to persuade the Iranians to accept these terms was like "selling the same carpet twice." Europe has long supported Iran's WTO application, but it has been consistently vetoed by the US. In December 2004, the Americans brushed aside European objections and once again prevented the WTO from starting accession talks with Iran. The EU as a whole, along with some European states individually, has already declared the People's Mujahideen, a once-popular left-wing Muslim organization hostile to Iran, to be a terrorist organization. The Iranians seek the extradition of Mujahideen members that are currently being held by the Americans in a camp in eastern Iraq. In 2003, the US turned down an Iranian offer to exchange some of these Mujahideen members in return for suspected al-Qaeda operatives who are in Iranian hands. There is no sign that the American position has changed since then.

There is no clear reason to suppose that a further round of talks on Iran's nuclear capacity will be successful. Earlier talks floundered over Iran's failure to change policies that the Europeans find objectionable, particularly in the fields of human rights and foreign affairs. Since then, Iran has become, if anything, more intransigent. Its commitment to democracy was further compromised by the parliamentary election in February 2004, in which more than two thousand reformist candidates were disqualified from running for office. Its commitment to free trade has been called into question by the isolationist tendencies of the hard-liners who won that election. Notwithstanding the demands of Europeans, Iran has not improved its record on human rights or reduced its support for militant groups that oppose peace between Israel and the Palestinians.

Of all the European incentives, the most tempting may be the offer of a light-water reactor. Iran has one such reactor, which has almost been completed by Russian contractors at the Persian Gulf port of Bushehr. Iran would like more, but other countries are reluctant to incur US wrath by supplying them. It is far from certain, however, that the Iranians are willing to abandon their heavy-water reactor program in return for the chance to purchase light-water reactors that would provide a significant boost to their civilian power programs.

What is clear is that the US, not Europe, can offer the incentives that are most attractive to Iran. The Americans have the Mujahideen in their custody and can approve Iran's entry into the WTO. US sanctions against trade with Iran have had a debilitating effect on the Iranian economy, and the Iranians would like that policy reversed. Most important of all, the Europeans cannot offer Iran the security guarantees that it seeks. The US can.

Iran's evasions and ambiguous responses concerning its nuclear programs are often portrayed as aggressive in design, but I infer from conversations I have had with officials that the Iranians see their tactics as a deterrent—against both Israel, their nuclear-armed regional rival, and the US, a hostile superpower that has invaded two of their neighbors over the past three years. The Iranians do not seem to have given up on their ambitions to have a fuel cycle. If Iran's leaders are to change definitively their policies and abandon their efforts to have a fuel cycle, they must be convinced that their own security, and the future of the Islamic Republic, will be better protected as a result. But the Bush administration, which loathes the Islamic Republic and wants it to fall, has not absorbed this unpalatable truth.

That much was underlined over the course of a few days in January 2005, when Bush pointedly did not rule out the possibility of using force against Iran and Condoleezza Rice refused in the Senate to discuss the possibility of dealing with Iran even if it changes its nuclear policy. Seymour Hersh claimed, in *The New Yorker* of January 24, 2005, that the US "has been conducting reconnaissance missions inside Iran at least since last summer," with a view to identifying dozens of nuclear sites that "could be destroyed by precision strikes and short-term commando raids."

The Pentagon dismissed much of Hersh's report. Equally predictably, Iranian officials sounded insouciant; whatever the truth of Hersh's assertions, they would not willingly admit that a violation of their borders had taken place. It is possible that Iranian unease at such reports will help the Europeans extract concessions during their negotiations. In the long term, however, they will only entrench the EU's gloomy conviction that the US, having effectively sabotaged the talks by refusing to join them, intends to use their failure as a pretext to increase pressure against the Islamic Republic.

During his first term, Bill Clinton tried to isolate Iran with tougher sanctions and with diplomatic efforts, only partially successful, that were aimed at stopping it from buying nuclear technology. In 1996, as Pollack recounts, the two countries nearly went to war after the bombing of a US military housing complex in Saudi Arabia by agents that were believed to be backed by Iran. Shortly after the attack, Congress passed the Iran-Libya Sanctions Act, which gave the president the authority to impose secondary sanctions on companies in third-world countries that invest in Iran's energy sector. The following year, the unexpected election of the reformist Iranian president Mohammad Khatami seemed to indicate the possibility of a new Islamic Republic, relatively moderate and less vehemently opposed to US interests. Clinton spent the rest of his term modifying his policy in the Iranians' favor. Pollack describes how Clinton encouraged "people to people" contacts, relaxed some bilateral sanctions against trade, and let it be known that he would not invoke the Iran-Libya Sanctions Act, passed in 1996. He also allowed Madeleine Albright to apologize for America's history of meddling in Iran's internal politics.

Clinton's concessions, as Pollack recalls, were designed to coax Khatami into making overtures of his own, but the Iranian president was losing a struggle for influence against a conservative establishment that felt threatened by his attempts to promote democracy and his softer tone toward the US. By the end of the Clinton presidency, it was clear that Iran's hard-liners were in the ascendant. Still, following al-Qaeda's attacks of September 11, 2001, Iran enthusiastically contributed to George Bush's efforts to defeat its loathed eastern neighbor, the Taliban government. State Department officials began talking to the Iranians about a broader détente. But early in 2002, the Israelis intercepted a ship carrying arms that were widely thought to have been obtained from Iran and intended for the Palestinian Authority, allegedly in violation of accords between the Palestinians and Israel. The situation was transformed.

A few weeks later, Bush included Iran in the "axis of evil" along with Iraq and North Korea. Since the invasion of Iraq he has been trying to pressure North Korea to dismantle its nuclear installations, but his approach to Iran is so far opaque. By refusing diplomatic and economic relations, the US government makes it clear that it does not consider the Islamic Republic a legitimate country. At the same time, the US demands that Iran cooperate in its efforts to stabilize Iraq and oppose the insurgency there.

The Islamic Republic, for its part, would like a stable Iraq. Democratic elections in Iraq will ensure that power is held by their Shiite coreligionists. On the other hand, it does not want Iraq to be a US client, or for Iraq to become a model for ideologues in Washington who think that pro-US democracies should be installed throughout the Middle East. The Iranians have long sought guarantees that if they adjust their foreign policies to America's advantage, their security will not be imperiled, but the Bush administration has rejected these overtures.[5] As a result in Iraq, the Iranians are helping the Americans in some ways and hindering them in others. The Iranians have

---

5. On the sidelines of academic conferences, through their envoy to the UN, and through intermediaries, Iran has expressed its willingness to try to achieve a "grand bargain" to end hostilities with the US. According to a recent article by Barton Gellman and Dafna Linzer in *The Washington Post* ("Unprecedented Peril Forces Tough Calls," October 26, 2004), ElBaradei told Bush in October 2002 that "he had spoken to Iranian leaders and believed they could still be dissuaded from enriching uranium. According to sources with access to written accounts of their meeting, ElBaradei said that Iran wanted to talk and offered to help open a quiet channel. Bush demurred." According to the same article, John Bolton, the State Department's hawkish undersecretary for proliferation, dismissed later overtures with the words, "We're not interested in any grand bargain."

encouraged their Shiite allies in Iraq to compete in elections that are expected to be held early in 2005. At the same time, the Americans and the British say that Iranian agents using arms and money have cultivated many Iraqi groups, not all of them Shiite, including several that are active in the Sunni Triangle. No one doubts that Iran is capable of creating more chaos in Iraq—in retaliation, say, for an Israeli or American assault on its nuclear facilities.

Pollack's starting point in *The Persian Puzzle* is his belief that Iran's leaders are obsessed with America for historical reasons, and that "the history of US-Iranian relations holds many lessons for the future conduct of American policy." Pollack spends some 140 pages summarizing the history of Iran and of US–Iran relations up to the revolution of 1979. He pays particular attention to the CIA-organized coup that toppled Mohammad Mossadegh, Iran's nationalist prime minister, in 1953, and to the widespread Iranian perception of the Shah as an instrument of American policy. Pollack believes that the wrongs, real and perceived, committed by America in Iran before the Islamic revolution have had an enduring influence on Iranian policy, and he attributes much of the Iranians' subsequent hostility to the national desire to avenge them.

Pollack's historical survey is often inaccurate[6] and he sometimes writes awkwardly. In his account, actions do not elicit reactions; they "solicit" them. The Iranians were able to "ingratiate themselves quickly into Lebanese society." Concerning the Iran–Iraq War of the 1980s, in which the US gave considerable support to Iraq, Pollack speaks not

---

6. For example, the Achaemenid emperor Darius's complex at Persepolis was not exactly the "imperial capital" that Pollack says it was. It was a center for ritual; the empire was administered and foreign envoys were received elsewhere. The Medes, who were superseded by the Achaemenids, did not, as Pollack writes, dominate Iran "for many centuries." Their empire lasted barely sixty years. Mullah is not, as he writes, "a Persian term for cleric"; it is an Arabic word for "teacher." Rastakhiz, the name of the single party allowed by the pro-Shah political party founded in 1975, does not mean "resurgence," as Pollack says, but "resurrection."

of the resumption of aerial bombardment, but of its "iteration." Pollack took just three months to write his book, and it shows.

In his final chapter, "Toward a New Iran Policy," Pollack lists the Iranian policies that the US finds most abhorrent:

> its support of … international terrorism, its violent opposition to forging a just peace between Arabs and Israelis, its pursuit of nuclear weapons of mass destruction … and its poor record of human rights.

Pollack's list is reasonable, except that it conflates Iran's ambiguity about its strategic nuclear ambitions—in other words, to remain within the NPT, while protecting its ability to make nuclear weapons on short notice should it want to—with the actual production of the weapons themselves. (Pollack observes that the two amount to the same thing in strategic terms; in legal terms, of course, they are worlds apart.) Pollack's subtitle is "The Conflict Between Iran and America," not "The Problems That America Has with Iran." But he does not provide a similar, Iranian, list of complaints. Such a list might read as follows:

> US support for Israel's brutal suppression of Palestinian demands for a viable state; the US failure to pressure Israel to declare and give up the nuclear weapons that it is known to have; the killing by American soldiers of many thousands of Iraqi noncombatants, and (as illustrated at Abu Ghraib and elsewhere) its shameful record on human rights.

Pollack is right that Iran's leaders are obsessed with America, but history is not the main, or even a major, reason why. If its history were an important determinant of Iran's policy, the Islamic Republic would not have tolerable relations with Britain, its former neo-imperial tormentor, or good relations with Russia, another Great Power that tried to control Persia. The dispute between Iran and the US is over America's efforts to determine the future of the Middle East and to promote its own policy there, and the threat that this poses to a revolutionary state that was founded on principles that are antithetical to those of the US. No Western country pursues its own interests more vigorously in the Middle East than America; naturally, Iran regards America as its biggest threat. Iran's enmity for Israel is mainly based on its view that Israel is an American proxy. It is inconceivable, Iranian officials believe, that Israel would commit its atrocities against the Palestinians without American approval.

A clue to Pollack's thinking is his statement that "it has largely... been Iran that has set the tone and direction of the relationship" between Iran and the US. It is odd, and perhaps an expression of hubris or just a blind spot, that Pollack does not seem to regard America's large and active presence throughout the Middle East as having much influence on the "tone and direction" of its relations with Iran. After all, it is widely recognized that the Iranians had no part in the attack of September 11, 2001, and Bush's "strategic vision" has involved invading Iraq and supporting Ariel Sharon. Iran is no longer strong or confident enough to try to export its revolution. Its behavior, good and bad, is almost completely reactive.

It may be helpful to think of Iranian tactics, of which Iran's pursuit of nuclear ambiguity is an example—no matter how aggressive they are in themselves—as the underpinning of an essentially defensive strategy. The Islamic Republic is on the defensive in several ways: against a disenchanted population at home; against a hostile America on its eastern and western borders. The US has established new military bases close to Iran, in Kyrgyzstan and Uzbekistan, in addition to its forces stationed in Iraq and Afghanistan. To most knowledgeable outsiders, it is clear that Iran's leaders are trying to stem the tide of history, which tends, sooner or later, to submerge inflexible ideologies and their autocratic proponents.

When he is describing the situation in Iran, Pollack can be astute. He is right to warn US policymakers not to count on the generally pro-American feelings among many Iranians and he is right to see these feelings partly as a reaction to the vitriolic anti-American sentiment of their unloved rulers. As a member of Clinton's NSC, he was right to identify President Khatami as a sincere proponent of reform. Although they came to nothing, his efforts to encourage Khatami were honorable ones. I found his account of these efforts the most interesting part of the book.

Pollack believes that Iran's leaders "can convince the Iranian people to endure heavy sacrifices in the pursuit of abstract notions such as 'resisting foreign influence,'" but a few days in Tehran would probably convince him otherwise. Iran's leaders know that the abstract notions they promote in Friday sermons now enjoy little popular support. They fear that a period of economic hardship will provoke people to express their unhappiness in unpredictable ways. Iranian politicians, particularly those who control the nation's finances, are wasting Iran's oil surplus on populist spending sprees. They have fostered a culture of consumerism that contradicts the egalitarian values that they claim to uphold. They are unwilling to risk higher unemployment in order to reform their astonishingly inefficient economy, which is dominated by a corrupt state sector protected from competition. Iran is a state that, for all its apparent stability, is unsure of its people.

If Iran attains not only a fuel cycle for peaceful purposes but the ability to make nuclear bombs quickly, it may feel more secure, but it is unlikely to reactivate its old, highly combative foreign policy. If, on the other hand, it begins to assassinate opponents abroad, striking directly at Western targets, Iran will certainly force America and its allies—even the Europeans, who are likely to be primarily concerned about their interests—to take strong action. Iran is vulnerable to moves to isolate it still further. Sanctions by the EU, its main trading partner, or even the threat of sanctions, could have an acutely desta-bilizing effect.

After the 2003 agreement between the Europeans and Iran, I rashly predicted that Iran would hold to its new commitments.[7] But the Iranians flouted their spirit. During subsequent talks, Iran's nego-tiators infuriated their foreign partners by making unexpected demands at key moments in negotiations—as happened at the end of Novem-ber 2003, while the resolution on Iran's nuclear program was being drafted by the IAEA's governing board. Eventually, in return for with-drawing the demand that they be allowed to experiment with twenty centrifuges, the Iranians secured wording that, in their view, would make it easier for them to restart their enrichment and reprocessing activity in the future.

In the absence of reliable opinion polls, many foreign observers believe that most Iranians would support Iran's acquisition of nuclear weapons. They reasonably assume that Iranians resent the fact that neighbors and near neighbors such as Pakistan, India, and Israel have nuclear weapons, and they do not. It is not surprising that Iranians should question the motives of nuclear-armed states that guard sensi-tive technologies. But foreign observers also seem to assume that, to some degree, large numbers of Iranians identify with their leaders and the decisions they take. This may not be the case.

Over the past year, I have visited the scenes of two Iranian dis-asters. The first was at the southeastern town of Bam, where an earth-quake killed more than 26,000 people in December 2003. The second was Pakdasht, a poor neighborhood outside Tehran, where a man was recently sentenced to hang for the murder (and, in many cases, rape) of twenty people, mostly young boys. Delayed by incompetence, departmental infighting, and alleged corruption, Bam's "reconstruc-tion" is a national disgrace. So is the response to Pakdasht, where,

---

7. See Chapter Four, "Big Deal."

over a period of more than a year, the local authorities showed apparent indifference as, one by one, the children of ordinary people disappeared. I found that the inhabitants of these places abandoned Iranians' customary reluctance to curse the authorities in front of strangers. They are so fed up with the state, so distrustful of its motives and dismissive of its claims to competence, that they no longer regard it as their own.

These are extreme examples of the bad relations between rulers and ruled that are reflected in urban Iranians' growing skepticism about politics. (Voter turnout in the elections of February 2004 was barely 30 percent in many big cities, including Tehran.) The impassioned Iranian newspaper editorials that have been written in favor of the nuclear program do not reflect a national "debate" on the subject but the rhetoric of competing groups within the country. The program is domestically important only for a small group of politicians who score points off one another. (On November 16, 2004, for instance, Iran's parliamentarians, who have no say in formulating foreign policy, summoned Iran's chief nuclear negotiator and castigated him for the agreement with the Europeans, which, they said, required too many concessions by Iran.) But for most Iranians, the price of food, and the government's failure to lower it, are more important.

Iran's nuclear programs, and whether they are pursued, have become central to the Islamic Republic's wider ambition in foreign affairs. It is unlikely that Hersh's report will shake the belief of most Iranian officials that the Israelis or the US do not intend to launch an attack on their nuclear installations. But they and the Europeans know that the November 2004 agreement will amount to little unless the Americans join the negotiations, offering advantages such as security guarantees, a deal on Iranian assets in the US, and the prospect of normal economic relations. The Americans are wary of committing themselves to such policies unless the Europeans and others, especially Russia and China, consent to taking punitive action if Iran progresses further toward a fuel cycle that could produce nuclear weapons. What is needed to deal with Iran and its nuclear ambitions is the formation of an international coalition that includes the US, and that is not George Bush's strong point.

8

NEW MAN

July 2005

IRAN'S PRESIDENTIAL ELECTION, which was held in two rounds, on June 17 and June 24, 2005, ended in triumph for an Islamist ideologue, Mahmoud Ahmadinejad. The vote raised important questions. Have Iranians, by electing a hard-line conservative, turned their backs on the ambition of encouraging the rule of law and promoting the pluralism that was pursued by the outgoing president, Mohammad Khatami? Since voters favored a candidate who promised to set up a pure "Islamic government" over others who promised social and economic policies more in line with those of the liberal West, has the prevailing American view of Iran's politics, as a struggle between a freedom-seeking people and their repressive clerical rulers, been exposed as false? The answer to both these questions is yes—but only up to a point.

I know of no Iranian active in public life or in journalism, let alone a foreign diplomat or reporter, who predicted Ahmadinejad's win. Most political commentators, both conservative and reformist, expected the next president to be one of three men (in descending order of probability): Akbar Hashemi Rafsanjani, a former president who presented himself to the electorate as a moderate in all things; Mohammad Baqer Qalibaf, a conservative who said he favored modernizing the economy, and whose expensive campaign was aimed at attracting young voters; and Mostafa Moin, a former higher education minister who was viewed as Khatami's ideological heir. Ahmadinejad's chances were considered so remote that he spent much of the campaign deflecting pressure from allies to step aside to help unify the conservative vote. Two reformist candidates, Mehdi Karroubi and Mohsen Mehralizadeh, and a third conservative, Ali Larijani, were expected to do badly.

Popular discontent was a strong factor in the election. Many Iranians that I spoke to during the campaign said that they would not vote because the president, although he is Iran's highest elected official, is humiliatingly subordinate to the unelected Supreme Leader, Ayatollah Ali Khamenei. (During his eight-year presidency, Khatami has struggled in vain to take over some powers from Khamenei and from the officials Khamenei appoints; the prestige of the president's office has declined as a result of his failure to do so.) These Iranians said that they regarded holding elections as a fig leaf to protect an authoritarian conservative establishment made up of unelected clerics who guard their authority to dictate binding "national" policies on matters such as Iran's contentious nuclear program. Shirin Ebadi, a human rights lawyer and Nobel peace laureate, who had been briefly imprisoned in 2000, declared her intention not to vote. Iran's most famous political prisoner (who happens to be Ebadi's client), Akbar Ganji, called for a boycott of the election. Some analysts predicted that barely 40 percent of the electorate would vote, and that the Bush administration would have an easy time deploring the shortcomings of Iranian democracy.

As polling day approached, Mostafa Moin seemed to be doing well. He held a successful rally in a large stadium in Tehran. On the next-to-last night of campaigning, the northern section of Vali-Asr Avenue, the capital's main north–south artery, was thronged with young Moin supporters, some of them arguing volubly with Rafsanjani supporters. I spoke to many people who said that, having originally decided to boycott the election, they would, in fact, vote for

Moin. They seemed to be animated less by enthusiasm for Moin than by a desire to preserve the limited liberty of expression and social freedoms—to mix with members of the opposite sex, for instance— that have been tolerated under Khatami's presidency.

A few days before the election, I visited one of Rafsanjani's advisers. He told me that the Qalibaf campaign, despite the vast sums that had been reputedly spent on advertising, was faltering. He predicted that Rafsanjani and Moin would have to engage in the two-man runoff that the Iranian constitution provides for if no candidate wins more than 50 percent of the vote.

The following day, Ayatollah Khamenei's representative in the Islamic Revolutionary Guard Corps (IRGC), the best-equipped and most ideologically conservative part of the armed forces, publicly urged guardsmen and members of the Basij, a militia controlled by the IRGC and estimated to have between four and six million members, to vote for a conservative candidate who "puts himself sparingly in the public view while campaigning, and who refrains from extravagant spending." The Supreme Leader's message was unmistakable: the basijis should vote neither for Rafsanjani nor for Qalibaf. A few days later, according to the same Rafsanjani adviser, Basij officials began a "massive and concerted" campaign, mostly by telephone, to persuade basijis to vote for Ahmadinejad.

For what happened next, we must turn to another candidate, Mehdi Karroubi. Educated Iranians had derided this mildly reformist cleric, a former parliament speaker, for promising every adult Iranian a monthly handout of $62 if he was elected. After the polls closed on June 17, it became clear that, among poor Iranians, Karroubi's offer of a bribe was a vote-getter. Semiofficial results and private projections suggested that he would join Rafsanjani in the runoff. That, at least, was Karroubi's impression when he went to bed at 5 AM on June 18; he awoke two and a half hours later to find that "in one leap...[Ahmadinejad] had accrued a million votes" and overtaken him. When official results were announced, Karroubi was in third place—with a little over five million votes, compared to Ahmadinejad's 5.7 million votes and Rafsanjani's more than six million votes.

Karroubi presented his grievances at a press conference. (For a former high official to make public complaints is a provocative act; "family" disputes are usually solved behind closed doors.) The gist of Karroubi's argument was that the presence of basijis among some 300,000 election monitors appointed by the Council of Guardians was illegal and conducive to electoral fraud. "Money passed hands," he announced, giving rise to speculation that some voters had been paid to vote for Ahmadinejad. Karroubi also indirectly (but unmistakably) accused IRGC and Basij leaders of pressuring voters in Ahmadinejad's favor, and of encouraging some voters in provincial towns to vote more than once. In a letter that he sent to the Supreme Leader, Karroubi claimed that ballot boxes had been stuffed and that Khamenei's own son had interfered in the election. Two other candidates, Moin (who came in fifth, with a little over four million votes) and Rafsanjani himself, corroborated Karroubi's claims that serious irregularities had taken place.

Without the "irregularities" would Ahmadinejad have won his place in the runoff? There are reasons, though not conclusive ones, to suspect not. In some big provinces which Ahmadinejad won handsomely, the official turnout was far higher than most people expected. In Isfahan, for instance, the figure was 60 percent, almost double the turnout for last year's parliamentary elections. The officially announced nationwide turnout, 62 percent, was also surprisingly high. Some remote provinces produced odd figures. In South Khorasan, for instance, which is home to many members of Iran's disgruntled Sunni minority, the official turnout was an improbable 95 percent. Even though he was the candidate most associated with intrusive Shia Islamism, Ahmadinejad came in first in the province.

* * *

Ahmadinejad's popularity soared during the week that elapsed between the two rounds. He was a convincing winner in the runoff, defeating Rafsanjani by more than seven million votes. The first reaction of many Westernized Iranians was embarrassment. Ahmadinejad is a professor at Tehran's University of Science and Technology, but his special subject, traffic planning, does not promise imaginative leadership. These Iranians contrasted the president-elect's short stature, dreary clothes, and occasionally coarse language with Khatami's good looks, refined manners, and impeccable mullah's robes. (Appropriately, the two men do not get on. Khatami, it was said, was disturbed by Ahmadinejad's appointment as Tehran's mayor two years ago; fearing that Ahmadinejad would report to his conservative allies the proceedings of cabinet meetings, Khatami went against convention and did not offer the mayor an honorary cabinet position.) Khatami's conciliatory rhetoric in foreign affairs, his attentiveness to attractive women, and his admiration for Western writers have impressed many of the foreigners who have met him, especially Europeans. What, the Westernized Iranians wondered, would the Europeans make of this new man, a self-proclaimed "servant of the people" who created a controversy when he proposed turning municipal spaces in Tehran into graveyards for fallen soldiers in the Iran–Iraq War?[1]

---

1. Ahmadinejad, who is forty-nine, was born in the provincial town of Garmsar, the son of a blacksmith. When he was a small child, his family moved to Tehran. In 1976, he entered Tehran's University of Science and Technology to study civil engineering, and became active in Islamist politics. Notwithstanding recent claims to the contrary by some former US embassy hostages, Ahmadinejad is not thought to have participated in the 1979–1980 US embassy takeover, though it is possible that, like many others, he visited the embassy while it was in the students' hands. (Even if Ahmadinejad had been involved in the embassy takeover, it would hardly be shocking. Several prominent reformists, including the former head of parliament's foreign affairs committee and a current, female, vice-president, both had important roles in the takeover, and there was little US reaction to their appointments. Discussions in America over Ahmadinejad's past seem designed to sully the new president's reputation.) He spent part of the Iran–Iraq War of the 1980s serving in the Islamic Revolution Guard Corps, while continuing with his postgraduate studies. After the war, he took a series of official positions, serving as governor of the northeastern province of Ardebil. In 2003, following the conservative victory in municipal elections, he was appointed by the new Tehran municipality to be the capital's mayor.

Painful though it is for some to accept, Ahmadinejad may broadly reflect Iranians' collective desires—just as Khatami did in 1997, when he was elected to bring about liberalization and strengthen the rule of law. The fate of Khatami's reform movement is well known. Most of his legislative reforms were blocked by unelected conservative institutions such as the Council of Guardians. His cause was further set back at the 2004 parliamentary elections. Conservative candidates won control of the chamber after more than two thousand reformists were barred from running. The reform movement has been marginalized and many Iranians have come to regard its ultimate goal, democracy, as being of more interest to intellectuals and newspaper editors than to ordinary people.

Moreover, conservative Iranians associate "moral corruption"— the dramatic rise in prostitution, marital infidelities, and drug addiction during recent years—with the reformists' laissez-faire social policies. Under Khatami, it became common to see unmarried men and women walking hand in hand, and people wearing Western fashions—at first in well-to-do urban neighborhoods, more recently in modest ones. Some of Ahmadinejad's supporters are deeply concerned by these developments.

After the first round of voting, I borrowed two videos of Ahmadinejad's campaign speeches. One of them was an event in a crowded sports hall in Tehran. The other was a speech that he had delivered in the company of clerics in the seminary town of Qom. Before Ahmadinejad began his speech, a professional narrator of religious stories sang homilies to Zeynab (the sister of the third Shiite imam), whose birthday it happened to be. Young men in the segregated audience clapped and waved green flags that had Koranic verses on them. The women swayed demurely.

Once the audience had been warmed up, Ahmadinejad got to his feet and delivered a series of millenarian and vague promises which, in effect, dismissed most of the efforts toward political reform of the last century. He took no account, for example, of the Constitutional

Revolution of 1909, when democratic forces toppled the despotic Mohammad Ali Shah in the name of parliamentary democracy, or of Prime Minister Mohammad Mossadegh's nationalization of the Anglo-Iranian Oil Company, in the face of opposition by the then shah, Mohammad Reza Pahlavi. Such events apparently did not interest him.

Ahmadinejad believes that the two key developments in Iranian history are the advent of Islam and the revolution of 1979. He uses them as rhetorical references, ignoring other events that are tainted with Western notions of democracy. (He distinguishes between the Islamic Republic under Khomeini and the Islamic Republic after Khomeini's death in 1989, when he believes that revolutionary ideals were subverted.) If he were not so clearly an earnest religious zealot, you might accuse him of manipulating history and of treating his constituents like simpletons. But from all appearances, Ahmadinejad is sincere and, for many of his constituents, that quality validates his message, which is pious, reactionary, and seems genuinely unsophisticated.

During his Tehran speech, Ahmadinejad promised his audience a government whose "every project, every method, and every administrative mechanism has been extracted from the heart of Islam." He offered a clean administration, where "there is no room for personal or family profit." He repeatedly used the word "justice," which reminds Shiite Iranians of the five-year caliphate of Ali, the Prophet's cousin and son-in-law, and the first Shiite imam. (Shiites regard Ali's caliphate as the most fully realized example of Islamic rule.) During his speech, he touched on economics only to castigate the "rentiers" who profit from high interest rates and the banks that offer these rates. "If we return to the culture of Islam," he predicted, "you'll see tomorrow what kind of heaven this place becomes."

To Ahmadinejad, there is nothing very complicated about good government. What is required is trust between the ruler and the ruled, hard work, and faith in God. During his speech in Qom, he described how he had built up trust with his constituents in Tehran, and how corruption was being detected there—he described citizens approaching him after Friday prayers and informing on officials. The municipal government, he said, had used indigenous talent and minimal resources to dispose of a mountain of lethal waste that had accumulated over years on the city's periphery. Ahmadinejad may have wanted his audience to read in this mountain a metaphor for today's Iran.

If so, there would be near unanimity on who built the mountain—Ahmadinejad's opponent in the runoff, Akbar Hashemi Rafsanjani. This seventy-one-year-old cleric, a former confidant of Ayatollah Khomeini and a modernizing president between 1989 and 1997, campaigned as a patriarchal figure who personifies the Islamic Republic. But the Islamic Republic has become polarized—between a middle class keen on acquiring consumer goods and the conservative poor; between city residents and migrants from the villages. (According to UN figures, Iran's rural population has been dropping since 1996, while the urban population is rising by 3 percent a year, with dramatic social and economic consequences.) In the eyes of many, this polarization is the result of the uneven development associated with Rafsanjani's presidency, when Iran's economy became partially modernized and corruption also increased. Many people attribute to Rafsanjani (and his family) not only fabulous wealth but also boundless guile and a tendency to put expediency over principle.

I saw Rafsanjani deliver a speech in the run-up to the election. The audience was carefully chosen, consisting mostly of people associated with a network of very profitable private universities that an associate of Rafsanjani started in the 1990s. Rafsanjani does not care for unscripted criticism or heckling. (This is why he did not campaign in the provinces.) He did not stand up to deliver his speech, but remained seated, every inch the Brahmin mullah. He spoke about how he would be liberal and moderate in all things, but did not explain why his previous tenure had ended in hyperinflation, cronyism, and a series of horrific political murders that remain unsolved.

Rafsanjani's campaign went wrong from the start. Rather than try to sell himself to the electorate, he gave seemingly endless dull interviews to the foreign press, in which he portrayed himself as a man who could end more than a quarter of a century of enmity with the United States. (*Time* assumed he would become president and put him on the cover of its international edition, while Iran's relations with the US were hardly an issue during the campaign.) He repeatedly emphasized his reluctance to run for office—he had only done so, he said, out of a sense of duty. In the end, the voters saved him the trouble.

A few days before the runoff of June 24, I was in Tabriz, a northwestern city that is dominated by Iran's Azeri minority. Visiting Ahmaghieh, a poor suburb, I got my first inkling that Rafsanjani would lose. Ahmaghieh has a population of around 60,000 people. Roughly half of these people arrived there from the surrounding villages in the past few years. I was told that around three thousand people in Ahmaghieh live on government handouts. If they have a job, the men can make around $10 per day either working on building sites or in local factories. Until a few years ago, most local women wove carpets at home. Now Iran's former position as a major carpet exporter has been undermined by foreign competition, and the looms of Tabriz are mostly still.

In Ahmaghieh, I met two young men, members of the Basij militia who run a shop offering basic computer services. One of them told me that he had recently dropped out of a local university; he had despaired of getting a steady job in a government department because he did not have the necessary personal connections. His friend told me that the key election issue would be "saving us from unemployment." A poster on the wall outlined ways that people could help the destitute families of men who were in jail.

In common with many other residents, the two young basijis had not heard of Ahmadinejad until a few days before the first round of voting. Then Ahmadinejad supporters distributed a film showing the Tehran mayor in his modest house, and in his office dealing with people's problems with the city. After seeing the film, many in Ahmaghieh decided to vote for him.

The two men took me to the grimy office of a local doctor. He was an educated man, about forty years old, and he told me that he had been working in Ahmaghieh for the past eighteen years. He, too, had been impressed by Ahmadinejad's campaign, especially by his promise to solve the country's housing problems. (The doctor said that many of his patients were too poor to pay for consultations and he himself had not saved enough money to buy a house.) Diseases resulting from poor sanitation were frequent in Ahmaghieh, he said, and the township suffered power cuts for around three hours per day. (This was happening, he observed, in the second-biggest oil-exporting country in OPEC.) When I asked him about the fears, exploited by the Rafsanjani campaign, that Ahmadinejad would restrict social freedoms if he became president, the doctor replied, "Do you think that I, who have to spend the weekend at work in the hope of seeing a patient or two, have time to worry about social freedoms?"

That evening, I was back in Elahiyeh, a well-to-do district of north Tehran, stuck in election traffic. Some of the houses near where I live had been taken over for the Rafsanjani campaign. A well-connected young man had told me that young members of Rafsanjani's family had asked his friends to distribute flyers and campaign CDs, and that people were being paid to plaster their cars with Rafsanjani stickers. The street was packed with handsome young people wearing expensive clothes. Some shoved flyers through the windows of passing vehicles; others swayed to the Rafsanjani campaign jingle. The song blared from a parked car, an SUV that had been imported from Dubai, and everyone seemed to be having a good time.

Most of the 27 million Iranians who voted in the runoff election (49 percent of the electorate) live better than the people of Ahmaghieh and more modestly than the hedonists of Elahiyeh. But I suspect that lots of people had the two extremes in mind when they went to vote. Of the ten million people who voted for Rafsanjani, many did so because they believed that under his presidency, they would stand a better chance of preserving the upscale lives that they have enjoyed since the oil price hike of 1999 led to a dramatic rise in foreign exchange receipts. (According to the deputy governor of the Central Bank, foreign exchange receipts in the Persian year ending in March 2006 are expected to exceed $46 billion. Last year, imports soared 24 percent; consumer goods accounted for a sizable proportion of the increase.) Some feared that if Ahmadinejad became president, he would live up to his conservative reputation, segregate the sexes in universities, and order baton-wielding basijis to discipline any young woman who dressed daringly.

Many of Ahmadinejad's supporters feared that a Rafsanjani presidency would benefit a privileged few. It is not that Iranians are becoming worse off; most statistics show that poor Iranians are becoming less poor, better fed, and better educated. But life is hard for the millions who live on the edges of Iranian towns. For those who recently came from villages, urban customs can seem shockingly irreligious and frivolous while they struggle hard to make a living. Inflation in Iran is running well above the official rate of 15 percent. Ahmadinejad's economic adviser laments that a third of Iranians in their twenties are unemployed. The public university system is ill equipped to accept more than a fraction of applicants. (This summer, some 1.4 million young people will take university entrance exams to qualify for the 200,000 places available.) For many of Iran's first generation of city dwellers, urban life is a brutal assault on their traditions and their dignity. And it is dignity, not democracy, that Ahmadinejad has promised them. During a campaign speech in Tabriz, he declared, "We didn't raise a revolution to institute democracy. Democracy was insignificant next to our goals in this revolution."

* * *

The real victor of the 2005 elections was the Supreme Leader, Ayatollah Ali Khamenei. Having spent the past eight years trying to obstruct Khatami's reform movement, he can now reassure himself that besides the institutions—such as the Council of Guardians and the judiciary—that are directly answerable to him, the government and parliament, which are elected by universal suffrage, are also in conservative hands. Unlike the outgoing reformists, the newly chosen legislators and officials are committed—in public, at least—to the theocratic system that all but guarantees Khamenei his position for life.

Before the elections, George Bush was Khamenei's main adversary. Khamenei is known to be incensed by Bush's disdain for Iran's semi-democracy, and he is reputedly sensitive to taunts that the Supreme Leadership is not an elected position. Before the elections, Iranian conservatives worried that a low voter turnout would validate Bush's criticisms and that more countries would come to agree with him. If only a small proportion voted, they feared that Bush's hand would be strengthened in his effort to muster support for referring Iran to the United Nations Security Council because of its refusal to abandon its ambitions to produce nuclear fuel—an ability that Iran could, if it wanted, exploit to make bombs.

Khamenei helped ensure that the turnout was respectable. A month before polling day, the Council of Guardians issued the names of candidates that it had barred from standing.[2] Mostafa Moin, the main reformist candidate, was among them. Khamenei could hardly have been surprised by this decision, for he has considerable influence over the council. Amid accusations that the conservatives were fixing the elections in advance, Khamenei ordered the council to reinstate

2. Around a thousand candidates were disqualified, mostly because the Council of Guardians did not consider them to be well-enough known. The council disqualified all women candidates on account of their sex. A small number of candidates were barred for holding unacceptable political views.

Moin. The reformists were embarrassed; they are opposed, in principle, to ad hoc interventions by the Supreme Leader, which they consider unconstitutional. Some reformists urged Moin to spurn Khamenei's decision and boycott the election; if Moin rejoined the race, they argued, he would seem beholden to the very system he wants to change.[3]

In the end, Moin announced that he would run; the result was the most pluralist election campaign in Iran's history. That does not, of course, mean that the process was exemplary; it is hard to ignore Karroubi's allegations that the first round was rigged, or the judiciary's banning of a newspaper that dared to print Karroubi's allegations about Khamenei's son. All the same, in the first round, there was a wide range of views and a wide range of votes; according to the official results, no fewer than five candidates won more than four million votes apiece.

Amir Mohebian, a conservative newspaper columnist, expects the Supreme Leader to restrain Ahmadinejad's radicalism after he takes over as president in August. Khamenei does not always sit comfortably on top of the conservative establishment. He is more flexible than his public pronouncements suggest, and his primary concern is the Islamic Republic's survival, not its ideological purity. My guess is that Khamenei will advise Ahmadinejad to avoid exacerbating the existing divisions between traditional and Westernized Iranians, and to concentrate on fighting corruption and distributing Iran's oil revenues more equitably. Since his election victory, Ahmadinejad has distanced himself from suggestions that he plans to tighten dress codes—an issue that, in any case, he hardly mentioned during the campaign.

---

3. Moin's dilemma exemplifies an unresolved dispute that has sapped the energy of reformists ever since powerful conservatives prevented Khatami from introducing his reforms. Radicals such as Akbar Ganji argue that reformists should not compete for office but should instead build a popular movement for constitutional change. Moderates regard this idea as impractical, not to say dangerous; they argue that reformists must continue to work within the system. Now that reformists are no longer in government, the debate is bound to intensify.

But much depends on the ministers that he appoints. A hard-line culture minister, for instance, could increase censorship of the press, as well as book publishing and the arts, all of which have benefited from Khatami's relatively liberal approach. In any event, no one expects civil society to prosper. During the campaign, Ahmadinejad spoke disparagingly of Western-style NGOs and approvingly of traditional foundations and charities. It is unlikely, furthermore, that Ahmadinejad will undertake the structural reforms that the economy needs. Although he claims to favor the private sector and foreign investment, he comes from a political tradition that is paternalistic, distrustful of foreigners, and dirigiste in economic policy. (Ahmadinejad's economic spokesman has already announced that the government will reduce interest rates—against the advice of market economists.) Mohebian expects Iran's bloated state sector to grow further.

Few people think that Iran's policy toward Iraq will change under Ahmadinejad. Iran's leaders feel that they have done well in Iraq. They have cultivated to varying degrees all major Shia groups, including the secular ones, as well as the two major Kurdish factions of northern Iraq. Iran has considerably more influence over Iraq than it did when that country was being run by Saddam Hussein, and the US worries that this influence is harmful to its interests.[4] Although the

---

4. Iran agrees with the US that democracy should be strengthened in Iraq, but the two countries have different ideas about what that democracy will bring. Iran hopes that its Shia coreligionists will gradually introduce a pious reading of private morality; the Iranians are believed to be helping clerics in the southern (and overwhelmingly Shiite) city of Basra impose Islamic dress and mores. The Iranians are helping economically; Basra's electricity may soon be supplied by Iran. During a recent trip to Iran by Iraq's defense minister, his Iranian counterpart said that the two countries would cooperate on "modernizing Iraq's army." It is unlikely that this cooperation will amount to much, especially while the US continues to supervise the Iraqi army, but Iran's gestures are carefully targeted. By flaunting, even exaggerating, their influence across the border, the Iranians are reminding the US that any hostile moves on its part—for example, to knock out Iranian nuclear installations— could be fraught with consequences for Iraq.

Iranians enjoy American discomfort across the border, they would not stand to benefit if the current insurgency turned into unmanageable chaos.

Most Western governments, especially those involved in the current nuclear negotiations, had hoped for a Rafsanjani victory. As a veteran statesman and the head of an influential mediating body, Rafsanjani has considerable influence over Iran's negotiating positions. He would, it is thought, favor Iran developing a nuclear fuel cycle, but not at the cost of having its case referred to the Security Council. It may be that, having been humbled at the elections, Rafsanjani will lose some of his influence over the ongoing nuclear negotiations. If so, the balance may tip in favor of radicals who regard a nuclear fuel cycle as an indispensable shield against American aggression. Although Iranian presidents do not have much influence when it comes to formulating nuclear policy, Ahmadinejad can be expected to add his voice to those of the radicals—in favor of principle, against expediency. Ahmadinejad, whatever else he is, is a man of principle.

9

LIFTING THE VEIL

October 2005

AN IRANIAN WOMAN pauses in front of a huge Picasso, *Painter and His Model*, on view at Tehran's Museum of Contemporary Art. Standing in his studio, illuminated by subdued pools of colored light, the artist is depicted as an extension of the inanimate objects around him. He has been reduced to a series of mostly straight lines; his arms, palette, and easel merge into one another, and the rest of his body into the floorboards and wall paneling. To the model, on the other hand, Picasso has given a stark voluptuousness. With her expanse of stomach, distended breasts, and clublike limbs, she imposes herself on the scene in a way that the painter, who is part of the scene, cannot. For a few minutes, the Iranian woman is absorbed by this rich autobiographical painting, with all its intimacy and ambiguity. Then, rearranging her headscarf, she moves on to a Braque still life.

It is hard to decide what to marvel at—the Picasso, or the fact that it hangs here, in the capital of the Islamic Republic of Iran, part of a big show of modern Western art. In Tehran, any big exhibition is scrutinized before it begins by censors from the Ministry of Culture and Islamic Guidance. What, you wonder, did they make of the Picasso? Are the model's breasts too removed from conventional anatomy and her genitalia, paraphrased by an inky sliver, too figurative for her to be considered a proper (and therefore impermissible) nude? Perhaps they were flummoxed by the phallic limb protruding from her side? Whatever the reason, they let the Picasso through but acted decisively when they came to Francis Bacon's *Two Figures Lying on a Bed with Attendant*, a few rooms farther on. The censors sheared this triptych, whose gorgeous passages of paint evoke a terrible solitude, of its central panel. That panel—as visitors to Tate Britain, where it was on loan until the summer of 2005, will recall—depicts two naked men lying on a bed. It was deemed too gay for the Islamic Republic. (A little bit gay is too gay for the Islamic Republic.) The Bacon is now a diptych partitioned by a phantasmal smudge.

Of all the ironies raised by the current exhibition, titled simply "Modern Art Movement," none is more dramatic than this: arguably the finest collection of modern Western art outside Europe and America is owned by a country that, ever since the 1979 Islamic revolution, has prided itself on expressing contempt for Western culture. The Tehran show is the first exhibition of the whole collection since the revolution.

The fact that it is being staged at all owed much to the cultural glasnost that was pursued by the man who was president until the summer of 2005, Mohammad Khatami, and by the outgoing museum director, Ali-Reza Sami-Azar. Iran's conservatives delight in showing that even broken taboos can be revived, and now, after eight years of reformist government, they are back in power. Khatami's successor as president, Mahmoud Ahmadinejad, who was elected in June 2005, is an Islamic hard-liner who shows little appreciation for Western culture. The new museum director is an unknown quantity. Art enthusiasts who want to be sure of seeing these remarkable pieces should go to Tehran before the show ends on October 22, 2005. For Iran's hard-liners, these works are an unwelcome reminder of a morally corrupt, monarchical past; they may refuse to bring them out of the vaults again soon and fears are already being raised that some of the best pieces may be sold off.

In the exhibition catalog, Sami-Azar alludes to the collection's origins by thanking Kamran Diba, the museum's architect and first director, who negotiated the purchase of many of the works on display. (Diba left Iran when the revolution started; he now lives in France and Spain.) This may be Sami-Azar's elliptical way of thanking Farah Diba, Kamran's cousin and the wife of the former shah. While her husband poured money into buying the latest military hardware, Farah thought of preserving and developing Iran's artistic heritage. She set up several museums, which survive today, and started Iran's equivalent of the National Trust. She bought collections of Iranian art that had been in Western hands and put them on public display. And she persuaded the Shah that it would be a good idea, commercially and culturally, to build a collection of modern Western art and put it in the museum that Kamran was building (again, at her behest).

The times were propitious. Iran was swimming in foreign money after the oil price hike of the early 1970s. For the same reason, the Western art market was suffering, and masterpieces were going relatively cheap. According to Parviz Tanavoli, one of Iran's most distinguished sculptors and a former cultural adviser to the Queen, the collection was amassed for "tens, not hundreds, of millions of dollars," from dealers such as Ernst Beyeler in Basel and Leo Castelli in New York. At the time, the Queen used to joke that the collection cost less than one of the Shah's beloved Tomcat fighter planes. A few years ago, it was valued at $2 billion.

Most Iranians interested in modern Western art will never make it to New York's MOMA or the Pompidou Centre in Paris. MOCA (the wannabe acronym for Museum of Contemporary Art was Sami-Azar's idea) is the next best thing. The thrill of cultural exchange, of finding yourself among artists who speak a different visual language, is palpable when you enter the very first gallery, filled with Impressionists and Pointillists, not least from the chorus of beeps triggered by excited students as they cross infrared barriers installed to keep visitors and works apart.

Iran's traditional pictorial art, miniature painting, inclined to formalism, rigid convention, and the respectful portrayal of kings, is very different from a shimmering Pissarro depiction of peasant homes or a Toulouse-Lautrec lithograph of a jockey dominated by a horse's posterior. A tour group gathers before a Gauguin still life that contains a Japanese print and a carved Tahitian head. As a riposte to the Islamic Republic's official distrust of foreigners and to the equation of contact with contamination, it could hardly be bettered.

The show takes you through Kamran Diba's varied spaces, past a rare Léger from 1913 and Picasso's synthetic Cubist masterpiece *Fenêtre ouverte sur la rue de Penthièvre*, to a marvelously inventive late bronze by the same artist, of a baboon and her young. The curators have given deserved prominence to a trio of circus performers by the Fauvist George Rouault; its robust central figure, with her striking arrangement of Mesopotamian wedge nose and saucer eyes, might have been unearthed at Ur.

Every room has its own ironies. Particularly striking is a watercolor by the German Dadaist George Grosz, called *The Unexpected Guest*. It shows a gluttonous burgher gorging himself, surrounded by the cracks and tumors of his own ruin, while Death appears at the door. Grosz painted this picture as a Communist in the 1920s, but it could just as easily represent the perception that Iran's revolutionaries had, half a century later, of the elite they were supplanting.

There are three big omissions from the European part of the collection up to 1939: Cézanne, Matisse (except for one lithograph), and Mondrian. But such absences seem trifling when you enter the large, well-lit gallery that is devoted to Abstract Expressionism, the movement that proclaimed America's cultural primacy after the Second World War.

Far away at the United Nations, the US and Iran trade insults;

Iran's nuclear dossier edges closer to the Security Council. But here, art shouts louder than politics. Visitors contemplate two trembling Rothkos and a magnificently vivid Pollock drip painting (*Mural on an Indian Red Ground*) that seems to unite the balletic and the calligraphic. (The dealer Ernst Beyeler considers this Pollock to be one of the finest works that has passed through his hands.) The collection's sole de Kooning, a dark and vehement abstract work called *Light in August*, reminds us of one that got away. In 1994, before Sami-Azar's directorship, the museum swapped a painting from de Kooning's monumental Woman series for a rare volume of illuminated Persian miniatures, then part of an American collection. That series marked de Kooning's apostasy from abstraction, and a split in the movement; the chance of seeing *Light in August* and *Woman* side by side is gone.

Several rooms of exuberant Pop Art mark another high point in the show. Warhol, Lichtenstein, and Oldenburg are ill served by these small spaces, but there is no denying the pedigree of the art—or its relevance. Iran's new consumer culture, an unstoppable reaction to fifteen years of revolutionary austerity, means that Tehran is a good place to revisit Pop Art's mixture of celebration and irony, of childlike appetites and social blindness. What a shame that Sami-Azar never managed to rescue the silkscreen that Warhol executed of Farah while on a visit to Tehran. It entered the Queen's modest private collection, and now languishes in a damp basement underneath one of the former royal palaces.

Everyone agrees that the collection's later works are not its best. For every luscious Bacon (the collection has two, though one is currently on loan) or teeming Dubuffet, there are half a dozen modish duds. The collection takes us up to 1977. And then there is silence— a silence that is, for all Iranians, filled with screaming, convulsive politics. The 1979 revolution and the Shah's flight; the US embassy hostage crisis; eight years of war with Saddam and his backers in Europe and America; for many Iranians, these events seemed to augur permanent conflict between them and the West. And this was reflected in attitudes toward Western art and its champions. In the eyes of the revolutionaries, the deposed queen—who had fled into exile—symbolized a kind of moral sickness, masquerading as culture.

That so much of Farah remains, even today, is testament to the humane good sense that underpinned many of her public endeavors. As queen, she was charitable, progressive, and (unlike so many at court) uncorrupt. Nevertheless, she was prone to bad lapses of judgment. Farah was the Shah's willing accomplice in a grotesquely vainglorious commemoration of Iran's monarchy, staged in the ruins of Persepolis, the ancient Achaemenid shrine city, in 1971. (She and her husband played host to some sixty potentates and presidents. The event cost tens of millions of dollars, at a time when a shameful number of Iranians had no electricity or running water.) Equally damaging was her patronage of an arts festival whose most notorious performances featured nudity and live pigs. Pious Iranians did not forget these affronts. After the revolution, fanatics set out to tear down Persepolis. (They were stopped.) Royal palaces were thrown open as examples of degenerate living. And there were rumors that the nation's modern art collection would be sold off to Kuwait.

The art was saved, probably for commercial reasons, but it remained mostly unseen, while the museum put on edifying shows of religious and revolutionary art. Acquisitions were out. Only under Sami-Azar's directorship were these trends challenged. Sami-Azar helped to reduce artistic censorship and he promoted Iranian artists abroad. His tenure was marked by increased foreign contacts and loans; in 2004, the museum collaborated with the British Council to stage an ambitious exhibition of twentieth-century British sculpture. But the conservatives needled him. An appointed upper house vetoed a parliamentary bill that would have enabled the museum to purchase works from abroad. (Sami-Azar wanted to fill those pre-1939 gaps and invest in British art.) The hard-liners prevented him from sending works from the museum's Western collection, along with examples of contemporary Iranian art, to an ambitious festival of Iranian culture that was being planned by the Swiss dealer Beyeler. The festival never happened.

You can still catch some wonderful art in Tehran, and a shy nostalgia in the corridors of the Contemporary Art Museum. Picture the museum rising in the 1970s—at a time, in Tanavoli's words, when Tehran was "an international capital" and the streets teemed with foreigners. Imagine the inauguration, on a sweltering night in 1977, when Iran's beau monde gathered to celebrate the Queen's birthday and view parallel shows of modern Western and Iranian art. Amid performance and music, the Shah and Farah were feted by some of the world's most important patrons and curators, among them Nelson Rockefeller and the director of the Guggenheim. Amid the glittering company and self-congratulation, who could have imagined that revolution was less than two years away? But that's not the story of an art collection. It's the universal story of an elite too busy gorging itself to notice the unexpected guest, standing at the door.

10

THE PERSIAN DIFFERENCE

November 2005

TONY BLAIR SAID recently that the Islamic Republic may pose a "threat to our world security"; he also mused that he might one day be called upon to "do something" about Iran. Other Western leaders have criticized Iran's development of an ambiguous nuclear program, its influence in Iraq, and its venomous language toward Israel, and concluded that the Iranians have ambitions outside their borders.[1]

If Blair and others are right, and Iran has expansionist intentions, this would be a fascinating change. Since 1600, the Iranians (or Persians, as the Europeans knew them) have been largely confined to the same plateau, located between several mountain ranges, the Persian Gulf, and the Caspian Sea, that they occupy today. As nationalist ideas arrived from Europe in the nineteenth and twentieth centuries, the Persians proved to be the best prepared of all Middle Eastern peoples to build a nation-state on the Western model, and among the least likely to invade their neighbors.

---

1. Blair was responding to a speech by Iran's conservative president, Mahmoud Ahmadine-jad, on October 26, 2005, in which he described Israel as a "disgraceful blot" that deserves to be "wiped off the map." In Iran, embarrassed officials explained that Iran has no intention of attacking Israel. But the diplomatic damage was considerable; the President was widely condemned, Kofi Annan canceled a trip to Tehran, and Iran's efforts to avoid referral to the United Nations Security Council for refusing to abandon its plans to produce nuclear fuel suffered a setback.

Now, despite periodic displays of unhappiness by Iran's Kurdish and Arab minorities, there is a strong belief among many modern Iranians that they, as Persian-speaking Shia Muslims of Indo-European descent, have a unique identity. (Iran's biggest minority, the Azeri Turks, are better integrated into mainstream society than the Arabs and Kurds.) Since the Muslim Arab conquest of the mid-seventh century, Iran has been repeatedly invaded. To a striking degree, the Persians' cultural identity helped them to avoid being assimilated by successive occupiers, but it also restricted their ability to expand their own political orbit to include neighbors who do not share the same identity.

The last time that Iran was a world power was when it was ruled by the monarchs of the Sassanid dynasty, who came to prominence at the beginning of the third century AD. They installed Zoroastrianism as the state religion, and were overthrown in the seventh century by the Arabs. In important ways, the Sassanids were successors to the greatest Iranian empire of all, the Achaemenid empire, which stretched, at its peak around 500 BC, from the Indus to North Africa. The Achaemenids' administration was both multicultural and multilingual; its provincial governors, called satraps, tended to promote religious diversity. In fact, it is hard to see much common ground between the sprawling Achaemenid empire and the centralized, doctrinaire state of Iran in this or the last century, either before or after the Islamic Revolution of 1979. The closest that the Islamic Republic has come to empire-building has been in its efforts to export its revolution to other Muslim countries in the 1980s, and these have failed badly. Not surprisingly, the revolutionaries found it hard to sell a political philosophy that is based on Shia exclusiveness and informed, despite Iran's claims to be advocating supranational ideas, by Persian chauvinism.

One of the strengths of Neil MacGregor, the well-regarded director of the British Museum, is his interest in exploring ideas of continuity and change. He has said that an "Enlightenment institution" such as the British Museum should aim to change the way that people think about society, and examining the relationship between the past and the present seems to be a part of this. At the same time, he is not afraid of political controversy. His support for Donny George, the head of the Iraq National Museum in Baghdad, helped George to fend off American insinuations that he had been involved in the looting of the museum that followed the fall of Saddam Hussein's regime in 2003. Early in 2005, John Curtis, the head of the British Museum's Ancient Near East Department, said that US forces in Iraq had caused "substantial damage" to the remains of ancient Babylon. In 2004, the museum staged a provocative debate on how ancient Mesopotamian civilizations and Saddam Hussein's claims to be their spiritual heir were relevant to Iraq's current attempts to create a national identity.

In conceiving the museum's exhibition "Forgotten Empire: The World of Ancient Persia,"[2] MacGregor and Curtis, the show's main curator, and co-editor of its very good catalog, seem to have set themselves two main goals. The first is to answer the Greek chroniclers of the Greco-Persian wars whose accounts created what MacGregor calls "those stereotypes of the freedom-loving, tough European versus the servile, luxurious, effeminate, despotic Asian." The second is to draw attention to the link between ancient Persia and modern Iran—in other words, to remind people that Iran's Islamic theocracy, which is now accused of trying to develop nuclear weapons, is descended from a great pre-Islamic civilization. In its desire to encourage an urgent contemporary debate, the museum has simplified some complex arguments and historical experience. Nonetheless, "Forgotten Empire" is an important event that deserves to be remembered.

Cyrus the Great was the scion of an Iranian dynasty that was related to, and dominated by, the Medes, an Aryan people whose empire,

---

2. September 9, 2005–January 8, 2006. Catalog of the exhibition edited by John Curtis and Nigel Tallis (University of Calfornia Press, 2005).

based in what is now western Iran, flourished in the sixth century BC. Shortly after he came to power in 557 BC, Cyrus organized a revolt against his Median overlords. Within two decades, he had conquered not only the Median kingdom but also all of Asia Minor and Babylonia, and much of the eastern Mediterranean coast. Cyrus is remembered in the Bible for encouraging the Babylonian Jews to return to Jerusalem and rebuild the Temple of Yahweh. He is thought to have died in 530 BC, around the time of a campaign against Bactria, part of modern Afghanistan. Cambyses, his son and heir, continued the expansion of Iran into Egypt, but it was during the long and splendid reign of Darius I (522–486 BC) that the empire grew to its fullest extent, incorporating the western coast of the Euxine (Black) Sea. Darius's empire was the biggest the world had yet known. He left behind superb monuments, notably his palace complexes at Persepolis and Susa.

The wars between Greece and Persia lasted between 499 BC, while Darius was still king, and 479 BC, seven years after the accession of his son Xerxes. These wars, and the Greeks' famous victories at Marathon, Salamis, and Plataea, did much to form the emerging Greek national identity. The interest shown in the wars by Greek writers and the absence (so far as is known) of a written literary tradition in Achaemenid Persia, have produced a historiographic oddity. Most of the information that we have on the history and mores of the Achaemenids was written by their intermittent subjects and foes, the Greeks. This history, moreover, is often appended to accounts of the Greco-Persian wars—hooked, as it were, to a mere twenty years of the empire's life, and to military convulsions far from its center. Taken on its own, the Greek version of events can skew perceptions. One effect, as MacGregor lamented, is that "people still have it in their heads that [the Achaemenids] are the people that the Greeks defeated. It is like thinking of the British Empire as those people whom the Boers defeated."

The stereotyping to which MacGregor has referred is evident in the salacious *Persica*, a notoriously inaccurate book of history by

Ctesias, the Greek doctor of Artaxerxes II (404–359 BC). Following the defeats of the Achaemenids, there was a hubristic vogue in Greek art for scornful portrayals of Persians. Aeschylus' *The Persians*, a triumphalist stage account of the Persian court's reaction to a military defeat by the Greeks, portrays the Persian elders as weak and indecisive and the defeated King Xerxes as reckless and arrogant, but neither as monsters. In fact, some Greek writers strongly praised the Persians. Rather than advocate Greek-style democracy, Xenophon, in the *Cyropaedia*, his hagiographic account of Cyrus the Great, writes admiringly of the Great King's benevolent despotism.

Above all, we are lucky that the judgments of Herodotus, the most important Greek chronicler of the Persian empire, are far from being uniformly or reflexively negative. There is surely more to Herodotus's *Histories* than the promotion of a "negative yet still dangerous image of the Persians," as the museum's exhibition catalog puts it. Although he is biased, as one would expect, and strongly dislikes Cyrus's heir Cambyses, Herodotus finds much in the Persians to praise, including their aversion to lying and their prohibition of capital punishment for a single crime. The London show does not make the point that Greek portrayals of the Persians are more varied than many people think.

In the *Histories*, Herodotus comments on the readiness of Persians to adopt foreign customs. It is not surprising that the Achaemenids' administrative and artistic culture was diverse and eclectic, in view of the vastness of their territories and the fact that many of the societies under their control were advanced and worthy of emulation. The Achaemenids did not build a new civilization in the way that the Sumerians and Egyptians had; they adapted and refined the civilizations that they found.

Nor did they impose their languages on their subjects. Old Persian, the antecedent of the language that is spoken by modern Iranians, was the least used of the empire's three official languages, the other two being two non-Iranian tongues, Elamite and Akkadian, a Semitic language. (Aramaic was the lingua franca for communication between the satrapies.) From the Medes, the Persians borrowed institutional and ceremonial traditions. From the Egyptians, Cambyses took the title of pharaoh; his soldiers adopted Egyptian breastplates. "From the Greeks," writes Herodotus, "they...learned to lie with boys."

The Achaemenids fostered a hybrid art. Their vast columned audience halls—called apadanas—were conceived by Persians, but these and other buildings were constructed by artisans from throughout the empire. To build Darius I's palace at Susa, the Great King employed Ionian and Sardian stonemasons and Median and Egyptian goldsmiths. Babylonians made fine reliefs using glazed bricks. (There are two in the British Museum exhibition.) Looking at the colossal human-headed bulls at Persepolis, one is reminded of the winged bulls that the Assyrians, whose empire had long been swept away, used to support entrance arches.

It was in the Achaemenids' interest to be religiously tolerant; it would have been foolhardy to try to impose a single set of beliefs and practices on so huge an empire. There is still debate over what the Achaemenid kings believed. In the Cyrus Cylinder, a propaganda inscription that was found in Babylon and is held by the British Museum, Cyrus the Great claims to his Babylonian subjects that Marduk, the city-god of Babylon, chose him to occupy the city. The biblical book of Isaiah says that Cyrus was "anointed" by Yahweh to let the Babylonian Jews rebuild the Temple. Cambyses, Cyrus' successor and the conqueror of Egypt, favored Egyptian cults. Despite the later Achaemenids' veneration of Ahuramazda, the Wise Lord of the Zoroastrians, many scholars do not believe that they fully accepted Zoroaster's teachings. In the Persian heartland, Iranian and Elamite gods were worshiped side by side. Herodotus writes that the Persians offered sacrifices to Zeus.

Curtis's exhibition, hindered by its cramped space, nevertheless conveys well the hybrid character of Persian art and history. It is disappointing to discover that some major pieces, such as a fine Egyptian statue of Darius that is adorned with hieroglyphs and representations of the Nile goddess Hapi, are plaster casts, and it is annoying, owing to the narrow space available, that an important relief (also a cast) of a lion biting into the hindquarters of a bull, from Persepolis, cannot be seen from a distance of more than a few feet.

Still, one can imagine the awe that visitors to Persepolis and Susa must have felt on approaching the royal complexes, and as one wanders through the architectural fragments on display, the scale and splendor of the Achaemenid buildings can seem wanton and overwhelming. It is unnerving to think that a massive stone lion's paw on the gallery floor was only a small part of a column capital more than fifty feet from the ground. (One wonders, too, at the destructive energy that Alexander the Great must have spent to lay waste to Persepolis— he committed this act of vandalism in 330 BC, by which time he was in control of most of the Achaemenids' possessions.) The show contains an evocative sculpture, in polished black limestone, of a seated mastiff, a superb physical specimen with a leonine snout and paws. Its expression conveys vigilance, calm, and utter obedience to the Great King.

Amid these suggestions of opulence and imperial control, it is pleasing to look at a tiny and exquisite statue made from lapis lazuli of a young man with a crown, which was found at Persepolis, although we don't know over what, if anywhere, he ruled. The exhibition expertly illustrates the religious cross-fertilization of the empire; a small gold sculpture of two figures in a horse-drawn chariot is adorned with the head of Bes, an Egyptian god who may have had a protective function; the piece was found in central Asia, thousands of miles from Bes's spiritual birthplace. Coins from the Aegean coast show Baal, a fertility deity, on one side, and what is generally thought to be the Zoroastrian Wise Lord Ahuramazda on the other; the Wise Lord has been stripped to the waist, presumably to make him attractive to the body-conscious Greeks. To illustrate trading links between

East and West, the curators have included a relief that comes from Lycia, on Asia Minor's Aegean coast. The frieze depicts a Lycian ruler surrounded by pages and reclining on a couch, under which his dog patiently lies. The king is drinking from a Persian vessel.

The tolerance for cultural difference on display in the exhibition suggests that the empire was not unduly repressive. But the show does not challenge the view, first expressed by Herodotus and propagated later by other Greek historians and tragedians, that the Greco-Persian wars were waged between a single Greek people fired by a heroic sense of national identity and a faceless Persian confederation united only by the promise of material rewards.[3]

From this exaggerated perspective, it is a short step to the disparaging tone used by some reviewers of the show when describing the ancient Persians. In a commentary that got much attention, Jonathan Jones of the London *Guardian* suggested that the Persian empire was "grandiose, luxurious and remotely despotic" and that the Persians themselves were "a void at the heart of the exhibition." Rather than appreciate the museum's plaster cast of a relief showing foreign delegations bringing presents to the king, which he found "static," Jones advised his readers to visit the Elgin Marbles, which are displayed in a nearby gallery. "The Greek masterpiece is full of motion and emotion," Jones wrote, "from horses barely reined in, to a heifer being led to sacrifice."

Jones is not the first to denigrate Achaemenid art. It is worth recalling the views of Robert Byron, the gifted and opinionated aesthete who visited Persepolis while it was being excavated in 1934, and recorded his impressions in his classic travel book *Road to Oxiana*.

---

3. In the *Histories*, Herodotus reports the stunned reaction of a Persian general to being informed that competitors at the Olympic Games competed not for money but for an olive crown. Later, the author describes the Athenians' response to an attempt by the Persians to split the Greek alliance: "We are one in blood and one in language; those shrines of the gods belong to us all in common, and there are our habits, bred of a common upbringing."

Byron objected to Persepolis' "cross-bred sophistication." He found its famous columns, "like mules," to be "infertile...they have no bearing on the general course of architecture, and hold no precepts for it." Of the reliefs, Byron wrote,

> They are not mechanical figures; nor are they guilty of elaboration for its own sake; nor are they cheap in the sense of lacking technical skill. But they are what the French call *faux bons*. They have art, but not spontaneous art, and certainly not great art. Instead of mind and feeling, they exhale a soulless refinement.

Byron, too, refers his readers to the British Museum—though not, significantly, to the Greek galleries. In contrast to Jones, who seems to regret that the Achaemenids were not more like the Greeks, Byron hates Persepolis because it shows that the Persian "artistic instinct has been fettered and devitalized by contact with the Mediterranean. To see what this instinct really was, and how it differs from this, one can look at the Assyrian reliefs at the British Museum."

No one would deny that the Persepolis reliefs on show at the British Museum—including an original relief fragment showing "Susian guards," and the members of tribute delegations—are very different from the Assyrians' pulsating narratives of battles and hunts and the Parthenon's intimate stories. With few exceptions, the Persepolis friezes repeat archetypical profiles, often of a soldier; one can search in vain for variations in pose, or for emotion on the identical faces. Although flawlessly executed, the processions do not have the visual charm of the Lycian frieze with its varied poses and its parabola of outstretched pages' arms. There is no attempt to show the Great King's affection for animals, or to describe him at leisure.

These friezes have a different function. They were architectural elements in the sense that they were part of an arrangement of long staircases and terraces by which one reached the apadana and the palaces. For the visitor, mounting broad flights of stairs on his way to an audience or assembly, the reliefs on either side must have been mesmerizing, and also unsettling—giving a sense of being honored and taken into custody at the same time. The friezes were designed to intimidate, not to seduce, or to tell a story, or to show that the Great King was a good fellow who liked a drink. Judged on their own terms, they are an artistic triumph.

On September 22, *The Guardian* published a commentary by Shahrokh Razmjou, who heads the Center for Achaemenid Studies at the National Museum of Iran, in which he described Jones's review of the London show as "propagandist." Other Iranians were also upset about Jones's article. In a contribution to an Internet forum that circulates views on Iranian studies, an Iranian living in Britain wrote, "Everything I believe in is represented upside down in this article and, I should confess, it's very heartbreaking." It is worth asking why an arcane argument about the distant past aroused such emotions, especially since awareness of the Achaemenids' achievements is relatively recent.

During the Sassanid period, between the third and early seventh centuries AD, the Achaemenid empire slipped from the national consciousness. An official history written in the sixth century AD ignores the Achaemenid kings. The ruins of Persepolis came to be known as the Throne of Jamshid, a legendary king. (Most Iranians still call it that today.) After the Iranians were converted to Islam in the seventh century, many came to believe that Cyrus's tomb near Persepolis was the tomb of Solomon, or Solomon's mother, and it was used as a mosque. Inspired by Solomon, or Jamshid, or both, Islamic rulers commissioned pious inscriptions at Persepolis. In 1617, Persepolis was identified as the ancient Achaemenid capital by a European traveler; two centuries elapsed before booty-hunters moved in. Many of the original frieze fragments that are on show at the British Museum were "acquired" during two British foraging expeditions at Persepolis in 1811. (In those days Europeans turned up without bothering to ask anyone for permission to dig for antiquities and put locals to work with picks and shovels.)

Iranian interest in the Achaemenids increased after cuneiform writing on clay tablets and stone inscriptions was deciphered in the mid-nineteenth century. Some prominent families adorned their houses with Achaemenid-style reliefs. The British Museum exhibition catalog notes that Nasir ed-Din Shah, the monarch of the Qajar dynasty who ruled between 1846 and 1896, was "interested in antiquities." It does not mention that his interest was primarily commercial. The author of a recent short history of Iranian archaeology writes that Nasir ed-Din did not sponsor digs "with a view to study and inquiry... but principally with the aim of acquiring gold and silver."[4]

This supports the view of Rene de Balloy, the French minister in Tehran, who, in 1895, secured for France a monopoly to carry out all excavations in Persia.[5] The Louvre, which had already built up a collection of French finds from Susa, some of which are in the British Museum show, was the main beneficiary of the concession, and it now has a large collection of Persian objects. The concession lasted until 1927, two years into the reign of the new monarch, Reza Shah, a former army officer who rose to power after mounting a coup. Under Reza Shah and his son and successor, Muhammad Reza, more efforts were made to prevent ancient objects from leaving the country.

Distrustful of Shia clerics and contemptuous of Arab culture, Reza Shah associated himself with the pre-Islamic past. (For example, he

---

4. Sadiq Malik Shahmirzadi, *Iran Dar Pish Az Tarikh* (Prehistoric Iran) (Tehran: National Heritage Organization, 2002).

5. The Shah, de Balloy wrote during negotiations, "is in a mood of advanced avarice." The French ingratiated themselves with the Shah by giving him some valuable Sèvres porcelain, but they did not endear themselves to the Iranians. French archaeologists were suspected of repatriating more finds than the government had allotted them.

named his dynasty after a language, Pahlavi, that was spoken by the Sassanids.) His son went even further. He replaced the Islamic calendar with one that was based on the supposed foundation of the Achaemenid empire. He crowned himself King of Kings, a title used by the Achaemenids, in the shadow of Cyrus's tomb. On the twenty-fifth anniversary of his accession to the throne, the Iranian parliament conferred on him the archaic title "Light of the Aryans."[6] In 1971, he organized a lavish reception for sixty of the world's leaders or their representatives in the ruins of Persepolis. By the time he was deposed in the 1979 revolution, many Iranians regarded any Iranian monarchy, Pahlavi or Achaemenid, as synonymous with oppression and megalomania.

After 1979, influential clerics denigrated the Achaemenids, and a mob set out to destroy Cyrus's tomb. (They were stopped by a local scholar.) The name of Persepolis soccer club in Tehran was changed to Pirouzi, which means "victory." The prerevolutionary vogue for Achaemenid and Sassanid first names died out; Islamic names rose in popularity. Iran's leaders rarely made use of anti-Arab propaganda during Iran's eight-year war against Iraq in the 1980s. Rather than call on the troops to avenge the Arab conquest of the seventh century, as the Shah would probably have done, they invoked Islamic notions of martyrdom and justice to encourage zeal.

For several years after the revolution, Iranians have told me, Sound and Image, the state broadcasting monopoly, banned references on air to the Achaemenid kings. As recently as 1999, Sound and Image gave much attention to a book, written by an Iranian, which claimed that the Achaemenids were despotic rulers whose achievements had been falsified by Jews, and that their inscriptions were

---

6. In a scholarly paper on the etymological origins of the title, written in 1966, Sadegh Kia, the then deputy culture minister, wrote that "the selection of a title for the shahs is a very ancient Iranian custom; by accepting this venerable and becoming Iranian title, [the Shah] has revived this ancient national tradition after thirteen centuries."

European forgeries.[7] When exiled Iranian opponents of the Islamic Republic spoke highly of Iran's pre-Islamic past, they often wanted to distinguish themselves from the revolutionary present.

All this explains why the Islamic Republic's decision to send some eighty works to the British Museum was seen as involving a change of policy. The loans were arranged under the previous, reformist government of Mohammad Khatami. After Mahmoud Ahmadinejad's election, there was a risk that the show would be canceled; but in the end, Ahmadinejad sent one of his vice-presidents to the opening. Iranian conservatives no longer openly show contempt for the Achaemenids. Pirouzi soccer club is again known as Persepolis—even by Sound and Image. Most intriguing of all, during his unsuccessful campaign to be elected president this summer, Ali Larijani, the former head of Sound and Image, appeared in an election poster in front of the ruins of Persepolis.

Clearly, the conservatives are yielding to the views of young people who are increasingly interested in the pre-Islamic past. This interest is partly a reaction to the emphasis that is placed on learning the Arabic language and Islamic culture in Iranian schools. There are now a large number of new books in Persian about the Achaemenids, the Sassanids, and Zoroastrianism, and pre-Islamic first names such as Darius and Yasna have become popular once again. Iran is also experiencing a revival, much remarked upon by Iranians I have talked to, of nationalist and anti-Arab sentiment. Larijani is now Iran's chief nuclear negotiator, and he uses nationalist appeals to rally public support for the nuclear program.

That the Iranian state is prepared to exploit the increasing interest of its citizens in the past does not mean that there is an "unbroken arc" linking ancient Persia to modern Iran, although these words

---

7. Nasir Purpirar, *Davazdah Qarn-i Sukut* (Twelve Centuries of Silence) (Tehran: Nashr-i Karang, 2000).

were the title of a recent panel discussion at the British Museum.[8] The discussion, in which I took part, was interesting and enjoyable, but it became clear that a great deal more divides modern Iran from the Achaemenid empire than unites them. There is no unbroken arc.

This may not please Iranian nationalists who draw inspiration from the Achaemenid and Sassanid achievements while dreaming of a new era of Persian greatness. It may not reassure those Israelis who fear that Iran, if it gets the expertise to make nuclear fuel, will lose no time in challenging Israel's presumed nuclear supremacy, and may even start a war. But modern Iran, unlike the Persian empires of the past, has a political and cultural orbit that is tightly defined, not least by its differences from the Arab world. The characteristics that make up the Iranian identity are shared by no other people, and this militates strongly against delusions of a new, expansionist Persian empire.

---

8. The round-table discussion, titled "The Unbroken Arc: What Ancient Persia Tells Us about Modern Iran," was held at the British Museum on October 18, 2005.

I I

HOW NOT TO BE OFFSIDE

March 2006

SHORTLY BEFORE THEY set off for the Berlin Film Festival last month, the six Iranian directors whose films were scheduled to be screened there were summoned by a senior official in Tehran. The Islamic Republic does not like being embarrassed by filmmakers speaking openly while they are overseas; the group expected to be told the official line on two subjects—Iran's nuclear program and the controversial caricatures of the Prophet Muhammad published in a Danish newspaper—that Mahmoud Ahmadinejad, the Islamic Republic's president, has made his own. "If they had told us what to say," recalls Mani Haghighi, one of the six directors, "we might have been tempted to disobey, but these guys are smarter than that; to our surprise, we were advised to speak our minds."

So in Berlin Iranian filmmakers who do not hide their tense relations with the authorities found themselves echoing, if not President Ahmadinejad's aggressive rhetoric, then certainly the gist of his positions. "I think that Iran has a right to its nuclear program," says Haghighi, "and I said so." Others, including Jafar Panahi, an outspoken critic of restrictions on freedom of expression in Iran, spoke out against the caricatures. For a country whose prospects in the medium term may include international isolation and even military attacks, the festival turned out to be a rare public relations success. Panahi's

Offside, an engagingly subversive film about six female football fans who are arrested after smuggling themselves, dressed as men, into the all-male environment of Tehran's Azadi stadium, won the festival's prestigious Silver Bear award.

It would be premature to suggest that the religious conservatives who run the government have abandoned their ambition to cleanse the country's film industry of the liberals who they believe infected it during the presidency of Ahmadinejad's predecessor, Mohammad Khatami. The authorities probably allowed *Offside* its run at the Tehran Film Festival, which ended a few days before the Berlin Film Festival started, only in order to deny Panahi, who wins a lot of sympathy abroad when his films are banned at home, the opportunity to present himself as a wronged liberty-seeker. (*Offside* is unlikely to be certified for general release in Iran.) As Iran's diplomatic position becomes more parlous, and the world becomes inured to frowning Iranian officials parroting the official view, the advantage of giving exposure to personable patriots such as Panahi and Haghighi becomes apparent.

Offside may not be as visually satisfying as Panahi's earlier masterpiece, *The Circle*, which devastatingly exposes the lot of women in the Islamic Republic, and its cast of nonprofessionals is not always convincing. Nonetheless, the filmmaker's idea of placing the young women in the custody of two bewildered and tradition-minded conscripts while Iran's most important match in years unfolds within earshot but out of view is telling. United by their obsessive desire for Iran to beat Bahrain and qualify for the 2006 World Cup in Germany but divided by their views on the proper place for women, the characters in *Offside* represent a society that is in the process of tumultuous and unregulated change. Iran's postrevolutionary film industry, which took off in the early 1990s under such directors as Abbas Kiarostami and Mohsen Makhmalbaf and has thrived in spite of increasing political and commercial pressure, shows in microcosm some of the difficulties facing Iranians—and the imaginative methods they use to circumvent them.

How *Offside* was made is almost as absorbing as the film itself. Looking at the Alborz Mountains from his apartment in Tehran, Panahi explains that, having in effect been banned from working by the Ministry of Culture and Islamic Guidance, he applied for permission to shoot the film using a dummy director and a scam synopsis. "Five days before the end of shooting," he goes on, "they got wind of the fact that I was making the film and that the synopsis was a fake. We shot the final scenes on the road to Qom, outside the jurisdiction of the Tehran police." He has not been prosecuted, so far.

At the Berlin Film Festival, *Offside* was in competition alongside Rafi Pitts's *It's Winter*, an elegant depiction of working-class life on the fringes of an Iranian industrial town. But the most enjoyable Iranian contribution, although it was not in competition, was Haghighi's *Men at Work*. In this film, four middle-aged men decide, for no very good reason, to devote considerable energy to dislodging an ancient and phallic rock that stands on a mountain bend. The film's idea and name were supplied by Kiarostami, Iran's most important filmmaker since the 1979 revolution, whom Haghighi has known since childhood. But the joy of this rich contemplation of male friendship lies in its execution.

Haghighi is a gifted scriptwriter. As they speak, his characters display a rumbustious wit that is peculiar to Persian as it is spoken in Tehran, but behind the banter flows a current of nostalgia. His direction approaches choreography. Joined and then abandoned by passersby driving cars with throbbing music systems, the friends pirouette away from the action to talk of love and the past and then return to apply themselves with renewed vigor to their absurd task. Haghighi's depiction of late middle age is all the more remarkable when you realize that the filmmaker is only thirty-seven, and that he left Iran as a teenager, returning only six years ago.

Haghighi's experience of life both in Iran and abroad has increased his awareness of the barbed distinction that Iranian filmgoers often make between fast-paced, technically proficient films that are aimed at commercial success in the domestic market and more esoteric offerings, filmed on a shoestring, that are ignored at home but do well at foreign festivals.

Kiarostami's *Taste of Cherry* epitomizes the latter. Adored by the glitterati at Cannes, where it won the Palme d'Or in 1997, this story of a man who drives around trying to find someone to help him commit suicide mystified or bored many Iranians who saw it. But it spawned a "school of Kiarostami"—young directors whose films tend to feature, in the words of one sardonic critic, "nonprofessional actors and improvised dialogue and plots in which nothing happens, very slowly."

Given the scant interest shown in *Men at Work* when it was premièred at this year's Tehran Film Festival, and Haghighi's failure to secure a domestic screen permit for his earlier film *Abadan*, you might expect him to concentrate on marketing his talents abroad. But he resists this temptation. Last year, he teamed up with Asghar Farhadi, known also for making highbrow films, to write a rollicking urban drama, *Chaharshanbe-soori*, that Farhadi went on to direct. The film topped a poll of cinemagoers' favorites at January's festival in Tehran, and is now in general release.

The film's name refers to the end of the Persian solar year, which Iranians celebrate, in an echo of their Zoroastrian past, by setting off firecrackers. Into a high-rise apartment steps a domestic help who has been engaged to do the spring cleaning. Amid the ghostly forms of furniture draped in sheets and accompanied by a barrage of explosions from the city below, she witnesses the breakdown of a family under the strain of infidelity and suspicion.

However, even a good script and fine performances by Hamid Far-rokhnejad and Hediyeh Tehrani as the film's feuding couple do not fully explain the popularity, especially among affluent Iranians, that this bleak film is enjoying. *Chaharshanbe-soori* has struck a chord because, in the words of one cinemagoer, it "holds a mirror up to the middle class." It depicts a world where traditional patterns of behavior and morality have given way to a tarnished modernity, where children are picked up from school by a different nanny every day; a world where moms pop pills, dads have affairs, and the old extended family has broken down. Forget blood relations—this family lives next door to the husband's mistress.

Chaharshanbe-soori, Farhadi says, is about lies and concealment, "two illnesses" afflicting Iranian society. He attributes a spate of recent films about marital infidelity to the spread of damaged relationships behind closed, middle-class doors. The married couple's reconciliation at the end is inconclusive. Only the maid, who still has a life grounded in traditional family structures, seems to stand a chance of being happy.

Why was *Chaharshanbe-soori*, with its depiction of infidelity, granted a screen permit, but not Panahi's *Crimson Gold*—on the grounds, apparently, that it briefly shows an impious party? What explains the authorities' decision to allow the screening of Kamal Tabrizi's *The Lizard*, a mischievous comedy about a thief who dresses as a mullah, but to ban Haghighi's tamer *Abadan*? These are the decisions of the Cinema Directorate at the Ministry of Culture and Islamic Guidance, but they are rarely explained. Iran's censors are more flexible than is often supposed, but they can also be imperious, quixotic, and, on occasion, pointlessly vindictive.

A filmmaker like Panahi is kept on a tighter leash because he trumpets his opposition to much of what the Islamic Republic stands for. He is not, as they say, "one of us." Nor, for that matter, was Haghighi —though he now seems to have piggybacked his way to acceptance by working with a producer who is. This year, the bureaucrat-heavy jury of the Tehran Film Festival announced the rehabilitation of a previously out-of-favor director, Ibrahim Hatami Kia, by awarding his mediocre latest offering, *In the Name of the Father*, the prize for best film.

Amid these contradictions, there is a perceptible trend toward films with Islamic themes. The culture minister has spoken warmly of *Very Far, Very Near*, about a materialistic, whisky-drinking doctor who discovers that his son is dying and roars off in his Mercedes to tell him the news. In the end, the doctor himself is saved from dying in a sandstorm by what appears to be a miracle—his epiphany, it is assumed, will make him a better Muslim.

Primed with state cash, producers can lavish resources on such uplifting films. (*Very Far, Very Near* was very expensively made by the Institute for Islamic Propagation.) But there persists, among arch-traditionalists, a lingering suspicion that all cinema, whatever its message, is alien and corrupting. This ambivalence, combined with low investment, explains why the province of Tehran, home to twelve milliion people, boasts fewer than fifty cinemas.

More encouragingly, a new generation of filmmakers is learning that technology can help them elude official supervision. Previously beholden to the state for their 35mm cameras and reels, directors and film students are discovering that by going digital, they can make films for a fraction of the price and without clearance from the authorities. This poses a dilemma. Should the censors legitimize illicitly made digital films by granting them screen permits, or risk driving their creators further underground? What they decide will greatly influence Iranian cinema in the future.

Is there a zeitgeist in these complexities—a current that informs Iran's creative minds at a precarious time in its history? A clue may lie in the remarkably similar conclusions of Panahi's and Haghighi's most recent films. *Offside* ends with Iran's triumph against Bahrain and the girls' blissful submergence, along with their former captors, in a sea of delirious street revelers. In *Men at Work*, the four friends, apparently defeated by the resilient rock, sit in their car listening to the radio commentary on another Iranian victory in a World Cup qualifier, this one against Japan. As the final whistle blows and the commentator congratulates the Iranian team on taking a step toward Germany, the men are astonished to hear the rock tumbling into the valley behind them.

Few Iranians would suggest that these images have much to do with football. They are expressions of a patriotic identity, transcending politics, to which Iranians attach themselves in times of uncertainty and peril.

12

GETTING IRAN WRONG

April 2006

DURING THE PAST few months, many nations have reached a consensus on the threat that Iran's nuclear program poses to international security. A similar consensus eluded the same nations in the debate over invading Saddam Hussein's Iraq in 2003. On March 8, the International Atomic Energy Agency (IAEA) in Vienna referred Iran's case to the Security Council. In public or private, but increasingly in public, senior officials from a wide range of countries—including the US, the EU states that vociferously opposed the invasion of Iraq, as well as India and Japan—speak of Iran's alleged pursuit of nuclear weapons with a conviction that suggests they regard it as an incontestable fact. Citing a series of deplorably anti-Israel statements by Iran's president, Mahmoud Ahmadinejad, officials from some of the same countries express the fear that once Iran has the bombs it is assumed to be seeking, it will threaten Israel with a new and reckless vigor.

There is less agreement on the US contention that citizens of the Islamic Republic are captives of the country's clerical elite, and that other countries should strengthen Iran's pro-democracy organizations so that Iranians can enjoy, in George Bush's words, the "right to choose [their] own future." But this view may be spreading. In a recent speech, Jack Straw, the British foreign secretary, declared his support for Iranians' "aspirations for a freer and more democratic...future."

As the Security Council debates what to do about Iran in closed sessions during the coming months, Iran's relations with many countries will continue to worsen unless its leaders give in to international pressure and abandon their plans to become producers of nuclear fuel by enriching uranium, which they could use to make bombs. Between October 23, 2004, and January 2006, Iran had suspended work aimed at achieving a nuclear fuel cycle using enriched uranium. Then it started work on enrichment once again, and reacted to the IAEA's strong condemnation of this move by telling the agency that it could no longer inspect sites other than those that Iran had declared to be nuclear sites. On March 29, the Security Council issued a statement repeating the recent demand of the IAEA that Iran again suspend its work on uranium enrichment and allow the IAEA to inspect installations where nuclear work is suspected of going on.

If Iran refuses to comply with such demands, as it has vowed to do, and continues the uranium enrichment program that it started in January, a senior British official expects it to have acquired "the technology to enable it to develop a nuclear weapon" by the end of 2006.[1] If the Iranians do not back down, the US, Britain, and France are expected to try to persuade the Russians and Chinese to support a subsequent resolution declaring Iran in violation of international law.

Having agreed that the Security Council discuss Iran's behavior, Russia and China, however, have indicated that they oppose putting heavy political pressure on the Iranians. In the Security Council they will most likely insist that the IAEA must have the main responsibility for dealing with Iran's program, and that other UN action be delayed, if it is taken at all. Russia and China have major interests in Iran. The Chinese recently agreed to purchase a large amount of Iranian oil

---

1. The official, who spoke anonymously to British newspapers following Iran's referral to the Security Council, was referring to Iran's impending mastery of the nuclear fuel cycle, a prerequisite both to generating electricity and building a bomb. But he acknowledged that even with this technology, it would still take several years for Iran to build a serviceable weapon.

and gas during the next three decades. Russia considers the Islamic Republic an ally in its efforts to counter America's influence in the Middle East. It has also sold Iran civilian nuclear technology, a new air defense system, and civilian aircraft.

It is true that Russian officials were irritated by Iran's policy of prevarication while responding to their proposal that it transfer uranium enrichment activities to Russian soil.[2] Nonetheless, they maintain that excessive pressure on Iran may impel it to opt out of the Nuclear Non-Proliferation Treaty (NPT) altogether, and end even the much-reduced access that inspectors now have to Iranian sites. The Iranians have not discouraged such speculation. Russia and China seem unlikely to join in the policy of sanctions against Iran that the US, Britain, and France hope that a coalition of countries will adopt should Iran refuse to comply with a putative resolution demanding that it stop its uranium enrichment program and accept more intrusive inspections.[3]

To judge from his comments during a press conference on March 8, 2006, it seems that Mohamed ElBaradei, the IAEA's director general, has some sympathy for the Russian and Chinese positions. He called on the parties to avoid an "escalation" and engage in more talks.

---

2. Talks on this deal, which would deny Iran the opportunity to enrich uranium to the level needed for use in bombs, and prevent it from keeping spent reactor fuel that could itself be reprocessed for military use, have dragged on since last autumn, amid American and European accusations that the Iranians are negotiating in bad faith. On March 12, 2006, apparently in response to Russia's support for the referral of Iran's case to the Security Council, the Iranians ruled out the Russian proposal, only for the Russians to call for a new round of negotiations, apparently not started, a few days later. But the Iranians have not abandoned their insistence that they retain a working uranium enrichment facility on Iranian soil; and that, European and American officials say, would render the Russian deal meaningless.

3. At the beginning of March 2006, Sergei Lavrov, the Russian foreign minister, warned against endangering "the ability of the IAEA to continue its work in Iran. . . . I don't think that sanctions as a means to solve a crisis have ever achieved a goal in the recent history." A few days later, in what was interpreted as a hint that Iran may opt out of the NPT, Iran's foreign minister said, "If we reach a point that the existing rules don't meet the right of the Iranian nation, the Islamic Republic of Iran may reconsider policies."

ElBaradei is said by diplomats to be deeply disappointed that after three years of intensive inspections and correspondence with the Iranian authorities, he can't say that the Iranian program is peaceful. In his most recent report, on February 27, 2006, he acknowledged that the IAEA has not seen in Iran "any diversion of nuclear material to nuclear weapons or other nuclear explosive devices." But he was troubled that Iran had provided inadequate information about its program to develop centrifuges to enrich uranium. He was, he said, concerned about the ambiguous "role of the military" in the program. He mentioned a document sent to the Iranians from a supplier of nuclear technology described as suitable for the "fabrication of nuclear weapons components." The Iranians said the document was unsolicited.

ElBaradei's agency has much to lose if Iran achieves a fuel cycle and the ability to build a bomb at short notice. The Nuclear Non-Proliferation Treaty, signed by 188 nations, has been undermined by countries such as India, Pakistan, and Israel, which refused to sign it and have nuclear devices. North Korea withdrew from the treaty in 2003 and then claimed to have a nuclear device. The NPT would lose what little credibility it still has if Iran were to quit or were allowed to stay a member of the group of signers while remaining elusive about its nuclear program. If the NPT collapses, the result could well be a nuclear arms race involving Saudi Arabia and other nations in the Middle East. ElBaradei's extensive dealings with Iranian leaders, and particularly with its top nuclear officials, who answer to the Supreme Leader, Ayatollah Ali Khamenei, seem to have convinced him that the only solution is to negotiate a deal with Iran that will involve the US. On March 8, 2006, he called on the US to negotiate with Iran and stressed the need for "a comprehensive political settlement that takes account of all underlying issues."

As the Bush administration sees it, the main "underlying issue" is that Iran's fanatical and unpopular regime is secretly trying to build a bomb with which to threaten Israel and other countries. Only by asserting the possibility of sanctions or preventive war—the "meaningful consequences" to which Dick Cheney has referred—can the US and other influential nations stop this from happening. This reading of the Islamic Republic's position is misleading, however. First, it ascribes to a fractured and secretive state a transparency of intent and an ideological rigidity that it does not have. Second, it absolves the US of any responsibility for Iran's refusal to abandon its ambitions to have a fuel cycle, and of any obligation to use diplomatic means to persuade its leaders to change their mind.[4]

The Iranians' ability to behave with startling pragmatism was first displayed during the Iran-contra scandal of 1986, when they were found to be cooperating with their American enemies to buy arms from Israel, whose right to exist they contested. After the death three years later of the Ayatollah Ruhollah Khomeini, the Iranians developed relations with Saudi Arabia, a kingdom that Khomeini himself had loathed. The Iranians also indicated that they would take no action to implement the death sentence that Khomeini had passed on Salman Rushdie. After the attacks on America of September 11, Iran provided valuable support for the US-led invasion of Afghanistan and for the new Afghan government.

Iran's enmity toward Israel is more nuanced than Mahmoud Ahmadinejad's statements suggest. The President's declarations that Israel should be "wiped off the map" and that the Holocaust is a "myth" understandably aroused fears that Iran might be considering an attack on Israel. But Iran's senior civilian and military officials have insisted that Iran will strike Israel only if Israel strikes first.[5] More significantly, the

---

4. Other countries, particularly Britain, France, and Germany, which have spent the past three years in negotiations aimed at persuading the Iranians to abandon their fuel cycle ambitions, have repeatedly and futilely urged the Americans to negotiate directly with Iran. The proposed meeting concerning Iraq would be limited, both sides insist, to discussion of Iraq.

5. In November, 2005, Khamenei, who controls Iran's foreign policy, declared that Iran "will not commit aggression toward any nations."

President and the Supreme Leader have both reiterated Iran's long-standing demand for a referendum on the status of Israel that would involve all Palestinian refugees. This official position would not seem to be consistent with an ambition to destroy Israel by force, least of all by using nuclear arms, which would endanger the very Palestinians whom the Iranians claim to be protecting. Several senior Iranian officials, including Akbar Hashemi Rafsanjani, a former president who heads a powerful arbitration council in Tehran, have not disguised their irritation with the President's comments. But Ahmadinejad has benefited from the furor. By raising his prestige among hard-line Islamists around the world, the President has made it harder for his domestic opponents, who include Rafsanjani, to undermine him.

Iran's nuclear crisis centers on the Islamic Republic's ambitions and fears, and these are hard to identify when we consider the largely hidden decision-making process in Iran, where an elected president and parliament are subservient to an unelected Supreme Leader and other appointed bodies. All are in competition with one another and it is hard to know exactly how decisions are made. Seeking clues, one could do worse than review the deterioration in relations between Iran and the US since early 2002, when Bush included the Islamic Republic in his "axis of evil." At the time, I was told by Iranians connected to the clerical elite that this speech had convinced Iran's leaders that Bush intended to bring down the Islamic Republic. Iranian insecurities were subsequently heightened by the American invasion of Iraq, even though it got rid of one of Iran's worst enemies—and by the US's stated ambition to democratize the Middle East.

Unsurprisingly, Iran has obstructed Bush's mission of regional transformation. The Iranians have been asserting their influence over neighboring Iraq, while doing nothing to help the US out of its predicament there. Iran has been channeling cash and arms to Iraqi Shiite groups, and it encourages commercial and philanthropic work in Iraq by Iranian citizens. In spite of Western pressure, the Iranians have not changed their support for other regional adversaries of the US, including Syria and such groups as Hezbollah (which Iran co-founded with Syria) and Hamas. Some Iranian leaders went out of their way to whip up religious anger against the West during the recent controversy over caricatures of the Prophet Muhammad that were published in a Danish newspaper. "Iran's aim," observes an experienced analyst in Tehran, "is to ensure that the Americans are too harassed to be able to threaten it."

Achieving a nuclear fuel cycle and the ability to build a bomb would give Iran's leaders a different degree of protection altogether. It would be in a position to deter attacks by any hostile power. Acquiring a fuel cycle, however, is a perilous undertaking. In a speech that he delivered to senior officials at the end of 2004, whose contents were recently made public, Hassan Rohani, then Iran's chief nuclear negotiator, spoke of the intense diplomatic pressure being felt by Iran. "If we can one day complete this [uranium enrichment] cycle and present the world with a fait accompli," he said,

> the situation will change. The world didn't want Pakistan to get an atom bomb or Brazil to get a fuel cycle, but Brazil achieved a fuel cycle and Pakistan a bomb, and the world came to an accommodation with them ... but we haven't yet achieved a full fuel cycle, and that, as it happens, is our main problem.

Iran's leaders are unlikely to abandon their plans to achieve a fuel cycle unless they believe that they will be more secure as a result. On February 15, 2005, after Condoleezza Rice asked Congress to allocate $75 million to promote democracy in Iran, a senior US official, briefing journalists anonymously, predicted that the money would help Iranians "who wish to see a different type of Iran." Another official referred to Iranians' desire to live in "a different system." For Iran's leaders, the two main "underlying issues" that ElBaradei says should be discussed are their own security and America's readiness to coexist with an Islamic theocracy that it finds repugnant. The Bush administration has apparently adopted a policy of regime change toward Iran, although there seems no way it could accomplish this by military force. At the same time, the administration has been talking about possible meetings with Iranians concerning cooperation on achieving stability in Iraq—meetings that have yet to take place. When it comes to Iran, the administration doesn't appear to have a coherent idea of what it is doing.

Congress allocated $19 million less than Rice asked for to promote Iranian democracy. If we count the $10 million that had already been budgeted for this fiscal year but not yet spent, the administration has $36 million available for improving and increasing the propaganda it transmits to Iran, and $20 million to give to human rights organizations, NGOs, and labor unions, and to help Iranians who want to study in the US. This is a big increase over the $3.5 million that was allocated last year for similar purposes. The State Department is also greatly increasing the number of officers who work on Iran. For the first time during his administration, Bush is devoting much attention to Iran.

That is good news for exiled Iranian opposition groups, many of which are based in the US. According to Connie Bruck's comprehensive report on these groups, which was published in *The New Yorker* on March 2, 2006, a potential recipient of funds is Reza Pahlavi, the forty-five-year-old son of the former shah and the proponent of a referendum that would let Iranians set up a constitutional monarchy, with him as shah, or a secular republic. The twenty-five Persian-language TV and radio stations that broadcast to Iran from Los Angeles, home to 600,000 Iranian exiles, may also apply to the US government for funds.[6] Supporters of another group, the People's Mujahideen

---

6. The broadcasts are viewed by many Iranian city dwellers who have access to satellite dishes. Programs range from Persian pop videos to hostile political analysis of the Islamic Republic and pre-revolutionary films about cabaret artistes being wooed by lovable

Organization of Iran, are pressing the State Department to lift its designation of the Mujahideen as a foreign terrorist organization. If that happens, the Bush administration will be free to consider giving it money.[7]

It is hard for American organizations, even private ones, to have direct relations with Iranians inside the country. That was shown by the trial in 2002 in Tehran of Abbas Abdi, a prominent reformist, on charges of espionage. Abdi's crime was to organize opinion polls on behalf of the Gallup organization, one of which indicated that 74 percent of people living in Tehran wanted Iran to start an official dialogue with the US. (Abdi recanted in court, in response, it is now known, to judicial threats against his wife. He was jailed.) According to one of the Iranian officials who spoke on March 12, 2006, the Bush administration intends to use international NGOs and other organizations as go-betweens. This frank admission is likely both to make life harder for non-Iranian NGOs that have links to Iran and to increase the dangers facing Iranians who are in contact with them.

Before the invasion of Iraq, US government officials were misled by some Iraqi opposition groups and their American supporters into thinking that these groups had popular support at home, and that they had good information about the country. Similar claims are now

---

rogues. During Khatami's presidency, when popular dissatisfaction sometimes led to demonstrations in Tehran, television hosts and their guests, including Reza Pahlavi, called on people to take to the streets. But no serious protests have taken place in Tehran since mid-2003, and my impression is that viewers increasingly favor light entertainment over political programs. The authorities generally tolerate ownership of satellite dishes, although they are illegal. State TV tries to counter the effects of the L.A. stations by making programs that mock dissident presenters.

7. According to a European official who recently briefed US officials about Iran, the Americans do not plan to exploit discontent among Iran's dissatisfied minorities. Over the past year, there have been riots, bomb blasts, and attacks on the security forces in Iran's Arab- and Kurd-inhabited border regions with Iraq. One explanation for the Americans' reluctance to incite minorities is their fear that Iran would reply in kind in Iraq. Another is that the principal opposition groups stress the importance of Iran's territorial integrity.

being made about the Iranian groups. For her *New Yorker* piece, Bruck spoke to Raymond Tanter, a former member of the US National Security Council and a visiting professor at Georgetown University. Tanter is urging the administration to lift the Mujahideen's designation as a terrorist organization. He believes, in Bruck's paraphrase, that the Mujahideen is "the only opposition group capable of overthrowing the regime."

That would be news to the regime. The Mujahideen lost its credibility as a military force when its Iraq-based militants launched a suicidal attack on Iran at the end of the Iran–Iraq War in 1988; they expected to provoke popular rebellion but were crushed by Iran's forces. The organization's 3,500 remaining members have been disarmed by the US and live in a camp near the Iranian border. The Mujahideen's alliance with Saddam Hussein turned most Iranians against it. Indeed, in more than five years of living in Iran, I have yet to hear an Iranian praise it.[8]

Reza Pahlavi is less easy to dismiss. Some Iranians feel nostalgia for the prosperity and carefree hedonism of the time of the Shah, and they have a reflexive allegiance to his son. However, these sentiments do not seem widespread among the young people who make up most of the population; I have met plenty of young Iranians who favor a secular republic, but few who want a restoration of the monarchy. Pahlavi's association with some of his father's most reviled former

---

8. After the revolution, when it waged civil war against Khomeini's supporters, the Mujahideen advocated a mix of Marxism and Islamism. Its founder, Massoud Rajavi, has now disappeared from view, and his wife, Maryam, who advocates democracy, has been put forward as the group's spokesperson. The Mujahideen does not seem to be run on democratic lines; former members describe it as a personality cult centering on Rajavi. Its political wing, the National Council of Resistance of Iran, came to prominence in 2002 when it revealed sensitive information about Iran's nuclear program, information said to have been supplied by Israeli intelligence. The administration has not made clear if it would consider lifting the Mujahideen's designation as a terrorist organization if it renounces violence, which Maryam Rajavi has so far refused to do.

allies and his reliance on American largesse have not enhanced his reputation. His main handicap is that of the exiled opposition as a whole; he has not seen Iran in twenty-seven years, and Iran has changed enormously in that time.

The exiles' understanding of their own country is occasionally delusional. Take, for example, Pahlavi's chief adviser, an Iranian businessman called Shahriar Ahy. He expects Iranians to begin a campaign of civil disobedience after a "national congress" of opposition groups that is being planned this summer in the US. "All have to cooperate to bring the regime down," Ahy told Bruck. "We would have five, six, seven clusters inside, coordinated for unity of action. So, at the same time, the Kurds would be doing this! The oil workers striking over here! So the wolves are not running after different zebras."

Ahy's fantasy illustrates the gulf between perceptions of Iranians in the US, where many believe that conditions for regime change have never been more propitious, and the reality in Iran. In the words of a leading literary dissident in Tehran, "For the first time since the last shah's accession, in 1941, Iran is bereft of any effective opposition, legal or illegal."

Eight months after Khatami stepped down as president and his reform movement came to an end, there is no progressive political movement to take its place. This is not surprising, for the reform movement attracted a generation of brilliant public figures—officials who worked for Khatami, writers, editors, student leaders—who have since, for the most part, been silenced. They have been jailed, driven into exile, or intimidated into staying quiet. The once-active student movement is moribund.

Bush has contributed to the sense of torpor and pessimism that now afflicts many politically imaginative Iranians. By including Iran in his "axis of evil" and repeatedly praising pro-democracy activists during periods of unrest, Bush gave conservative judges and their hard-line supporters in the press and television a pretext to label all reformists as traitors and the lackeys of America. Abbas Abdi's trial is only one example among many. Khatami has made it clear that he regards Bush as partly responsible for his failure to reform Iran. Since Ahmadinejad's election and the subsequent worsening of Iran's diplomatic relations with many countries, it has become even harder for Iranians to express views in favor of more freedom of expression.

US officials have portrayed the Islamic Republic and its citizens as being monolithically opposed to each other. Again, this view is inaccurate. Iran's conservative leaders have presented their refusal to give up a fuel cycle program as an act of resistance against foreigners' efforts to deprive Iran of its rights. The success of this approach was apparent on February 11, 2006, when President Ahmadinejad addressed a huge crowd, estimated by foreign news agencies to number several hundred thousand people, that had gathered to celebrate the anniversary of the revolution. It was the biggest such crowd in years. Sentiments in favor of the regime and strongly opposed to the US are stronger now than at any time since I first visited Iran, in 1999.

If Iran's leaders do not change their nuclear plans, some countries, including EU member states, will probably impose sanctions on the Islamic Republic later this year. At first, these will try to block help to Iran's civilian nuclear program—partly with the aim of preventing Iran's single, Russian-built, nuclear reactor from becoming active—and to stop Iranian officials from traveling abroad. European restrictions on investment may follow.

The threat of sanctions is already deterring investors in Iran, especially in the oil and gas industries on which the country's economy depends. Some foreign energy companies have postponed plans to develop Iran's liquid natural gas. Oil ministry officials fear that a lack of foreign investment in the oil industry may hinder Iran's chances of meeting its OPEC quota; they will soon launch a scheme to cut wasteful gasoline consumption.

The Iranian authorities reassure the public that sanctions will not threaten the high economic growth that the economy has enjoyed since the big oil price rise of 1999. Ahmadinejad's budget for the coming Iranian year, which parliament ratified on March 14, 2006, has been criticized as extravagant and inflationary in its handouts to the poor, especially in the provinces. Khamenei has reminded Iranians that the sanctions that were formerly imposed on Iran, which included an oil embargo, stimulated the country to achieve self-sufficiency in many fields.

If that embargo were repeated, the inevitable collapse in revenues would threaten the Islamic Republic's survival. World oil prices would also soar, with threatening consequences for many of the world's economies. Iran has hinted that in response to sanctions it might block tanker traffic through the Strait of Hormuz, off its southern coast, further destabilizing the international economy.

The anticipated reluctance of many nations, including Russia and China, to impose such an embargo, and Iran's continuing progress toward a fuel cycle, increase the likelihood of attacks by the US or Israel on Iran's known and suspected nuclear sites. According to several recent analyses, including one by the International Crisis Group (ICG), only a major air campaign, entailing many civilian casualties, could do lasting damage to Iran's nuclear facilities.[9] Iran might retaliate using its missiles, which can probably reach Israel, and it would certainly encourage its regional allies, including Shiite leaders in Iraq and its friends in Syria and Lebanon, to cause trouble in Iraq and Israel. (Hezbollah and Hamas have both pledged to retaliate on Iran's behalf in case it is attacked.) If Iran's leaders feel that the US is determined to destroy the Islamic Republic, they will not hesitate to cause chaos.

It is not unthinkable that an imaginative solution will be found to

---

9. See the ICG's "Iran: Is There a Way Out of the Nuclear Impasse?," Middle East Report No. 51, February 23, 2006.

the immediate diplomatic impasse. (The ICG, for instance, proposes that the Iranians be permitted to have a small and heavily monitored enrichment facility, but to commission it only after several years of building confidence with the IAEA and the EU countries, among others.) That would be good news, but the underlying issue would still need to be addressed. That issue is what Iran's conservative leaders need to do to save themselves from being overwhelmed by George Bush's administration, whose plan to transform the Middle East has no room for undemocratic ayatollahs.

13

UNDER THE CYPRESS TREES

July 2006

IN THE SPRING of 2006, during the Persian New Year's holidays that lasted from March 21 to April 2, an estimated 32 million Iranians—almost half the population—left their homes to travel, exploring distant provinces, making pilgrimages, revisiting villages they had abandoned in their youth. Tehranis went north to the Caspian Sea. Isfahanis flocked to the desert town of Yazd. Around four million pilgrims visited the northeastern shrine city of Mashhad, where they generated some 15,000 tons of garbage—empty bottles, plastic cups, pistachio shells, watermelon seeds, used diapers, illicit beer cans. Across the country, parks and riverbanks were full of families cooking meat on skewers, young women playing badminton, and fat men asleep in the shade. My Iranian family and I were not among the 32 million. We stayed in Tehran, where spring storms dispelled the smog to reveal the Alborz Mountains behind the city. We spent ten days visiting friends and relations and being visited by friends and relations—and not once during this interlude of mirth and joy did I hear the words "bomb," "attack," or "run."

After the holidays were over and Tehran was pale and choking again, I wondered if Iraq had been like this back in 2002, before the invasion, and it struck me that there is an important distinction to be drawn between the two countries. Whereas Iraqis had been impoverished and worn down by sanctions, Iranians feel a degree of comfort, even protection, because their country is OPEC's second-largest oil exporter and the cost of a barrel of Brent crude recently cleared $70. Soaring oil export revenues—$24 billion in 2003, $32 billion in 2004, an estimated $47 billion in 2005—have given Iran the means to protect its citizens from capitalism's sharp edges. The government controls the price of bread, rice, meat, and cement. It prevents money-losing factories from going under. It keeps gasoline so outrageously cheap—a liter costs around ten cents—that few gasoline pumps have anti-spray nozzles, and the shallow lakes that form around them cause attendants to complain of nausea. The World Bank estimates that Iran's energy subsidies are the world's second highest (only Iraq's are higher). But that's all right; Iran can afford it.

Until when? It's simple, really: until the price of oil falls. Then what? Nobody knows. In the meantime, the imports continue to flood in, the foreign exchange reserves grow, and the subsidies go up, up, up. The public's confidence in the government's ability to spend its way out of disaster seems intact. In April a prominent Iranian Web site claimed that the state-owned Melli Bank, Iran's largest, was some $4 billion in debt to the Central Bank, but neither the government nor the Melli Bank responded publicly, and there was no rush to withdraw savings. Many of the Melli's debtor institutions are government ministries and other state entities. Iranians simply assumed that rather than fine the bank heavily, as the law requires, the Central Bank would quietly reschedule Melli's debts. Among some Iranians, the crisis over Iran's nuclear program has fostered perverse expectations of further windfalls. The worse the crisis gets, the higher the price of oil rises and the richer Iran becomes. Let the bad times roll.

That, at least, is how things appear on the surface. Tentatively, however, some Iranians of my acquaintance have started discussing the relationship between the nation's financial good fortune and a tension in foreign relations that may not ultimately be controllable; they wonder, as the treasury swells, how long this situation can go on. Most of these people are middle-class professionals, and many of them profited from the eight-year presidency of Mohammad Khatami, who left office in the summer of 2005 after completing his second term. Khatami's failure to reform the country politically has obscured the small but significant steps he took toward economic liberalization—steps that endeared him to those Iranians who wanted an end to the state planning of the past. Khatami's government stopped supplying foreign currency to favored individuals at a subsidized rate of exchange, passed a law to encourage local investment, and established an oil stabilization fund for excess oil receipts, partly as a hedge against a fall in oil prices and partly to finance private sector projects. Khatami's economic managers accepted the inevitability of eradicating subsidies and began privatizing state assets.

Although some poor Iranians got richer under Khatami, middle-class Iranians were the conspicuous beneficiaries of his presidency. They invested in property, in Tehran's bullish and notoriously under-regulated stock market, in cell phone infrastructure. Their bank savings gave them real returns of as much as 8 percent a year. There was also a moral edge to the question of liberalization. Some of the newly rich drank bootleg booze and held un-Islamic parties. They drove expensive cars and wore flashy clothes. Recalling the egalitarianism that animated their leaders following the 1979 revolution, many poorer Iranians looked on disapprovingly, enviously. When Khatami's tenure ended, they elected the most populist candidate on the ballot to replace him, Mahmoud Ahmadinejad.

During Khatami's reign, when Iranians repeatedly showed that they favored reform and the unelected conservative establishment responded with repression, many journalists and analysts convincingly argued that the Islamic Republic was experiencing a crisis of popular legitimacy. In some ways, Ahmadinejad has deepened that crisis; in other ways, he has lessened it. Authoritarian in politics, dirigiste in economics, Ahmadinejad may not be a democrat, but he is a highly effective populist—he has connected with ordinary Iranians more successfully than most people expected.

Ahmadinejad does not believe that Iran's oil wealth should benefit middle-class rentiers, or that it should be put aside for a rainy day. He thinks it should be spent now, to help the poor, in pursuit of a "model Islamic society." Ahmadinejad's contempt for market economics and for the diplomatic niceties that traditionally guide the affairs of nations has alienated him from the middle class and in particular from the private sector. The stock market has not recovered from the sharp fall it suffered following the President's suggestion, in October 2005, that Israel should be wiped off the map—a suggestion that won him worldwide opprobrium. The property sector is stagnant, and privatization has ground to a halt; the recent auction of three public companies attracted a total of one bid. In April the President allegedly ordered banks to shift their loans from big institutions to private borrowers. "There is a discrepancy," an economist friend of mine observed, "between running a country and pursuing transformative ideals."

There is also a discrepancy between Ahmadinejad's egalitarian pose and the state's treatment of some of its employees. In January, Tehran's bus drivers struck for the right to nominate their own representatives to deal with their employer, the Tehran municipality, and for improvements in pay and working conditions. Several hundred were briefly arrested, and many of them were prevented from returning to work. Details of the strike and of the state's response were kept from the Iranian public.

In the expansionary budget that he presented to parliament in February, the President pledged much extra money for public works, education, and those entities, such as the state broadcasting monopoly and the Institute for Islamic Propagation, that peddle the official ideology. The budget that the parliament eventually passed the following month was trimmer, but the government pledged to push through many of its original proposals by submitting supplementary budgets. Normal Iranians are waiting for the benefits that Ahmadinejad has promised them: jobs, housing loans, pension increases. The affluent are looking for evidence of pragmatism, for a sign that they can start investing once again. Rich, unsure, all of Iran is waiting.

Around the time of the New Year's holidays, several reports and articles appeared in the United States and elsewhere about President Bush's military plans regarding the Islamic Republic and the growing likelihood of their being carried out. Seymour Hersh's article "The Iran Plans," which appeared in *The New Yorker* on April 17, 2006, provoked the most comment, mainly because it contained allegations that the administration was considering the use of nuclear weapons to destroy Iran's underground uranium enrichment facility at Natanz, south of Tehran, but also because it alleged that US special forces had entered Iran "to collect targeting data and to establish contact with anti-government ethnic-minority groups," such as the Kurds, Arabs, and Azeris. Although Bush dismissed this as "wild speculation," a series of resolve-stiffening articles by such sedentary militarists as *The Washington Post*'s Charles Krauthammer and *The Weekly Standard*'s William Kristol seemed to confirm Hersh's view that the American right is indeed readying itself to fight another good fight—but almost certainly by conventional means.

Two papers on the subject, Anthony Cordesman and Khalid Al-Rodhan's "Iranian Nuclear Weapons? The Options if Diplomacy Fails," published by the Center for Strategic and International Studies (2006), and "Iran: Consequences of a War," by Paul Rogers of the Oxford Research Group in Britain (2006), described the military objectives that, short of an invasion or nuclear strikes, the United

States can choose from.[1] The US could confine its attacks to Iran's air defenses and a score of declared or suspected nuclear development sites, with the aim of setting back the Iranian program. But such a restricted campaign would not hamper Iran's ability to respond by disrupting tanker traffic through the Strait of Hormuz—the narrow passage through which some 20 percent of the world's oil passes—or by intervening directly to worsen the chaos in Iraq. With preemption in mind, the US also could strike at Iran's missile production facilities and naval bases, and at installations used by the Islamic Revolutionary Guard Corps (IRGC), the best-equipped and most ideological branch of Iran's armed forces. This approach would, Cordesman and Al-Rodhan wrote, inflict "much broader military losses—losses [that Iran's] aging and limited forces can ill afford."

A third US option would be to extend strikes to include Iran's civilian infrastructure—in the hope, long nurtured by American neoconservatives, that if the Islamic Republic is weakened, a popular revolution will sweep it away and usher in a liberal democracy. At their most extensive, US strikes could, in Cordesman and Al-Rodhan's words,

> cripple Iran's economy by striking at major domestic gas production and distribution facilities, refineries, and electric power generators.... If the US chose to strike at the necessary level of intensity, it could use conventional weapons to cripple Iran's ability to function as a nation.

Rogers's paper was interesting because some of his predictions

---

1. Neither report expected that the American armory of bombers, cruise missiles, long-distance precision weapons, and teams of saboteurs would be greatly impeded by Iran's meager defenses, although the Iranians, having learned from Israel's successful attack on Saddam Hussein's nuclear reactor at Osirak, in 1981, are thought to have hardened and hidden many military facilities.

contested the premises—anti-proliferation, pro-democracy—that the Bush administration might use to justify an attack. "The key response from Iran," Rogers wrote, "would be a determination to reconstruct a nuclear programme.... This would require further attacks. A military operation against Iran would not, therefore, be a short-term matter but would set in motion a complex and long-lasting confrontation." He predicted that attacks would rally Iranians behind the Islamic Republic and "inevitably increase the anti-American mood in the region and beyond." In April, Zbigniew Brzezinski, who was Jimmy Carter's national security adviser during the Iranian revolution and US embassy crisis, told David Ignatius of *The Washington Post*,

> I think of war with Iran as the ending of America's present role in the world.... Iraq may have been a preview of that, but it's still redeemable if we get out fast. In a war with Iran, we'll get dragged down for 20 or 30 years. The world will condemn us. We will lose our position in the world.

It is striking, given the intensity of the arguments in America—among policy elites if not among the general population—and elsewhere, how little public discussion the talk of attacks elicited in Iran. This can be ascribed partly to restrictions on freedom of speech. The narrowing of Iran's public space by the conservative establishment started with the banning of pro-Khatami newspapers in 2000 and 2001 and intensified after rigged elections handed control of the parliament to hardliners in 2004; it has continued since Ahmadinejad came to power. Rather than report Hersh's assertions, which might have caused doubts among the public, Iranian newspapers merely carried the reaction of Ali Larijani, the head of Iran's National Security Council, who dismissed Hersh's article as "psychological warfare" and said that it underlined America's "impotence" in the face of Iran's determination to become a producer of nuclear fuel.

The same newspapers trumpeted Ahmadinejad's announcement on April 11 that Iranian scientists had for the first time succeeded in enriching experimental quantities of uranium. "Iran's Entry to the Nuclear Club" blared one headline. "The West, Checkmated" read another. Neither of these newspapers nor the slavishly pro-establishment TV monopoly dwelt on the fact that the nation's scientists have much work to do before they can enrich enough uranium to power a reactor or, if ordered to, build a bomb. According to a recent intelligence review by the US government, Iran will almost certainly not have this capability before the end of the decade, and probably not until 2015. To all strategic intents and purposes, Iran is still a long way from becoming a member of the nuclear club.

Following Ahmadinejad's announcement, I started canvassing the opinions of Iranians I came across in Tehran. Since the summer of 2002, when the startling extent of Iran's nuclear program first became widely known, and the EU, led by France, Britain, and Germany, started trying to persuade Iran to abandon its plans to become a producer of nuclear fuel, my casual questioning of people had taught me to be skeptical of claims, often heard inside and outside the country, that the Iranians are passionately committed to the nuclear program. Being able to make nuclear fuel is a technical achievement that carries ill-defined political and strategic benefits. It is not so potent a symbol as, for instance, taking the oil industry out of foreign hands and making it publicly owned—which is what Muhammad Mossadegh, a nationalist prime minister, did in 1951, setting in motion events that led to his toppling by the CIA two years later. But that is how the Iranian authorities present it: as a brave bid for independence.

The question is what Iran plans to do with its nuclear fuel. It might run reactors to make electricity—which is all the government says it wants to do. It might run reactors and make a nuclear bomb, but also decide, for fear of the diplomatic consequences, against testing. It might claim to have made an arsenal of nuclear weapons, and no one would be sure if it is telling the truth. And so the line between membership and nonmembership in the nuclear "club" becomes fuzzy. Supposing you are an Iranian who is "passionate" about your nation's nuclear program, it's hard to know at what point you should rush into the streets in triumphal ecstasy, as millions of Indians and Pakistanis did after their respective countries' tests in 1998. It's hard to say when the world might reconfigure its assumptions to reflect a "nuclear" Iran. In the absence of incontrovertible proof that Iran has developed a bomb, or seeks to do so, the crisis is about intentions, and no outsider knows Iran's intentions, or how the country is changing as a result of international pressure and threats. Who can tell if Iran has a nuclear doctrine and, if so, what is written in it?

The picture is complicated by the ambivalence that many Iranians feel toward the elite running the country. Affection for the Islamic Republic has waned since the Iran–Iraq War of the 1980s, when most Iranians were united by their reverence for Khomeini, their extreme religiosity, and their hatred for Saddam and his Western backers. Now there is no Khomeini, less religiosity, and, instead of specific hatreds, a generalized cynicism toward those who hold political power— whether in Iran or elsewhere. In the eyes of many, Ahmadinejad, who portrays himself as a man of the people, is an exception, but Iranians know that all major decisions are made not by him but by Khomeini's successor as Supreme Leader, the Ayatollah Ali Khamenei.

These ifs and buts are essential background to the conversations I had with Iranians following Ahmadinejad's declaration that Iran had enriched uranium. I had been struck by the contrast between Tehran's quiet streets after that announcement and the joyful celebrations in the same streets that marked a famous victory by the national football team in June 2005. The evening after Ahmadinejad made his announcement, I went to my weekly poetry class, which is held in the flat of an affluent, middle-aged woman and attended (mostly) by other affluent, middle-aged women—and where we have sat, for the past two years, at the feet of a magnetic Kurdish mystic. During a break for tea and baklava halfway through the class, there were short conversations about the traffic in Tehran (it keeps getting worse), grown-up children (one misses them so much when they go abroad to study and work), and prophetic dreams (everyone has had them except me). Of politics or the nuclear program, not a word was said. I sidled up to a young man, a reserved and bookish fellow who is doing his military service, and asked him how his fellow conscripts had greeted Ahmadinejad's news.

"With indifference. It doesn't change their lives. They don't think that this dispute has much to do with them."

"No elation? No delight?" The young man raised his eyebrows, an Iranian "no."

And so it went in the days that followed, as I listened to people talking in the city. In the sauna of a state-run sports club where I go to swim, sweating among red-faced bureaucrats; riding a shared taxi to the city center; among family and friends, gathered for dinner at someone's house—in none of these settings did I hear more than cursory references to the nuclear dispute.

When I asked, people told me, without passion, what they thought of the "situation." (No one utters the word "crisis.") Many expressed support for the nuclear program and described the opposition of the United States and other nuclear countries as hypocritical and discriminatory. Some said that they wished Iran's leaders had proceeded more cautiously; they felt that the Security Council could have been avoided. The more cynical ones predicted that the clerics would cave in as soon as it looked as though attacks were a real possibility.

I got the impression that everyone I spoke to, whatever his or her opinion, was observing the crisis from a distance, dolefully aware of being irrelevant to the decision-making process. A woman told me: "It doesn't matter what we think; our leaders will do what they want to do regardless." I replied that her words had reminded me of my own country's prime minister, Tony Blair, and his decision to participate in the invasion of Iraq even though he knew that the majority of Britons opposed him. She nodded as if she knew exactly what I was talking about.

In mid-April 2006, two days after Mohamed ElBaradei, the head of the UN's nuclear watchdog, the International Atomic Energy Agency, left Tehran after failing to persuade Iran to suspend uranium enrichment, I took my car to be repaired and chatted with the mechanic as he lay underneath it.

"Do you think there will be war?"

"No. They might have attacked, but not now that we've enriched uranium. That's what counts. They won't attack a country that has enriched uranium."

"There's lots of talk over there about an attack."

"If they attack, they know we'll fire off some missiles to Israel. We've got some good weapons. They won't attack." He emerged grinning from under my car and wrote me an excessive bill.

The same day, I learned from a Tehran newspaper that the price of a *Bahar Azadi*, a gold coin that the Islamic Republic first minted fourteen years ago and a common refuge for investors in times of uncertainty, had climbed to an all-time high. In the same paper, a columnist criticized the government for lowering interest rates when tensions over the nuclear program precluded investment in "productive" sectors, such as construction. Some economists predicted that people who withdrew their deposits would invest them in gold, foreign currency, and illegal high-interest deposit accounts of the kind that flourished during the Iran–Iraq War.

Here in north Tehran, where the gardens are white with blossom, the idea of attacks seems impossibly remote. I look around and wonder how the people who live and work near our home would react— the Azeri grocer in his corner shop, the street sweeper asking for tips, the American-educated doctor and her two sons who live a few doors away.

But attacks, if they come, will not be remote at all. They will be terrifyingly close. The Tehran Research Reactor; the Isfahan Nuclear Technology Center; the Nuclear Research Center for Agriculture and Medicine, in Karaj, west of Tehran; Iran's sole, almost completed, nuclear reactor, at Bushehr on the Persian Gulf Coast; the big military complex at Parchin, south of Tehran, where, according to the United States, Iran is running a weaponization program—these and dozens of other probable targets are situated in or near Iranian cities.

The people who work in these places are not all scientists or IRGC officers. There is a youthful grandmother who cleans the floors before going home to make dinner for her large family. There is a conscript, longing for his twenty months to end so he can return to his fiancée in some distant province, standing guard at the gate. There are cooks, drivers, night watchmen, gardeners, and odd-job men. Then there are the houses all around, the taxi stands and small businesses, and perhaps a landscaped park with its spread-eagled addicts and forbidden lovers. If there are air strikes, surprise will be a big factor; these people, too, will be deafened, traumatized, injured, or killed.

Thinking of attacks, trying to predict how people might respond, I remembered an act of unspeakable violence that paralyzed part of the government and killed large numbers of people. In the early hours of December 26, 2003, an earthquake razed three quarters of the southeastern city of Bam, killing about a third of its 80,000 inhabitants and wiping out the local administration. The state's response was slow; thousands of survivors spent two freezing nights without tents that they had been promised. Bereaved and homeless, some survivors succumbed to a desperate opportunism and started looting the possessions of their dead neighbors.

Like Hurricane Katrina half a world away, the earthquake in Bam showed how unerringly calamities can fray the decency of normal people. It also showed how fragile the contract of power and subservience between the state and its citizens is. From quite early on, survivors of the earthquake regarded the authorities as guilty: guilty of not enforcing building regulations that would have made their houses safe, of behaving as if the earthquake had been a challenge to security and not a humanitarian disaster, of delaying reconstruction through departmental infighting and graft. More than three months after the earthquake, rioters in Bam gutted official buildings out of frustration at the slow pace of reconstruction and were shot at by police.

Finally, Bam showed how ill equipped an inflexible bureaucracy is to conceive of, let alone plan against, the unexpected. In the earthquake's aftermath, politicians and commentators urged that the disaster should serve as a reminder that Greater Tehran, a province of twelve million people that lies on a major fault line, is unprepared for the earthquake that many seismologists regard as long overdue. For a few weeks, there was lively debate. The government appointed a High Council for Disaster Management, chaired by a vice-president, to devise a template to guide the authorities in the event of another big earthquake. The plan was to resolve departmental overlaps and show who in the government should answer to whom in times of crisis.

And then: nothing. The template was not finished. It is still unclear which officials and institutions would assume control over emergency relief and security if there were to be a big earthquake in Tehran. I wonder if the authorities are any more prepared for military attacks.

In 1988, near the end of the Iran–Iraq War, Saddam Hussein launched a wave of Scud missiles against the Iranian capital. The military effectiveness of these missiles, with their light warheads, was slight, but they were loud and blew out plenty of glass, and they caused panic and a mass exodus from the city. What now, if the Americans attack? If we assume that military strikes would incapacitate, to some degree, the Iranian security forces and damage the civilian infrastructure, would there be an exodus? If so, would poor people take advantage of the vacuum to steal from those who have fled?

"In traditional areas," I was told in April by an Iranian disaster expert, "people have tended during crises to gather around the mosque. Older, respected members of the community issue orders, and things are fairly disciplined." But Tehran's traditional communities have long been under assault as a result of migration to the cities from the countryside and two widespread concomitants, unemployment and drug addiction. No one can be sure how people would react in the hours and days following major military strikes.

After that, predictions become easier. Order would be restored, because Iran's security and paramilitary forces are too vast to be overwhelmed for long, and then political reverberations would be felt, though not in ways that the US neocons expect. Rather than embolden Iranian democrats to launch a popular rebellion, military strikes would strengthen the state by uniting the majority of Iranians, whatever their domestic loyalties, against the foreign enemy. "If there is an attack," an Iranian who works to promote civil society told me in April, "the Islamic Republic and its popularity will no longer be under discussion; the question will be the nation of Iran, and its survival, and Iranians will gather to protect it." Acquaintances of mine, many of them hostile to the Islamic Republic, agreed. They accused Bush of confusing Iran, a country whose national consciousness goes back thousands of years, with the cut-and-paste nation to its west. "We are not Iraq," several told me, wagging a finger.

Their words reminded me of Bush's view of Iranians as a people irreversibly divided from its leaders—a view that lay behind the adminstration's recent request to Congress for $75 million for anti-regime propaganda and pro-democracy activism. Bush and many others seem to assume that the gap, such as it is, cannot be bridged, and that anyone seeking to exploit it, including the United States, will be thanked by Iranians. But the situation, as Ahmadinejad's election and continued popularity have shown, is more complicated than that. In a country where between 60 and 70 percent of the economy is publicly owned, millions of citizens are dependent on the state in the most basic ways imaginable. So far, Bush's efforts to exacerbate tensions between Iranians and Iran's authorities have not been a success. Furthermore, they have undermined the very democrats he purported to be helping.

The US president did not cause Iran's reform movement to fail. It was flawed by the timidity of its leaders and their followers. But it is no coincidence that the movement went into terminal decline immediately after Bush included Iran in his 2002 "axis of evil." That speech, and the subsequent invasion of Iraq, convinced Iran's clerical leaders that Bush was determined to try to topple the Islamic Republic. One of the ways they reacted was by intensifying their assault on liberalizing, reformist Iranians. The hard-line establishment depicted all democracy advocates as traitors; they were discredited, tortured, or jailed. Iran's pro-democracy movement could not survive in the atmosphere of protracted crisis that Bush helped create.

If there are attacks and a national emergency, things will get worse. Pro-democracy newspaper columnists, striking bus drivers, dissenting students—all will be smashed with an iron fist. Military action will herald a crisis of the kind that, during the Iran–Iraq War, Khomeini's followers used in order to limit democracy and eliminate their opponents. The Islamic Republic will become more fanatical, and anti-American feeling, strikingly absent in many Iranians, will grow.

I know all this in my head. In my heart, I am more like the people about me. "Crisis? What crisis?" As the air warms and my wife lumbers into her final smiling month of pregnancy, it seems too vile to imagine that sometime soon, a nice American boy may press a button or open a chamber and rain destruction down around us.

14

CHILDREN OF THE REVOLUTION

September 2006

IN THE SUMMER of 2006, I visited the village of Jasp, in central Iran. Situated on a broad plateau, protected by mountainous folds of rock, it is idyllic and still. To be precise, Jasp isn't one village but a cluster of seven villages known for their cool climate and plentiful rainfall—a relief from the heat of the plains below. Jasp in the summer is green from the almond and walnut trees that sway in the wind along with tall poplars and scraps of cloth that serve as scarecrows. Water gurgles in irrigation channels running through small garden plots. An old woman leans on a stump, a donkey brays, and a tractor shaves the side of a ruined tower, made of mud and pierced with musket slits, that once protected the inhabitants from aggressors. Then the villages of Jasp subside once more into drowsiness and silence.

Driving out of Jasp, I offered a lift to a policeman who had leave to return to his home on the plains. The police here, he told me, don't have much to do. Jasp's four-hundred-odd inhabitants, most of them elderly, are not lawbreakers. (With the exception, he added, of the village's opium smokers, to whom the police in Jasp, as in thousands of other Iranian villages, turn a blind eye.) He told me that the peace is only disturbed on weekends, when townspeople from the plains come in their cars to barbecue kebabs of minced meat and commit "recreational excesses"—by which he meant that unmarried boys and girls laugh loudly and listen to pop music, and the girls smoke cigarettes, and everyone enjoys being far from their disapproving parents.

The road we took from Jasp to the plains followed a spectacular gorge. As we descended and the temperature rose, it occurred to me that this, rather than the newer highway I had used to get to Jasp, was probably the route that Ahmad Maleki took when he left his home village in 1962 to make a new life in the capital, Tehran.

At the time, Ahmad's departure was unusual; the majority of Iranians still lived in villages. Now, according to the United Nations, some 68 percent of Iranians are urban dwellers, a figure that is expected to rise to more than 75 percent by 2020. Iran has a strikingly youthful population—more than 70 percent of its seventy million people are under thirty—and the young tend to converge on the towns and cities. In the six years that I have lived in Iran, I have visited scores of villages around the country. In almost all of them, I have been struck by the absence of young people. The villages are served by a narrow road or path, and the traffic is overwhelmingly headed out.

I had gone to Jasp to learn about the origins of Zeinab, the twenty-seven-year-old daughter of Ahmad and his wife, Farhang, who also comes from Jasp. Ideally, Zeinab, who visits her ancestral village with her parents most summers, would have accompanied me, but being a pious young woman from a conservative background, she had placed limits on the interaction that she was prepared to have with a Western male stranger. Traveling to her parents' village and back again, although permitted under the laws of the Islamic Republic of Iran, was way outside those limits.

"I have never been out alone with a man who is not related to me," she had told me as we sat in the Mehr News Agency in central Tehran, where she works. "I am not going to start now." And she pulled at her chador, which was slipping, so it pressed against her pale, angular face.

Skirting the enormous mausoleum of Ayatollah Ruhollah Khomeini, the leader of the 1979 revolution, I approached Tehran from the south. The city shimmered through the filthy haze and heat and the dust raised by a thousand public works in progress. An overpass without any signs had been flung toward the city. I hesitated, took it, and, as usual, entered south Tehran unsure of which road I was on, and where I would end up.

I got directions to Mowlavi Street, from which I would take my bearings—it follows the bazaar's southern axis. Porters pushed overloaded carts; a young junky wiped windshields with a rag; children sold poems that told you if you were destined to be happy. At the side of the road, from speakers installed near a mosque, hymns in praise of Fatemeh Zahra, the Prophet Muhammad's daughter, whose birthday it was, blared into the sky.

It was here, in this dense old neighborhood, that Ahmad Maleki settled back in the 1960s, and where he started the grocery store that he owns and runs to this day. In the house that Ahmad built, in the same area, the Malekis raised and educated nine children, of whom Zeinab is the fifth. The results, when you consider that Ahmad reads slowly and his wife is barely literate, are quite impressive. The majority of the Maleki children either attended university or, in the case of the younger three—whose ages range from seventeen to nineteen—are studying hard to gain admittance. (Zeinab has a degree in religious studies from Tehran University.) Slowly, the Malekis are consolidating their position in the metropolitan middle class. In 2005, more than forty years after he got to Tehran, Ahmad bought his first car.

Here was Zeinab's neighborhood, but where was Zeinab? She had consented to see me only in the white-walled conference room of the Mehr News Agency, an organization aligned with the ruling clerics, where we sat underneath big photographs of Khomeini and his successor as Supreme Leader, Ayatollah Ali Khamenei. I met Zeinab there four times. After each of our conversations, I would try to persuade her to invite me to meet her parents. I cajoled and argued; I asked her to give them a bag of cherries from my garden. Each time,

Zeinab would smile her rare, surprisingly warm smile, and shake her head. What was it she had said when we first met? "We have to build our lives on firm foundations."

For her those foundations are faith in God and unquestioning obedience to his laws, and a belief, too, in the sacredness of the Islamic Republic, which Khomeini set up to realize God's will. Family values are a natural concomitant; during our conversations, I sometimes got the impression that Zeinab identifies her interests seamlessly with those of her family as a whole. She helped her mother raise her younger siblings, and she tutors the youngest two, seventeen-year-old twins. Then there is the wider network of kith and kin, for Ahmad and Farhang were not the only members of their respective families to move to Tehran. Zeinab has six aunts and uncles and forty first cousins in Tehran alone. Two of her siblings are married; she has five nieces and nephews. The various families gather to eat lunch on Fridays, the Muslim day of rest. Together, they observe the mourning periods and religious holidays that punctuate the Shia Muslim calendar. They go to the cinema, eat pizza. Once, I asked Zeinab if she had ever felt lonely; she laughed as if she found the idea ridiculous.

In 1984, halfway through the eight-year war that Iran fought against Saddam Hussein's Iraq, the Malekis' eldest son, sixteen-year-old Muhammad-Baqer, was declared missing, presumed dead. He had joined the Basij, an Islamic militia whose fighters were known for their reckless courage in combat. I asked Zeinab if her parents had approved of Muhammad-Baqer's going to fight at such a young age. She nodded; there was no reproach in her eyes.

At least one weekend every month, Ahmad and Farhang, and whichever of their children want to come, pile into the family car and head for Tehran's huge war cemetery, Zahra's Heaven, near Khomeini's shrine. There, in a section where unidentified soldiers have been buried, they pray for Muhammad-Baqer. Around them, thousands of mourners are cleaning the graves of their loved ones and laying flowers.

Around half a million Iranian soldiers are thought to have died in this terrible, futile war—in which the West supported Saddam's invasion of Iran, and continued to back him despite his repeated use of chemical weapons, until the conflict ended in exhausted stalemate. The scene in Zahra's Heaven is replicated in cemeteries across the country.

Zeinab's job, on behalf of the Mehr News Agency, is to keep memories of the war alive. She reports on remembrance ceremonies and on trips to Mecca that the government has organized for the widows of martyrs. She interviews the victims of Saddam's gas attacks and the heroes of famous victories. One of her sisters married a veteran. "I've spent my most productive hours with these people," she says, her eyes shining. "And you know what they all say, Mr. de Bellaigue? They say that if there is another war, they will fight."

Against whom? Against the US, they say, should it dare to strike the Islamic Republic's nuclear installations, and, if necessary, against Israel, an illegitimate state that has inflicted unparalleled suffering on Muslims. But there is a third, more abstract enemy: the values of the West—its moral equivocation and spurious claims to superiority and progress. Once, as we sat in the Mehr offices, Zeinab quietly attacked Westerners' "superficial" reading of Islamic laws, especially those pertaining to women; those laws that Westerners regard as discriminatory, she said, are in fact Islam's means of "protecting" women.

I asked Zeinab about the arrest and beating in June 2006 of some women's rights activists who were trying to stage a demonstration in Tehran. Her eyes hardened. "I don't think these people are interested in women's rights. Foreigners have incited them to create disorder. They should be dealt with severely."

Every Thursday afternoon, Zeinab attends a "morals" class in a nearby school. She and some four hundred other women are instructed by a woman, a mathematics teacher by profession, who is renowned locally for her knowledge of Islam. Drawing on the Koran and the sayings of the Prophet and the twelve Shia imams, she suggests ways to negotiate modern life within the framework of the faith—ways to be a better wife, mother, sister. Zeinab says that the classes have helped her control destructive emotions such as jealousy.

If you stroll around Mowlavi Street, you may better understand Zeinab's hankering for moral and political certainty. Everywhere there is evidence of tumultuous change. The older, more established families are leaving and being replaced by new arrivals, many of them poor and ill educated, from the provinces. The two-story brick houses with their gardens are coming down; apartment blocks built on the cheap are going up. The old bonds between neighbors who look out for one another are under threat.

This is the fallout from a political decision, made shortly after the revolution, to encourage Iranians to have more children. The idea was to build a strong and populous country, capable of standing up to outside threats. The people did their duty and the population leaped by more than 45 percent in a single decade, but Iran's new leaders hadn't thought things through. In around 2000, as the baby boomers started coming of age, it was clear that the nation's infrastructure was under severe strain.

There is hardly an area of Iranian life that has not been affected. There is a wide, albeit narrowing, disparity between the number of university applicants and the number of places available. Those who do enter university cannot be sure of finding a job after they graduate. Official figures—which most economists regard as conservative, if not misleading—put unemployment among young Iranians at 21 percent. Housing, especially in the big cities, is in short supply and overpriced.

A shocking number of Iranians have found solace in narcotics. According to the United Nations *World Drug Report*, Iran has by far the largest prevalence of opiate abusers in the world; in the cities, and especially among the young, morphine and heroin are replacing opium as the drug of choice. Divorce, homelessness, and prostitution have all soared over the past decade.

In Jasp, there are few signs of these ugly urban phenomena. There, human relations are warm and, no matter how poor you are, there is always enough to eat, growing and grazing in your midst. Islam in places like Jasp is profoundly felt, but not noticeably colored by political ideology; this distinguishes rural Iran from the shaken neighborhoods of the nation's big cities. In Tehran, religion and politics are barbed; they are barricades against the threat posed by outsiders. And that, I think, is why Zeinab Maleki never invited me to her home.

"The thing about Iranian girls," Niki Mahjoub said, "is that, if they're with a guy, they won't show interest in other guys, but the guys"—Niki rolled her big brown eyes—"they're always being unfaithful. The boys have a word for girls who have been in relationships before. It's an English word..." She curled her lip in distaste: "*Open.*"

Niki and I were in a coffee shop off Africa Street, in prosperous north Tehran. She was drinking a fruit milkshake using a squiggly straw, observing the world through long, looked-after lashes. She had unobtrusively made herself up and had on a short coat and a red headscarf that artfully revealed a lot of black hair. Like Zeinab Maleki, Niki is a twenty-seven-year-old journalist, but that is where the resemblance ends.

Several months before, after she split up with her fiancé, Niki had told me of her plans to go abroad to study. Now, feeling stronger, she had changed her mind. "I'm enjoying my freedom," she said, recalling a recent trip that she and some friends had taken to the Persian Gulf island of Kish. When she smiled, it struck me that Niki bears a strong resemblance to Nisha Pillai, a newscaster for BBC *World News*. I remarked on this and she smiled again. Niki is a smiler.

Niki is an assertive, independent woman. She speaks of the important decisions in her life as if she is the sole, or least the most important, determinant of her own destiny. Her conversation is infused with the development jargon that she has learned while dealing with such organizations as the United Nations Development Programme and the World Food Programme, whose activities in Iran she covers for *Shargh*, Iran's most prominent liberal newspaper. I have seen Niki get angry at the government for turning a blind eye to illegal child marriage, and at parliament for rejecting a bill that would have righted, just a little, the present bias against women in the child custody laws. Not, however, at the "enemy" in the West.

I met her in July 2005, shortly after Mahmoud Ahmadinejad, an Islamist ideologue, surprised the world by winning Iran's presidential election. Niki and her colleagues at *Shargh* were devastated by the results. Most had voted, in the second round of a fiercely contested contest, for Akbar Hashemi Rafsanjani, a former president who occupies the center of Iranian politics. These young reformists—the average age of employees at *Shargh* is thirty—had the uncomfortable feeling that a distance had opened between them and the millions of Iranians who had voted for Ahmadinejad. "We'd forgotten," Niki told me, "that for the poor it's the cost of living, not promises about democracy, which decides elections."

Niki's parents, Mahmoud and Lili, took news of Ahmadinejad's triumph phlegmatically. As middle-aged Iranians who experienced the 1979 revolution and the war with Iraq, they learned long ago how to live with political uncertainty. In 1979 and 1980, when the Islamic Republic was taking shape, the Mahjoubs watched as many thousands of Iranians, Westernized and well educated like themselves, emigrated to Europe and North America. But the Mahjoubs stayed. "Their love of Iran," Niki told me, "was stronger than any other emotion."

Over the 1980s, the family struggled to adjust to a new system that opposed their liberal way of life. Lili, a civil servant, was "retired" on account of her sex. Mahmoud changed his job several times. The Iran–Iraq War dragged bloodily on, but it wasn't really their war;

Mahmoud was too old to be called up and there were no sons to worry about. At the state schools they attended, Niki and her two sisters were taught the values of Shia Islam and the revolution, and encouraged to distrust the West. When Niki attained puberty, the school authorities ritually presented her with an Islamic hair covering.

It cannot be easy being a girl who feels alienated by the values she is taught at school. At home, she enjoys a relatively liberal environment. In public, she puts on a mask. I know many young Iranians who, as children, were asked by schoolteachers if their parents drank alcohol or watched Western films, and whether or not they said their prayers. These young people often developed into accomplished liars.

When I met her in 2005, Lili Mahjoub, a petite and thoughtful woman whom Niki regards as a vital confidante, told me that some children develop "dual personalities" under the pressure. Deceit, furthermore, cannot easily be switched off. Children develop a talent, and they bring this talent home, and their family life suffers as a result.

Perhaps Niki is an exception; she is remarkably disarming and open. Compared to many of her friends, she is lucky, she believes, that her parents have always trusted her to make her own decisions. There is, for instance, no pressure on her to marry quickly. "I know lots of young people who got married without thinking things through," she once told me. "They quickly fell out of love." To her friends, for whom she often acts as an agony aunt, Niki recommends a long courtship.

Although Niki acknowledges a debt to the West's ideas, she does not envy its human relations. From what she knows of the West, from the accounts given to her by her sister Nazli—who studied in Germany—and the American films she has seen, she has concluded that "everything there is for consumption. Everything has a sell-by date, even a human being. I don't want to be used, like tissue paper, and thrown away."

Niki and I stepped out of the coffee shop to walk the short distance to the *Shargh* offices. Gaggles of young men were hanging around a small shopping complex, talking into their cell phones and checking their hair in the shop windows. One had a plaster over his nose—evidence of recent plastic surgery. The boys exchanged glances with some rich girls trailing expensive perfume as they were admitted into a jeweler's store; they were accompanied by their mothers and carried dainty shopping bags. Eminem was pumping through the closed window of a Land Cruiser occupied by two young men. The driver mouthed something obscene to a prostitute speculatively rolling her hips as she sauntered to nowhere under the violent sun.

When Ahmadinejad came to power, many Iranians predicted that he would try to reverse the limited liberalization of mores and dress that had marked the tenure of his reformist predecessor, Mohammad Khatami. The streets, it was said, would soon be full of Islamist goons—as they had been in the 1980s and early 1990s—brutalizing women who dared to wear makeup.

That hasn't happened, and the reason is that the social changes of the Khatami years cannot be reversed. Poor boys and girls may not be able to afford the two dollars that a latte costs in an uptown coffee shop, but many of them take note of the carefully ripped jeans and the sunglasses, the heeless pumps, clipped eyebrows, and retroussé noses of the elite, and imitate them as best they can. On weekends, the aspirants converge by the thousands on a handful of north Tehran parks, where they flirt and eat ice cream. As likely as not, their parents do not know that they are there.

The *Shargh* offices are in a residential building at the end of a side street. I said goodbye to Niki and she headed off to the social affairs section, where she works. I went into the arts section to find Mehdi Yazdani-Khorram, who runs *Shargh*'s Persian literature pages. Mehdi was sitting at the big desk that serves as the section editors' work surface, dining table, and, occasionally, pillow. He was on the phone, taking what I guessed, from his jovial and appreciative tone, to be a congratulatory call.

A few days earlier, Mehdi told me after putting down the receiver, his first novel, *According to the Meteorological Office, Tomorrow This Damned Sun* . . . —for such is the book's daunting title—was officially cleared for release, a year and a half after he submitted it to the censors at the Ministry of Culture and Islamic Guidance.

I had seen Mehdi quite a bit during this year and a half. He had been dejected by Ahmadinejad's election and by the appointment of a hard-liner as culture minister; his novel would not be favored, he correctly predicted, by the new administration. He had complained at the opacity of the ministry's workings, and at the changes to the book, some of them trivial-seeming, that the anonymous censors insisted he make. It's possible that the authorities didn't know what to make of the dense and Surrealist-influenced *According to* . . ., which transports the reader into the mind of a Tehran student without the aid of a conventional narrative. Every time we saw each other, Mehdi seemed to have recently visited the ministry in a fruitless effort to push his application along.

Even now, permit in hand, his satisfaction was mitigated. One regret was that the book would appear with some two hundred changes. A second was that the ministry had approved a print run of only 1,650 copies; a separate permit, unlikely to be granted, would be needed for each reprinting. After Mehdi told me this, one of his colleagues called out from the other end of the big table: "Congratulations, Mehdi! Even before it's come out, your book is a collectors' item!"

Mehdi is twenty-six, but his heavy, ungainly build and the russet beard that he has let grow rampant and straggling make him seem older. His conversation is punctuated by a short, dry laugh that bears witness to the absurdity of his position. He is in love with books, and his encyclopedic knowledge of Western literature derives from his voracious reading of the Persian translations of every European and

American work of fiction, poetry, and philosophy that he can get his hands on. But his knowledge isn't just blandly there; it's a statement, a rebellion. His shambolic appearance too is a rebellion.

Mehdi's father is a retired military officer who spent much of the Iran–Iraq War at the front. One of Mehdi's abiding memories is being advised by a revolutionary friend of the family to pray for his father's martyrdom. A second is his childhood hunger for cultural nourishment. "At that time, in Iran, there were no books to speak of," he told me the first time we met. "There were only TV broadcasts from five to eleven at night." So he wrote: stories, poems, thoughts.

Gradually, a mutual incomprehension opened up, between a boy who longed to immerse himself in high culture and the revolutionaries around him; they saw the war and its ideals—the paraphernalia of martyrdom and mourning—as the only culture worth knowing. Even today, Mehdi becomes infuriated if an ignorant relative, as happened recently, informs him that a certain mediocre work by an Iranian theologian is the finest work of philosophy in the world. "Philosophy!" Mehdi spluttered as he recounted this to me. "My relative doesn't know the meaning of the word!"

Mehdi is acutely conscious of the place of Iranian intellectuals throughout modern Iranian history—misunderstood by the people and mistrusted by the government. He is a young man in a hurry; he is close to completing his second novel and is planning a third. He wants to be translated, to be famous. Perhaps, he thinks, he and his wife, Somayeh, should go abroad.

If you visit Mehdi and Somayeh in their suburban apartment, you will find a young couple who have distanced themselves from their environment. Somayeh has, like her husband, reacted against her traditional background, and has limited contact with her family. For a living, Somayeh translates French novels into Persian; this accentuates the sense that she has of being foreign in her own land, and her longing to be someone else. She chafes at the limited opportunities there are in Tehran to buy French books—they are barely available, except during the annual book fair. She dislikes the uncertainty that comes from translating books in a country where copyright is not observed. "You start translating a book and then you learn that someone else is translating the same book and they're a long way ahead of you."

Somayeh's particular resentments have merged to form a general antipathy toward the Iran she sees around her. She is fed up with talkative taxi drivers. She is fed up with her neighbors in the apartment building; they have boisterous children and are always banging on the door, asking for something, being nosy. "Don't they realize that you can't work—I can't work—in this environment? I need peace." She longs to go to France, the France she has read about, of rationalism and unobtrusive citizens. As I listened to Somayeh, I was reminded of something Lili Mahjoub had told me when I asked her about Niki's plans to go abroad: "So many young people imagine that outside Iran there is a life without pressure."

Somayeh is not alone in feeling alienated and in wanting to flee. Although no one can be sure—except for the authorities, who won't release the figures—it is thought that well over 150,000 Iranians emigrate every year, and most are young. Over the past year and a half, since I met Mehdi and Niki, I have heard of several employees of *Shargh* who have moved abroad—to Canada and Italy and other European countries.[1]

Of the vast majority of young Iranians that stay, many are thinking outside the box that the state has built for them. I know of university students who seek enlightenment from Buddhist philosophy. There are groups of hard-rock musicians practicing in basements. Mystical, anticlerical poets such as Jalal-ud-Din Rumi are winning devotees.

---

1. Shargh, *Iran's best newspaper, was closed down in September 2006. Niki and Mehdi both found work at other newspapers. In 2007, Mehdi's first novel was awarded a prestigious literary prize. [Added 2007]*

Young women attend private classes on the development of European painting. These activities and interests are not illegal, but neither are they encouraged. The Islamic Republic is accommodating an increasingly diverse populace—reluctantly, against its will.

What is the main preoccupation of young Iranians today? Democracy and its limits? The censorship of books and TV? The controversial nuclear program, which in 2005 saw Iran referred to the United Nations Security Council? The answer is none of the above. It's getting by—making enough to live in a little more comfort, or at least survive.

Thirty-year-old Majid Fadai is a colleague of Zeinab Maleki at the Mehr News Agency. He covers politics but his head is full of numbers. "In order for my wife and I to move into the flat that we're negotiating to rent," he told me in the summer of 2006, "I need to scrape together a deposit of 100 million riyals." (That's a little less than $11,000, the equivalent of four years' wages for the average Iranian.) "I've got a thirty million riyal deposit to collect from my current landlord and I'm expecting another thirty million in the form of a bank loan. Then there's the special loan that the government offers newlyweds; another ten million." Majid plans to make up the remainder with small loans from friends and nonprofit lending institutions linked to the mosque.

Majid and his wife of a little more than a year, Sediqeh, who is a nurse, have a combined monthly income of five million riyals, which comes to around $550, a little more than the national average. In Delijan, the provincial town where they were both born and raised, that might go quite a long way. In the capital, however, where life is costly, it means a precarious existence. The two of them work in central Tehran but live in a western suburb. On a busy day, the round trip to and from work takes four hours. When, one evening, they invited me to their home, they themselves arrived at around the time that I did, 8:45. "Now you understand," Majid said, "why we want to move closer to where we work."

Majid and Sediqeh's parents are poorly educated, working-class people, but they instilled in their children the importance of self-improvement. Now, rather than weave carpets in Delijan, as her mother does, Sediqeh is planning to get an MA in nursing. Her husband gets to cover the President's foreign trips; it's a source of pride back home. The Fadais' horizons have broadened, but they have a duty to keep looking back. They speak to their parents and visit Delijan regularly.

Tehran and the other big cities are full of Majids and Sediqehs, acting as a bridge between a limited provincial existence and a demanding metropolitan one. There are apprehensions, privations. But there is also, in the Fadais' home, a sense of anticipation, a sense that they stand at the threshold of an adventure.

They are the kind of Iranians whose lives Ahmadinejad promised to improve. The President ordered public banks to lend generously to private borrowers, but the move fueled inflation. In the summer of 2006, *Shargh* informed its readers that the price of property and household goods had risen by 20 percent and 40 percent respectively over the past year. "In a rich country like Iran," Majid said as we ate fruit and Sediqeh made dinner, "having a house should be considered a right." But he doesn't expect to be able to buy one before he is forty. "In ten years, after the demographics stabilize, Iran will be a good place to live. Nowadays it's tough."

Sediqeh is the strikingly attractive younger sister of Majid's aunt by marriage, and the two families know each other well. Speaking to me at his office, Majid had told me of the large number of young women, introduced to him by his mother and sisters, that he had refused to pursue. He had fallen for Sediqeh, he went on, because of her "beauty, piety, and for the fact that she is one of us." Once the couple had met several times, and Sediqeh had given her assent, Majid and his father formally asked for her hand.

Now, after a simple dinner, they both expressed themselves "very satisfied" with the match. "Majid has put on weight since he got married," Sediqeh announced proudly. She apologized for the slightly worn furniture we were sitting on, which dated from Majid's bachelorhood. When the couple move into their next apartment, Sediqeh will bring her trousseau, which includes furniture and kitchen appliances. Then, Majid went on, they plan to go on a pilgrimage to the shrine of the Imam Reza, the eighth Shia imam, in the eastern city of Mashhad, and ask for his help in their life together.

They are not overtly political but, like the majority of Iranians, Majid and Sediqeh are supporters of the country's nuclear program. Sediqeh in particular reacted sharply to my suggestion that Iran may have more to lose than it has to gain by insisting, in the face of strong international pressure, that it will not suspend its program of uranium enrichment, a program that could have both civilian and military applications. "It's our right," she said firmly. Majid agreed: "I didn't vote for Ahmadinejad, but I like what he says about the nuclear program. He's saying to all the Western countries who have a nuclear industry, 'You want to talk to us? Fine. But you're on a horse and I'm walking alongside. First I get on a horse, so we're equal, and then we'll talk.'"

As I left the Fadais' house that night and drove back to my own, I made a prediction: ten years from now, this resourceful couple will have achieved many of the objectives that they have set themselves. And what of the other young people I have come to know: Mehdi and Somayeh, Niki, Zeinab? It struck me that these Iranians, so different in the way that they live and see the world, share a determination to hope and to plan, even though they enjoy few of the certainties that I enjoyed at their age. What if inflation soars suddenly? What if there are sanctions, even military attacks?

"So what?" they reply in unison. You can't stop living your life because your country is being discussed at the UN, because someone has put you in an "axis of evil," because your President is a poor economist and hates Israel. In these young people there is an insistent optimism—even in Somayeh, with her bleak longing to leave. It's the beauty of youth.

15

THE DEFIANT IRANIAN

October 2006

AT THE BEGINNING of 2002, President George W. Bush tried to punish Iran for supporting anti-Israel militants, for refusing to adopt a Western-style democracy, and for allegedly trying to produce weapons of mass destruction. He included Iran, along with Iraq and North Korea, in the "axis of evil." Among foreign diplomats and journalists in Tehran, it became fashionable to speak of the coming "implosion" of the Islamic Republic, Iran's revolutionary state. Weakened by a power struggle between reformists and conservative hard-liners, Iran was now, or so it was said, acutely vulnerable to the sort of threat that the United States, whose forces had easily toppled the Taliban and scattered al-Qaeda, seemed to represent.

The fear of intervention by the US in Iran became more urgent among Iran's leaders when America invaded Iraq the following year. Indeed, it later became known that, in early 2003, the Iranian Foreign Ministry quietly sent Washington a detailed proposal for comprehensive negotiations, in which the Iranian government said it was prepared to make concessions about its nuclear program and to address concerns about its ties to groups such as Hezbollah and Islamic Jihad, in return for an agreement from the White House to refrain from destabilizing the Islamic Republic and start lifting long-in-effect sanctions. The US rejected this overture out of hand. It seemed that Bush didn't want to offer guarantees to a regime that he intended, at a later date, to try to destroy.

Nowadays, it is hard to imagine the Iranian government repeating this sort of offer. Such is their apparent strength and good fortune that they take a provocatively long time to respond to diplomatic overtures, such as the proposal that the US, Britain, France, Germany, China, and Russia offered them in June 2006, and which they rejected. The six powers had offered a series of incentives—including nuclear technology whose peaceful application can be verified, a very modest relaxation of US sanctions, and diplomatic support for Iran's bid to join the World Trade Organization—as an inducement to Iran to suspend its uranium enrichment program. If you ask an Iranian conservative what during the past four years has caused the upturn in Iranian confidence, he or she will probably dwell on the eclipse of the reform movement of the former president, Mohammad Khatami, and his replacement in last year's election by a hard-liner, Mahmoud Ahmadinejad, who has promised to return Iran to the state of unsullied revolutionary purity that he imagines existed during the rule of Ayatollah Ruhollah Khomeini.

Ahmadinejad's populism finds expression in dirigiste economics and nationalist rhetoric about Iran's right to nuclear power. Last year, in a private meeting that was filmed and made public, apparently against his wishes, he intimated that he enjoys the favor of Mahdi, the twelfth Shia imam, who disappeared in the eighth century. Most Shias believe that Mahdi will return after the world has been plunged into chaos, heralding a period of divine rule followed by the end of the world. Ahmadinejad's domestic opponents accuse him privately of being a member of a shadowy group whose aims apparently include generating chaos with a view to hastening Mahdi's return, accusations that his supporters have denied. The President's main domestic political promises, to redistribute wealth and better the lot of normal Iranians, owe more to socialism than they do to Shia eschatology.

Ahmadinejad has incensed many people outside the country with his extreme verbal attacks on Israel and the West and his widely denounced dismissal of the veracity of the Holocaust. In October 2005, the Iranian government organized a "World Without Zionism" conference for Iranian students, in which Ahmadinejad said that Israel should be "wiped off the map." In following months, he made a series of remarks in speeches and in interviews in which he challenged Western laws against publicly denying the Holocaust. In July, during the Israel–Lebanon conflict, he compared the Israeli offensive to the actions of Hitler. And in August, Ahmadinejad reiterated that "the main solution" to the Middle East crisis is "the elimination of the Zionist regime."

In his contemptuous indifference to the Holocaust and its place in the collective Western conscience, and in his argument that the Holocaust has been used to justify Israeli repression, Ahmadinejad reflects the views of many Iranians, who have hardly been exposed to historical literature about the Holocaust. For all the notoriety that his comments earned him, however, it is far from certain that Iranians share his apparent obsession with the issue, which seems to serve calculated political aims. In August, in avowed retaliation against the earlier publication in European newspapers of caricatures of the Prophet Muhammad, the government staged an exhibition of cartoons about the Holocaust. When I visited this exhibition, which featured some grotesquely anti-Semitic cartoons, a handful of Western journalists and I had the place to ourselves. More recently, in New York, when asked his opinion of the Holocaust by a *Newsweek* interviewer, he said, "We know this was a historical event that happened..."

For all his rhetoric of social reform and making the state more Islamic, the truth is that Ahmadinejad has not changed Iran very much. It is the same inefficient, partially democratic, near theocracy that it was during Khatami's presidency. Its economy remains, if anything, even more dependent on revenues from oil, by far the country's most important commodity. The prominent elements of Ahmadinejad's vague program of general "upliftment"—to spend oil revenues to help the common man and increase the state's already considerable control over the economy—seem designed mainly to reinforce the status quo that the reformists tried to challenge.

Why, then, do Iran's leaders speak with new confidence about the future? One answer is that as recently as 2003, after two neighbors, Afghanistan and Iraq, fell to American forces, Iran's region of the world seemed dark and foreboding. But now it is full of promise, and the reasons for this are the means the Bush White House has employed to pursue its ambition of reshaping the Middle East and, in particular, its disastrous occupation of Iraq. Bush apparently wanted to force the Islamic Republic to moderate its behavior dramatically and to weaken it internally to the point where it would collapse. On both counts, he has achieved more or less the opposite of what he intended.

Iran's hardening attitude toward Israel illustrates this failure. Around the time of Bush's proclamation of the "axis of evil," some Iranian politicians, including members of the reformist Khatami government that was then in office, regarded Iran's traditional refusal to acknowledge Israel's right to exist as an ideological relic that, sooner or later, would have to be scrapped. Within the Iranian establishment, which consists of unelected clerics who occupy senior positions, the elected government and parliament, and the armed forces, there were intense disagreements, of which the public was only partly aware, over the value of maintaining Iran's rejection of Israel's legitimacy.

In 2002, Iran's foreign minister offered guarded encouragement to Saudi proposals that Israel be offered peace in return for withdrawing to its pre-1967 borders. As recently as the beginning of 2004, Iranian officials said that Iran was on the verge of reestablishing full diplomatic relations with Egypt, whose peace deal with Israel and subsequent cooperation with it had been treated with contempt by Iranian revolutionaries. A reformist member of parliament's foreign affairs commission predicted to me early in 2004 that the Islamic Republic would soon undergo a "strategic realignment." It would, he said, establish closer relations with such countries as Jordan and Egypt, which have relations with Israel, to the disadvantage of Syria, its erstwhile partner in truculent opposition to a two-state solution in Palestine.

The debate in Iran was at its liveliest when the US seemed to pose a serious threat. Proponents of more pragmatic policies emphasizing diplomacy could argue that Iranian interests were being harmed by the efforts of radicals to thwart Bush. But as the ramifications of the war on terror became clear, the perceived threat to Iran receded and those radicals felt stronger. They were further strengthened by Ahmadinejad's election victory in 2005, although Iran had already decided to resume uranium enrichment before his inauguration and foreign policy was not much discussed in the campaign.

After having temporarily rid Afghanistan of the militantly anti-Shia Taliban, the US has stood by while Shia Iran expanded its influence in that country, especially among Persian-speaking Shia Afghans. Similarly, it is clear that Iran, by cultivating extensive links with the armed militias, clergy, and traders in Shia-dominated southern Iraq, has benefited from America's dislodging of Saddam Hussein, an oppressively anti-Shia Sunni leader. In the words of a new study of Iran's foreign relations by the Royal Institute of International Affairs in London, "Iran has superseded [the US] as the most influential power in Iraq."[1]

During the recent conflict between Israel and Hezbollah, the admiration of many Sunni Arabs for any government that stands up to what they see as Israel's callous behavior allowed Iran, a non-Arab Shia state that borders neither Lebanon nor Israel, to assert it had vital interests in the conflict. From the outbreak of fighting, Iran's conservative establishment celebrated Hezbollah's exploits as if they were their own. During and for some weeks after the conflict, the

---

1. *Iran, Its Neighbours and the Regional Crises*, a report edited by Robert Lowe and Claire Spencer (Chatham House, 2006).

streets of Tehran were festooned with photographs of Sheikh Hassan Nasrallah, who studied at the Iranian seminary in Qom; newspapers reprinted photographs of him genuflecting in a gesture of sub-servience to Iran's Supreme Leader, Ayatollah Ali Khamenei, during a recent trip to Tehran.

It cannot be said with confidence that Nasrallah was acting under Khamenei's orders when Hezbollah kidnapped Israeli soldiers. There is further room for skepticism if we assume that Hezbollah was surprised by the Israeli response, which seems to have been the case. It is unlikely that Hezbollah would consult Iran on particular operations; more likely they would do so on strategy. But the transport of Iranian arms to Hezbollah, often through Turkish airspace to Damascus and then across Syria's land border with Lebanon, has been well documented, and Western experts agree that Iranian backing has been crucial to Hez-bollah's military buildup on the northern border of Israel since the Israeli withdrawal from Lebanon in 2000. In part thanks to these arms, Hezbollah emerged from the recent fighting with its military reputa-tion enhanced. After the cease fire, more than two hundred deputies in the Iranian parliament thanked Khamenei, whom they elevated to "The Guardian of the Affairs of Muslims," for the vital moral "role" that he had played in the Hezbollah "triumph." In an interview with a Tehran newspaper on August 3, Ali Akbar Mohtashamipour, who, as Iran's ambassador to Syria, helped found Hezbollah after the Israeli invasion of Lebanon in 1982, boasted of the military experience that Hezbollah fighters gained while fighting alongside Iran during the Iran–Iraq War of the 1980s. Although Iran continues to deny that it is a major supplier of Hezbollah rockets, Mohtashamipour acknowl-edged that Hezbollah has medium-range Zelzal-2 missiles and short-range Katyusha rockets, which are both made by Iran. He also referred to the Hezbollah militia as Khomeini's "spiritual offspring."[2]

---

2. Mohtashamipour interview in *Sharq*, August 3, 2006.

The upshot is that this anti-American regime, its prestige rising in proportion to its refusal to do the US's bidding, does not seem likely to bow to the Bush administration and renounce its right, guaranteed in an international treaty to which it is party, to become a producer of nuclear fuel. In and out of Iran, few were surprised when the Iranians, on August 22, 2006, responded with a long-winded rejection of a United Nations Security Council resolution calling on them to suspend their uranium enrichment or face the possibility of sanctions. The Iranian communiqué contained a request for clarification of the incentives that the council's permanent members, along with Germany, had offered in return for a suspension. While ruling out the immediate suspension of enrichment that the six powers had demanded, the Iranian statement left open the prospect that a suspension might result from further negotiations.

This emboldened Russia and China, two permanent members of the Security Council, to reiterate their longstanding reluctance to impose sanctions that would threaten their commercial interests in Iran. Javier Solana, the EU foreign policy chief, started fresh talks with Iran's nuclear negotiator, and on September 17, France's president, Jacques Chirac, made it clear that the EU no longer regarded an Iranian suspension as a precondition for a new round of formal negotiations aimed at reaching a lasting settlement. During future negotiations, he suggested, the six powers could formally remove Iran's nuclear dossier from the Security Council's agenda, and the Iranians could simultaneously renew their suspension.[3] On September 21, the US agreed to extend an August 31 deadline the UN Security Council had set for Iran to suspend enrichment, to allow time for Solana's new diplomatic initiative. But by early October, even the most sanguine of the Europeans had all but given up hope that Iran would suspend

---

3. According to a European diplomat with wide Middle East experience, behind Chirac's conciliatory words lie his fears for the security of the French troops that are being deployed in south Lebanon, and French apprehensions that they are hostages to Hezbollah's and Iran's goodwill.

enrichment, and a discussion of sanctions in the Security Council seemed inevitable.

Among American and Israeli government officials, and some of their allies, there is a fear that Iran is playing for time. Iran's technicians still have several years' work ahead of them before they can produce enough fuel to run a reactor and, if ordered to, build a bomb. It seems likely that Iran's leaders have calculated that there is little appetite, even in the Security Council, for serious punitive action. Even if the US and its allies manage to impose sanctions, these will very likely be limited to the transfer of some nuclear and nonnuclear military technology, travel restrictions on senior officials, and the freezing of Iranian assets abroad—instead of the far more threatening possibility of restrictions on nonmilitary trade or an oil embargo. Iran, Ahmadinejad has said, will not give up "an iota of its nuclear rights."

For many in the US, Europe, and Israel, Iran's determination to produce nuclear weapons in defiance of the world's significant powers seems clear. Some go further, suggesting that Iranian leaders who have a bomb will be temperamentally inclined to use it. One proponent of this view is Bernard Lewis, a distinguished scholar of the Middle East who was influential in winning over US public opinion to supporting the invasion of Iraq. In a recent *Wall Street Journal* article Lewis argued that Ahmadinejad's millenarian beliefs should undermine any assumption that if Iran gets nuclear weapons, the Middle East will be protected from nuclear catastrophe by the doctrine of mutually assured destruction (MAD). According to Lewis, since Ahmadinejad and his followers "clearly believe" that the time for a "cosmic struggle" and "the final victory of the forces of good over evil" is nigh, MAD has no meaning. "For people with this mindset, MAD is not a constraint; it is an inducement..."[4]

---

4. See "August 22," *The Wall Street Journal*, August 8, 2006.

In fact, Ahmadinejad, and every other Iranian politician and official who speaks on the subject, takes elaborate, even ritual, care to reiterate Iran's long-standing claim that it has no intention of developing nuclear weapons, and that the program is exclusively peaceful. The US national intelligence director, John Negroponte, has predicted that Iran "might be in a position to have a nuclear weapon" at some time between 2010 and 2015.

The verbal attacks of Iran's leaders, Ahmadinejad in particular, on Israel and America have rightly received much attention and criticism. Equally, some Western analysts have noticed a tendency on the part of the US government and its allies to misrepresent Iran in order to generate support for tough action against the Islamic Republic. In the "ritual condemnation of Iran," laments Ali Ansari, the author of *Confronting Iran*, a new book on Iran's troubled relations with the US, "no rhetorical flourish, no level of hyperbole, seems excessive."[5] Iran is "not just a member of the Axis of Evil, but the founding member, the chief sponsor of state terrorism, or to use a more recent characterization, the central banker for terrorism." Ansari is a British academic of Iranian birth who is often invited by the press to comment on contemporary Iranian affairs. He is no friend of the Islamic Republic, but he regards many of these epithets as exaggerated or undeserved.

The Iranian leaders that Ansari describes in *Confronting Iran* are more predictable than the Islamic zealots often portrayed by neoconservatives. As much as its Islamist ideology, Ansari finds, collective memories of hurt and humiliation at the hands of foreign powers, nationalist sentiments, and the instinct of Iranian leaders for self-preservation shape the Islamic Republic's foreign policy. As a fellow of the Royal Institute of International Affairs, a prestigious British

---

5. Basic Books, 2006.

institution that has close relations with the Foreign Office, Ansari was privy to sensitive information when Britain, France, and Germany tried, from 2003 onward, to dissuade Iran from carrying through its plans to produce nuclear fuel, while the US skeptically stood aside. In Ansari's account, these efforts failed both because of opposition in Iran and the US's failure to support negotiations when they had a chance of succeeding. When the US finally threw its weight behind the talks, Ansari writes, it offered Iran no more than "technological scraps," for example, access to commercial aircraft parts.

"After all," Ansari writes, "Iran, unlike Iraq, had not invaded anyone, nor had it been defeated in war." Many in the West saw Iran's refusal to continue to allow intensive spot inspections as evidence that the Iranians were hiding a nuclear weapons program; Ansari understands it primarily as part of Iran's struggle to evade Western dominance, a struggle it has been waging since the end of the nineteenth century. Ansari does not ascribe Iran's opposition to the now-defunct Middle East peace process solely to ideology; "an underlying motive for Iran's...obstructionism," he writes, "was the fact that it had not been invited to the table."

In Ansari's analysis, Iran's pugnacious behavior is partly designed to underscore its claims to be a regional power that could, if treated respectfully, use its influence benignly. For example, in diplomatic meetings with the Europeans and others, Iranian officials have repeatedly suggested that they could use their influence over Hezbollah to secure peace between Palestinians and Israel. Iran has reportedly offered to help arrange prisoner swaps between Hezbollah and Israel.[6]

Ansari's belief that Iran's behavior can be understood by studying national ambition and self-interest, rather than the ideological proclamations of Ahmadinejad, is shared by another expert on Iran,

---

6. See "Iran Urges Prisoner Swap Negotiations," *The Jerusalem Post*, August 22, 2006.

Ray Takeyh, a senior fellow at the Council on Foreign Relations, in Washington, D.C. In his new book, *Hidden Iran*,[7] Takeyh writes that three elements, "Islamic ideology, national interests and factional politics," contribute to Iran's national policies; but even now, in the Ahmadinejad era, he believes that calculation and self-interest are more important than the religious fervor that was a driving force for Iran during its war with Iraq in the 1980s. As an example of Iranian pragmatism, he cites Iran's silence in the face of Russian atrocities against Chechen Muslims. In return for this surprisingly accommodating Iranian attitude, and for Iran's acquiescence in Russia's dominance over much of Central Asia, the Russians provide the Islamic Republic with diplomatic support, conventional arms, and nuclear know-how. (Russia has built Iran's sole, and still unused, nuclear reactor at Bushehr, on the Persian Gulf coast.)

As for Iran's nuclear program, which he believes is designed to produce weapons, Takeyh writes:

> The Islamic Republic is not an irrational rogue state seeking such weaponry as an instrument of an aggressive, revolutionary foreign policy designed to project its power abroad...for Iran this is a weapon of deterrence, and the relevant question is whether its possession will serve its practical interests.

According to Takeyh, "the unpredictable nature of developments in Iraq has intensified Iran's anxieties and further enhanced the utility of the nuclear option." Looking east, he says, Iran sees "a nuclear-armed Pakistan with its own strain of anti-Shiism." Most important of all, in my opinion, Iran, he says, may be able to "play the nuclear card to renegotiate a more rational relationship" with the United States.

---

7. *Hidden Iran: Paradox and Power in the Islamic Republic* (Times Books, 2006).

* * *

Underlying both authors' analyses of Iran's internal politics, and their relatively calm appraisals of its regional ambitions and abilities, is their sense of Iran's complicated power structure and Ahmadinejad's place in it. Some American commentators refer to Ahmadinejad as if he were synonymous with the Islamic Republic and its policies. In the US, where the president can veto laws and order invasions, that would be natural enough; in Iran, where he can be challenged and overruled by elected institutions such as the parliament as well as by unelected officials gathered around the Supreme Leader, Ayatollah Ali Khamenei, it is misleading. As head of the government, Ahmadinejad has broad control of the country's finances and many domestic policies. His influence can be seen, for instance, in the government's decision to set up a large fund to help needy Iranians, and in continuing the gradual purge of secular-minded professors from the nation's universities—itself a disturbing development.

In matters of internal security and public order, however, Ahmadinejad's authority is restricted by several supervisory bodies, the most important of which are dominated by representatives of the Supreme Leader. There is also the unofficial veto power of the senior clergy, theologically conservative grand ayatollahs who do not hold political office. They recently forced Ahmadinejad to back down on his pledge to allow women to attend soccer matches. Ahmadinejad officially presides over the powerful Supreme National Security Council; but here again Khamenei's word is final.

On major decisions concerning foreign and military policy, we can assume that Ahmadinejad's views are no more than advisory. He does not set the Islamic Republic's policy toward Israel any more than he would decide whether to use nuclear weapons should Iran eventually acquire them. Strategic and important tactical decisions are taken by the Supreme Leader and his advisers, who include Ali Larijani, Iran's chief nuclear negotiator, and senior officers in the Revolutionary Guard.

Despite Ahmadinejad's threatening anti-Israeli rhetoric, Iran's role in the Israeli–Palestinian conflict has long been defined by what Takeyh calls its "unwillingness to commit forces to the actual struggle against the Jewish state." That has not changed. Before the recent conflict in south Lebanon, Iran supplied rockets and other weapons to Hezbollah; but the Iranians conspicuously failed to dispatch to the front the "suicide battalions" that they had organized, with much fanfare, earlier this year. The batallions come under the command of the Revolutionary Guard, and were officially established for "defense," a defense that one volunteer told me could mean the defense of Islam —that is, Palestine or Lebanon if need be. The battalions were much covered in the Iranian press, but are generally regarded as an empty gesture—fat boys giggling for the cameras.

Khamenei is an inscrutable politician; his rhetoric can be extreme, but Iran has greatly moderated its foreign policy since he succeeded Khomeini in 1989. Iran's policies toward Israel remain opaque, somewhere, perhaps, between Ahmadinejad's most venomous anti-Israel comments and his assurance on August 27 that "Iran is not a threat to anybody, not even to the Zionist regime."

The deterioration of the US position in Iraq, and Hezbollah's ability to withstand Israel, have done much to free Iran's leaders from their old fear of Bush. They have also encouraged Ahmadinejad to develop his quixotic, pseudophilosophical worldview. Ahmadinejad is opinionated but not intellectually inquisitive, quite unlike his predecessor, Mohammad Khatami, whose presidency was symbolized by his call for a "dialogue among civilizations," and by his winning, gallant manners. Ahmadinejad has an ideologue's disdain for competing or alternative views. He defines his job in language that refers to the divine and the revelatory. On his provincial tours he touches sick children with a rapt look that is reminiscent of a religious healer. He sends discursive letters to the leaders of other countries on what is wrong with the world. These seem expressions of his belief in his own destiny and divine mission. He does not see himself as an ordinary president, and he is determined that his presidency should not be judged by mundane standards.

In the revealing long letter that he sent to Angela Merkel, Germany's chancellor, in July, Ahmadinejad suggests that the Germans, a proud people who have contributed much to "knowledge, philosophy, literature, art and politics," are being prevented from achieving their potential by efforts on the part of countries that defeated them in World War II to keep "a black cloud of humiliation and shame" hanging over their heads, and to ascribe to them responsibility for the "sins of their forefathers." In this letter, Ahmadinejad avoids questioning whether the Holocaust happened, but he positions Germany today in opposition to the powers that defeated it in the war, and to Israel, "the greatest enemy of humanity."

From here, Ahmadinejad leaps—as he has done in speeches in the past—to question the conditions in which Israel was established, and to ask why Britain and other supporters of Zionism, "if they felt responsibility towards the survivors of the Holocaust, did not give sanctuary to them in their own countries." He criticizes the control that the US and the UK, along with the other permanent members of the United Nations Security Council, continue to exercise over the affairs of the world. This, he says, has contributed to the spread of oppression, injustice, and weapons of mass destruction. Ahmadinejad goes on to propose a partnership between Iran and Germany, founded on shared "exalted visions" and aimed at instituting divinely sanctioned justice and ending "the distortions that are present in the world."

In directly addressing Western leaders and asking them to change their ways, Ahmadinejad is following a familiar Islamic path. In his letter to Merkel, and an earlier (also unanswered) letter to Bush, in which he berated the American president for his policies and for betraying the principles of Jesus Christ, Iranians are reminded of Ayatollah Khomeini's famous invitation to Mikhail Gorbachev to study

Islam, itself an echo of the letters that the Prophet Muhammad during his mission in the seventh century sent to three contemporary rulers, urging them to become Muslims.

If we assume that the Iranian president knows very little about Europe and the West, he must nonetheless have been advised that his letter, and its confiding, complicit tone, would shock the representative of a people that is, more than sixty years after the event, still trying to come to terms with the Holocaust. For more than a month after it was sent, Ahmadinejad's letter to Merkel was not made public in either country. The President's decision to release it, at the end of August, suggests that he was addressing it not only to Merkel but also to Iranian citizens. The day after the letter appeared in the Iranian press, Ahmadinejad announced that he was inviting George Bush to debate with him the best way to run the world. "The time has come," he told journalists, "for us to respect the intelligence and opinions of the peoples of the world."

There is little in Ahmadinejad's letter to Merkel to suggest that his political positions are based on his millenarian beliefs; rather, his attention seems fixed on changes that he believes should be made to the existing world order. Ahmadinejad does not seem to have a clear or coherent idea of what these changes should be, or how they might be brought about. Even if he did, the Islamic Republic has not given him the means to attempt the transformation that he proposes so vaguely. This explains why Ahmadinejad's pronouncements often have an illusionary, theatrical quality, and why most of them pass unnoticed in the West.

Ahmadinejad has been described to me by an experienced observer of Iranian politics as a man who "thrives in a crisis," often of his own making. Although many Iranians sympathize broadly with his anti-Israel feeling and his defense of the nuclear program, they are increasingly unhappy that, so far, they have received little of the oil revenues that he promised to distribute to them. Meanwhile, he seems to derive pleasure from the appalled bewilderment he elicits in the

West. In a recent interview with the German weekly *Der Spiegel*, he reiterated at length his doubts about the Holocaust. In the words of Hubert Kleinert, a German political scientist and former member of the Bundestag, whose comment accompanied the interview, this conversation was "without precedent: a living Iranian president—not some neo-Nazi or obscure fringe theorist—expounding in a lengthy interview about the alleged uncertainty of the Holocaust.... It's as if Mr. Ahmadinejad wants to position himself as a worldwide symbol of the neo-Nazi movement."[8]

It is likely that Ahmadinejad has different aspirations. He seems to covet a position of leadership among Islamists everywhere and, to achieve this, he is prepared to say what few other Muslim leaders, especially those who have relations with the US, dare to say. For Ahmadinejad, saying outrageous things wins him the admiration of Israel-haters everywhere, while concealing the fact that little of his fuzzy program of "upliftment," for Iran and the world, can be realized.

A recent opinion poll found that Ahmadinejad is the third-most-admired politician among Egyptians, after Hassan Nasrallah of Hezbollah and Hamas's leader, Khaled Meshaal. Among Lebanon's Shias, the prestige of Ayatollah Ali Khamenei, whose photograph is often displayed in Hezbollah-dominated areas, is higher than ever. This has led some commentators, including Vali Nasr, in his new book, *The Shia Revival*,[9] to observe that Iran's leaders seek "great-power status."

If they achieved that, it would upset the conventional view that Iran, as a Shia country dominated by ethnic Persians, cannot realistically aspire to lead a region that is, on the whole, run by Sunni Arabs. That seemed to be a lesson from the 1980s, when Khomeini's revolutionary

---

8. See *Der Spiegel*, May 30, 2006.

9. Norton, 2006.

government failed in its repeated attempts to foment revolutions elsewhere. But among the Shias of Iraq and Afghanistan, Iran's influence is strong and seems bound to grow. Many ordinary Sunnis, especially those living under pro-American governments, admire Iran for standing up to the common enemy. By supporting the beleaguered Hamas government of the Palestinian Authority, the Iranians have won thanks from the Sunni Palestinians who voted for it.

Iran's ability to retain the goodwill it has gained rests on its staying above the sectarian violence that is tearing Iraq apart. Shia groups supported and perhaps armed by Iran, such as the Supreme Council for Islamic Revolution in Iraq, are thought to be behind many sectarian killings. But Iran has not been directly implicated; and it has given no sign that it approves these murders. Iran's press, both government-run and independent, avoids inciting anti-Sunni feeling whenever there is a massacre of Shias in Iraq; it dwells instead on American neglect or perfidy. Iran may be reluctant to be perceived as being involved in Iraqi sectarian strife because of the effect that it might have on some of its own troubled peripheral provinces, some of which have large Sunni populations.

Even if Iran manages to avoid sectarian conflict, it is unlikely to become a "great power," for the same reasons that have prevented it from doing so in the past. If tensions between Israel and the Palestinians eventually diminish, and more voices are heard in favor of resuming the peace process, regional support for Iran's hard-line position will drop; and traditional divisions—between Persians and Arabs, and between Shias and Sunnis—will start to seem more important.

Right now, though, the Iranian government feels more confident than at any time since it was placed in the "axis of evil." The Iranian leaders calculate that Hezbollah's success in resisting Israel's attacks, assuming that it continues to be in a position to threaten Israel, may diminish the likelihood that America or Israel will attack Iran's nuclear facilities, as some commentators have suggested they intend to. Iranian officials have made it clear that if there are strikes, they will respond by attacking American interests in the region. American troops in Iraq and Afghanistan are obvious targets, though Iranian civilian and military leaders have also threatened to disrupt world oil supplies passing through the Straits of Hormuz.

By engaging itself militarily, politically, and morally across the Middle East, George Bush's America has become vulnerable. In the face of an overstretched competitor, Iran is less likely than ever to relinquish its nuclear program unless it gets something it wants in return. It is still far from clear that America's weakness will force it to accept Iran's demands, particularly the demand that the US relax its sanctions and end its efforts to destabilize the Islamic Republic. If the US does not, it is hard to imagine today's Iran suspending its enrichment program for very long.